Latino Orlando

Southern Dissent

UNIVERSITY PRESS OF FLORIDA

Florida A&M University, Tallahassee
Florida Atlantic University, Boca Raton
Florida Gulf Coast University, Ft. Myers
Florida International University, Miami
Florida State University, Tallahassee
New College of Florida, Sarasota
University of Central Florida, Orlando
University of Florida, Gainesville
University of North Florida, Jacksonville
University of South Florida, Tampa
University of West Florida, Pensacola

LATINO ORLANDO

SUBURBAN TRANSFORMATION AND RACIAL CONFLICT

SIMONE DELERME

UNIVERSITY PRESS OF FLORIDA

Gainesville / Tallahassee / Tampa / Boca Raton

Pensacola / Orlando / Miami / Jacksonville / Ft. Myers / Sarasota

25 24 23 22 21 20   6 5 4 3 2 1

Library of Congress Cataloging-in-Publication Data
Names: Delerme, Simone Pierre, author.
Title: Latino Orlando : suburban transformation and racial conflict /
    Simone Delerme.
Other titles: Southern dissent.
Description: Gainesville : University Press of Florida, 2019. | Series: Southern dissent |
    Includes bibliographical references and index. | Summary: "Latino Orlando" portrays the
    experiences of first- and second-generation immigrants who have come to the Orlando
    metropolitan area from Puerto Rico, Cuba, Mexico, Venezuela, Colombia, and other Latin
    American countries. While much research on immigration focuses on urban destinations,
    Simone Delerme delves into a middle- and upper-class suburban context, highlighting the
    profound emographic and cultural transformation of an overlooked immigrant hub.
Identifiers: LCCN 2019020694 (print) | LCCN 2019022120 (ebook) | ISBN
    9780813066257 (cloth : alk. paper)
Subjects: LCSH: Hispanic Americans—Florida—Orlando—History. | Latin Americans—
    Florida—Orlando—History. | Immigrants—Florida—Orlando—History. | Children of
    immigrants—Florida—Orlando—History. | Orlando (Fla.)—Emigration and immigration.
Classification: LCC F870.S7 D45 2019 (print) | LCC F870.S7 (ebook) | DDC
    975.9/2400468—dc23
LC record available at https://lccn.loc.gov/2019020694
LC ebook record available at https://lccn.loc.gov/2019022120

The University Press of Florida is the scholarly publishing agency for the State University
System of Florida, comprising Florida A&M University, Florida Atlantic University, Florida
Gulf Coast University, Florida International University, Florida State University, New College
of Florida, University of Central Florida, University of Florida, University of North Florida,
University of South Florida, and University of West Florida.

University Press of Florida
2046 NE Waldo Road
Suite 2100
Gainesville, FL 32609
http://upress.ufl.edu

DEDICATED TO MY PARENTS,

JOSEPH DELERME AND CAROL PIERRE DELERME,

WITH LOVE.

CONTENTS

FIGURES

TABLES

FOREWORD

Immigration and demographic change have shaped American history (and pre-history) and continue to do so. Much of this story has focused on the great European immigrations and forced African migration, from the colonial era through the early twentieth century. More recently, there have been significant Asian, Latino, and African immigrations, especially after the 1965 Immigration Reform Act opened up possibilities for non-European immigration. In the literature on American immigration, the South has been largely an outlier, often relegated to a few pages in general histories or ignored altogether. Over the past several decades, however, the realities of significant immigration into the American South have stirred scholarly and popular interest in charting, following, and understanding the immigration and migration of hundreds of thousands of people to the South to look for work, to escape from poverty and persecution, and to find a place to call home.

In the South, as elsewhere, such immigrants and migrants have not always been welcomed. In the long history of immigration to the United States, various groups have suffered rejection and violence at the hands of xenophobic native-born Americans. The nativists charged that such newcomers threatened to bring disorder, disease, and disloyalty and to take jobs away from Americans. Nativism ran strong in nineteenth-century America. This was especially the case in regard to Catholic Irish and Germans, Eastern European Jews, Italians, and Chinese. Much of this prejudice existed in the South. For example, the largest mass lynching the United States history occurred in New Orleans, where eleven southern Italians were murdered. In the early twentieth century, the Ku Klux Klan also beat the drums of immigrant, ethnic, and religious hatred to go along with its racism.

At the same time, the need for workers provided incentives for attracting immigrants to the United States to work in fields and factories. In some cases employers used immigrants to displace African American workers and foster divisions among working-class people as a way of preventing unions from forming. During the early twentieth century, the bracero program for Mexicans made agricultural expansion possible, just as similar programs have more recently made food processing and other industries possible. Meanwhile, political upheavals and poverty brought Cubans, Haitian and other Caribbean peoples, and refugees from Vietnam to southern states. Although often invisible in the histories of New Souths, immigrants and migrants from other parts of the United States became important members of new southern communities that stretch from Florida into the Carolinas.

Part of that population movement to the South included migrants from Puerto Rico and people of Puerto Rican descent from New Jersey, New York, and other northern states. Especially in the case of Florida, they came for work, a congenial climate, and retirement. In doing so, they created Latino places that reflected their cultures and interests and redrew the social map of the South. They also changed the black-white racial, cultural, and social dynamics of the South to multiethnic ones.

Currently the most influential migration pattern affecting and remaking the South involves not only people of Puerto Rican descent but also people from Mexico, Central America, the Caribbean, and South America. This migration has stimulated new political backlash among many native-born Americans. It also has heightened the new groups' awareness of their distinctive cultures and interests even as they adapt to or adopt some southern values and ways.

In *Latino Orlando: Suburban Transformation and Racial Conflict*, Simone Delerme investigates an important new aspect of this migration. Noting that since the mid-1990s more and more Latinos are settling in the Southeast, she focuses on Florida's greater Orlando area, where Latinos are predominantly from Puerto Rico or are of Puerto Rican descent. As American citizens and in some cases having lived in the mainland United States all their lives, they constitute a unique aspect of Latino migration and adaptation. They also are surprisingly understudied in their southern context. Delerme approaches them through a combination of personal knowledge, experience, and historical research to analyze their shifting patterns of settlement, class divisions, cultural conflict, and racialization. In central Florida, they are clearly dissenters from the dominant black-white cultural divide. The processes whereby Orlando is becoming Latinized suggest new patterns of identity formation and new definitions of what it means to be southern, with implications that extend beyond central Florida. Delerme's book, which tracks this history with keen insight, is a welcome addition to the Southern Dissent series.

Stanley Harrold and Randall M. Miller
Series Editors

PROLOGUE

When I was growing up, the place we called home—East Harlem, New York— was sometimes portrayed negatively in the media and in the academic literature. I was naïve about this fact. In the 1980s, when my brother and I walked to my grandmother's house a block away, we avoided the crack vials that spotted the concrete and passed the vacant lots and abandoned buildings that lined the streets. But I was desensitized to the landscape and jumping over crack vials became a game, no different than playing hopscotch. My immediate and extended family congregated at my grandmother's house almost daily, and El Barrio— East Harlem, or Spanish Harlem, as we sometimes called our community—was our home, as it has been for four generations of Delermes.

In October 1931, the New York & Porto Rico Steamship Company mailed a letter to Eusebio Delerme, my paternal grandfather, to confirm his second-class passage aboard the Coamo. At the age of 24, he was planning to migrate to New York City from Vieques, an island municipality off of Puerto Rico's eastern coast. Ten years later, he was a property owner and the proprietor of La Viequense, a bodega in Spanish Harlem on 22 East 112th street. My grandmother and their eleven children, my father included, made the operation of the bodega a possibility. The business operated out of the building they all lived in. The bodega was on the ground floor and my family lived upstairs.

My family's livelihood was connected to that bodega and the opportunities it afforded. For one, my uncles and aunts never had to go hungry with the constant supply of arroz (rice), Goya brand habichuelas (beans), and other staples. While my father's parents were both born in Puerto Rico, he was born in New York City. My mother was also born in New York City and identifies as Haitian American. My parents lived in New York City until the early 1990s, when they relocated to Wilmington, Delaware. I'm part of the Puerto Rican

Figure o.1. La Viequense grocery store.

diaspora and spent my childhood in a Puerto Rican–concentrated enclave. This is what prompted my academic interest in the Puerto Rican experience of migration and in the research that led to this book.

I never gave much thought to the socioeconomic conditions in Harlem while I lived there in my youth. We were an upwardly mobile middle-class family living in what was once a notorious ghetto. Decades ago there were allegations of homeowners burning down their properties to collect insurance money and urban poverty surrounded us. However, my parents, uncles, and aunts saw this area as a real estate opportunity. Several family members decided to purchase property in the area, making Spanish Harlem a place that my large Puerto Rican family happily called home. Real estate opportunities were important to my immediate and extended family's history of migration and kept us connected to Puerto Rico and New York and later brought us to Florida. My family is not unique. Thus, the book highlights the role real estate and homeownership opportunities have played in the massive Puerto Rican migration to the suburbs of Orlando, Florida.

Black, White, or "Mixed"

In the early 1990s, in the middle of my fifth grade year, my immediate family moved from Spanish Harlem to Wilmington, Delaware. The bank where my father worked in New York had undergone a series of mergers and he had decided to relocate to an office in downtown Wilmington. My father managed the bank's newly opened emergency recovery operation. In Delaware, I found myself living in a suburb and attending a school where I rarely encountered other Latinos. Whites were segregated in the suburbs and African Americans were concentrated in Wilmington's inner city. The population was clearly polarized and Latinos were too small a group to have much impact on race relations or social life in the region. At the time, state policy legislated forced busing to integrate students. In New York, I was surrounded by my Puerto Rican and Haitian family and interacted with non-Latino whites, African Americans, and a diverse group of ethnic and racial minorities at school and in my community. In Delaware, where I first faced a black-white racial binary, I was forced to make choices about where I belonged and my ethnoracial identity formation began. Delaware also prepared me for what awaited in Greater Orlando, where African Americans and non-Latino whites were polarized until Latino migration began to challenge the black-white racial binary that had prevailed for decades.

In middle school, students were constantly confused about my racial identity. The vast majority of students identified as African American or white, so they wanted to know if I was black or white. They understood categorization in terms of race; there was no discussion or awareness of other ethnic groups. Since there were practically no other Latino students in the school to be compared to, my classmates assumed that I was one of the "mixed" kids, the term used for students with one "black" and one "white" parent. Making sense of my race and ethnicity was confusing. My mother insisted that we were black because of our Haitian ancestry and would rattle off a list—Spanish, Italian, French, African, Caribbean—when I asked, "What am I?" My dad always stayed quiet about the subject of race. When I asked my father what his race is decades later, he responded, "Puerto Rican." His birth certificate says his race is white. These personal experiences made me interested in racial and ethnic identities, topics I explore in the book.

Researching Puerto Ricans

At the University of Delaware, I began to realize the extent of my placelessness. I lacked cultural knowledge about my heritage because I had spent so many years

in Delaware and I felt like I belonged nowhere. However, a small but active Latino and Latin American population was emerging and mobilizing on campus.
Under the guidance of a Colombian anthropologist, Juan Villamarín, I began
reading about Puerto Rican culture and identity in order to understand the history of the island and how identities are negotiated on the mainland. It was not
until I participated in the University of Delaware's Ronald McNair Program that
my personal explorations and confusing childhood experiences became actual
research, a process that continued over the next sixteen years.

I conducted a study of Spanish Harlem and compared the landscape to 4th
Street, the inner-city community in Wilmington, Delaware, where I found a
small concentration of Latinos who were mostly Puerto Rican. My primary research question about Spanish Harlem was simple: "How well does the community exemplify and portray Puerto Rican culture?" My second question was
an attempt to understand cultural preservation: "Is the community at risk of
becoming culturally extinct?" At the time, I did not have the vocabulary to
understand gentrification, urban revitalization, and assimilation processes in
Spanish Harlem. But I was struck by the landscape of Spanish Harlem and decided to photograph the many murals, flags, and other symbols of Latinization.
The Puerto Rican presence and influence on the community was undeniable.

I read *Divided Borders: Essays on Puerto Rican Identity* by Juan Flores and
was struck by his descriptions that explained the feeling the streets of Spanish
Harlem evoked for me: "Looking at New York, the Nuyorican [a Puerto Rican
from New York City] sees Puerto Rico, or at least the glimmering imprint of
another world to which vital connections have been struck."[1] He also talked
about the similarities between the Spanish-speaking neighborhoods of Los Angeles and New York, "where all of your senses inform you that you are in Latin
America, or that some section of Latin America has been transplanted to the
urban United States where it maintains itself energetically."[2] I was developing
a scholarly interest in Latino-concentrated communities and the migrants responsible for the Latinization of these areas.

My personal experiences and my subjectivities provided the motivation for
an academic career and for the research documented in this book, which is why
I have shared elements and anecdotes from my life. My interests all originate
with identity questions of a personal nature that went unanswered throughout
my early education and childhood. Conflicted notions of ethnic and racial identity, racialization, and otherness were my everyday reality and seem to have only
increased and become more complex with time. As I critically analyzed these

concepts in the book, I could not help but think of my own notions, definitions, and experiences. The anecdotes from my life are connected to the themes I explore in here. As a self-reflexive cultural anthropologist, I want to explain my subjectivities and positionality so my connections to the diasporic community are clear, in addition to the influences and experiences that drew me to this research in the first place.

From Spanish Harlem to Suburban Orlando

My immediate family always considered Spanish Harlem "home." My parents kept our building so we could come back on weekends and take a break from the isolation we felt in Delaware. How I looked forward to those special weekends with my Puerto Rican family, a time when I didn't have to question my identity because I was surrounded by people who looked like me. When I began my graduate education at Rutgers University, I decided to return to my childhood home to live. My brother soon followed, and I spent the next eight years living in Spanish Harlem. My initial intention was to conduct anthropological fieldwork in Spanish Harlem. I wanted to continue studying the Puerto Rican community that remained and the economic revitalization that was transforming the landscape I once knew.

It was clear that everything was changing. A mall had been built across the street from my building where an abandoned factory had once stood, a plethora of new luxury condos now occupied the vacant lots I once walked past, and a studio apartment started at $500,000. In contrast, my parents paid about $18,000 for their building back in 1977. Nearby 116th Street was now known as "Little Mexico" because of the influx of Mexican immigrants. However, another phenomenon was at work. United States Census Bureau data revealed an outmigration of Puerto Ricans from the island and from northeastern and midwestern cities such as New York and Chicago. Some of my family members were following national trends and moving South. A few settled in the suburbs of Greater Orlando. I decided I would document the process of Latinization that resulted from the influx of migrants to Orlando and identify how families preserved elements of their culture when they migrated to a new suburban destination in the American South.

Before I began the Florida research project, my only knowledge and memory of Greater Orlando derived from the vacations my family had taken to Orange Lake, a time-share resort my large extended family visited annually. For two weeks in August, my aunts, uncles, and cousins from New York City would pack into rented vans and make the drive to Orlando. We stayed at the time-share in Orange County or with my Tío Chichi and Titi Mindy, who lived in nearby Seminole County. Like so many other Puerto Rican families, Tío Chichi and Titi Mindy had moved from the Bronx to Greater Orlando in the late 1980s. I knew Orlando only as a tourist visiting the spaces of International Drive, the various theme parks, and downtown Orlando's bustling Church Street Station.

What caught my attention and appealed to me were the newspaper articles and the early academic scholarship about Orlando Puerto Ricans that pointed to a middle-class, suburban migration that differed from the earlier migrations to New York City. In 2005, anthropologist Jorge Duany and historian Felix Matos-Rodriguez participated in a Hispanic Summit sponsored by the Greater Orlando Chamber of Commerce to provide an assessment of the Puerto Rican population's historical background and current settlement patterns. In their policy report, they predicted that Puerto Ricans in Central Florida could follow a different path than previous waves of migration to the United States.[3] The earlier waves from Puerto Rico were characterized by a massive outmigration of working-class men and women who found low-wage employment in the industrial North. In Greater Orlando, the researchers noted the presence of a large number of well-educated professionals and managers, most of whom identified as white in the census; higher rates of homeownership and a stronger presence in suburban neighborhoods than in New York; and less isolation from non-Hispanic whites than in other settlements.[4] Additionally, Puerto Ricans have established numerous enterprises, primarily in retail trade, services, transportation, and communication. Duany concluded that "compared to earlier movements from Puerto Rico to New York or Chicago, the recent movement to Orlando is more strongly associated with efforts to maintain or achieve middle-class status."[5]

After reading social scientific texts that portrayed Puerto Ricans negatively as an undergraduate and graduate student, I had little desire to re-create similar representations by focusing on poor, marginal Puerto Ricans in Spanish Harlem who were being displaced due to urban revitalization and gentrification. I wanted to include the Puerto Rican middle class, the upwardly mobile professionals present in Greater Orlando, in my research study. I planned to move south to focus on migration to the suburb of Buenaventura Lakes, which housed a large number of Puerto Rican homeowners and was described as the largest Puerto Rican neighborhood in Central Florida, or "Little Puerto Rico." I planned to collect data about several questions: How were the social class identities and social status of Puerto Rican residents in Buenaventura Lakes articulated, interpreted, defended, and performed? How did the mortgage crisis impact them? Were they upwardly or downwardly mobile?

Two years of anthropological fieldwork led me in other, unanticipated directions. In addition to learning about social class identities and the development of the Buenaventura Lakes suburb, I ended up gathering data about migrant integration in the region, the process of Latinization, racial identities and racialization, and language ideologies. These are the themes I explore in the chapters of the book. Before I moved to Buenaventura Lakes, I was not focused on or fully aware of the local response to Latinos and the relationships (or lack of relationships) they had forged with non-Latino whites and blacks. African Americans were often invisible in the commercial and residential spaces I frequented and were a demographic minority. I only began to question race relations and relations among various ethnic groups more deliberately as the research design emerged and I learned more about the concerns of Latino and non-Latino white residents.

ACKNOWLEDGMENTS

I am grateful to the mentors, friends, editors, and reviewers who have inspired me and supported my research. Thanks to Ana Ramos-Zayas, Patricia Silver, Aldo Lauria-Santiago, Jorge Duany, Peter Guarnaccia, David Hughes, Hannah Gill, Marilyn Kerr, Randall Miller, Stanley Harrold, Kate Babbitt, and Sian Hunter for taking the time to read earlier drafts of the book and for providing invaluable feedback. Thanks also to the University of Mississippi Critical Race Studies Group and the participants in the Junior Faculty Working Group, who also provided feedback on chapters. I also thank the Center for Puerto Rican Studies (CENTRO) for providing financial support and valuable mentorship during the data analysis phase of my research.

Introduction

One of the most notable demographic shifts in recent decades is Latino migration to nontraditional destinations in the US South. These migrants are transforming the landscape, the soundscape, and cultural, political, and economic life of the communities where they settle. In 2010, the sheriff of Osceola County, Florida, a Central Florida native, told me that "we went from a rural county to mouse house, SeaWorld, and the large influx of Hispanics. Businesses had to adapt." His office had to change. "We needed Spanish speakers, receptionists, employees, and officers that could not only communicate with the people verbally, but that also understood their culture." In his mind, the tourist industry and the migration of Hispanics were the two forces that were transforming the county. He was right.

Latino Orlando: Suburban Transformation and Racial Conflict documents the migration and settlement of Puerto Ricans and other Latinos in Greater Orlando; identifies the transformations these migrants have made to the landscape and the soundscape and the local response; and examines how race- and class-based identities are constructed and represented. The book focuses on Greater Orlando, which consists of the four counties—Orange, Osceola, Lake, and Seminole—that are part of the Orlando-Kissimmee-Sanford, Florida, Metropolitan Statistical Area.[1] This book draws attention to the Puerto Rican population, diversifying the academic literature on the Latino migrants who have settled in the South.

Latino settlement patterns in the United States have historically been associated with urban life. Migrations to gateway cities—such as the movement of Mexicans and Central Americans to Los Angeles, Houston, and Dallas; Puerto Ricans to Chicago and New York City; and Cubans to Miami—are well documented.[2]

Since the mid-1990s, however, Latinos have dispersed in massive numbers, moving primarily to rural towns and large cities in the South and Midwest and to smaller cities in the Northeast. Added to rapid growth in particular rural areas is a shift toward the suburbs, areas where people have "little to no recollection of experience with Latino/a newcomers."[3] These settlements are much smaller than the communities in traditional gateway cities such as East Harlem. However, rapid population growth and community formation has increased the visibility of migrants in new destinations. It is speed, not size, that is defining Latino population growth in southern states. Table 0.1 shows the demographic changes in the ten states with the fastest-growing Latino population in the period 1990 to 2010, most of which are in the South. Table 0.2 shows the more modest change in the traditional settlement states in that same period.

Table 0.1. US states with fastest-growing Latino population, 1990–2000

	1990	2000	% Change	2010	% Change
North Carolina	76,726	378,963	+394	800,120	+111
Arkansas	19,876	86,866	+337	186,050	+114
Georgia	108,922	435,227	+300	853,689	+96
Tennessee	32,741	123,838	+278	290,059	+134
Nevada	124,419	393,970	+217	716,501	+82
South Carolina	30,551	95,076	+211	235,682	+148
Alabama	24,629	75,830	+208	185,602	+145
Kentucky	21,984	59,939	+173	132,836	+122
Minnesota	53,884	143,382	+166	250,258	+75
Nebraska	36,969	94,425	+155	167,405	+77
US total	22,354,059	35,305,818	+58	50,477,54	+43

Source: Social Explorer, "Census 1990 [Hispanic or Latino by Specific Origin, Alabama, Arkansas, Georgia, Kentucky, Minnesota]"; Social Explorer, "Census 1990 [Hispanic or Latino by Specific Origin, Nebraska, Nevada, North Carolina, South Carolina, Tennessee]"; "Census 2000 [Hispanic or Latino by Specific Origin, Alabama, Arkansas, Georgia, Kentucky, Minnesota]"; Social Explorer, "Census 2000 [Hispanic or Latino by Specific Origin, Nebraska, Nevada, North Carolina, South Carolina, Tennessee]"; "Census 2010 [Hispanic or Latino by Specific Origin, Alabama, Arkansas, Georgia, Kentucky, Minnesota]"; Social Explorer, "Census 2010 [Hispanic or Latino by Specific Origin, Nebraska, Nevada, North Carolina, South Carolina, Tennessee]."

Table 0.2. Change in the Latino population in traditional settlement states, 1990–2010

	1990	2000	% Change	2010	% Change
California	7,687,938	10,966,556	+43	14,013,719	+28
New York	2,214,026	2,867,583	+30	3,416,922	+19
Illinois	904,446	1,530,262	+69	2,027,578	+32
New Jersey	739,861	1,117,191	+51	1,555,144	+39

Source: Social Explorer, "Census 1990 [Hispanic Origin by Race, California, Illinois, New Jersey, New York]"; Social Explorer, "Census 2000 [Hispanic Origin by Race, California, Illinois, New Jersey, New York]"; Social Explorer, "Census 2010 [Hispanic Origin by Race, California, Illinois, New Jersey, New York]."

An examination of the geography and demography of new destinations in the South reveals that the initial population of Latino migrants who settled in nontraditional places tended to be born outside the United States. They also tended to be young, undocumented Mexicans who were attracted to employment opportunities.[4] Yet "in less than two decades, this migration has transitioned from a seasonal, agricultural migration of young *mexicanos* into Georgia and North Carolina to a regional settlement of Latino families from other US cities and towns, all parts of Mexico, [Puerto Rico] and much of Central and South America."[5] These shifts in migration patterns were driven by political unrest in Central America, southern employers' recruitment of labor, environmental disasters, the desire of immigrants to start over, and economic crises across Latin America.[6]

Focusing on the "new geography of Mexican migration," Vanesa Ribas points to the legalization programs of the Immigration Reform and Control Act of 1986, which "regularized the status of several million Mexicans." Many of these "legalized migrants left traditional settlement areas in the Southwest and California and made their way East and South in search of new opportunity structures."[7] Other factors drew millions of Latino/a migrants to the Southeast, such as "the militarization of the U.S.-Mexico border" and "the increasingly adverse context of reception in traditional destinations."[8] Latino migrants were drawn to the Southeast because of economic restructuring and the rise of the manufacturing, construction, and meat-processing industries.

I am not suggesting that Latino migration to the Southeast region is a completely new phenomenon. Particular places in the Southeast, such as rural Osceola County, have become new or maturing destinations of migration. Anthropologist Angela Stuesse points out that the "intensity and breadth of this growing trend is novel."[9] Historian Julie Weise argues that "when Latino migration to the U.S. South became visible seemingly out of nowhere in the 1990s, the newness of this 'Nuevo' South went unquestioned."[10] Weise, who recovers and compares earlier histories by documenting the experiences of Mexicans in New Orleans, the Mississippi Delta, the Arkansas Delta, rural southern Georgia, and the exurbs of Greater Charlotte found that a few southern planters "briefly recruited Mexicans in 1904, but in that and other cases the early immigrant experiments were short-lived."[11] Through her comparisons, Weise is able to show that the experiences of migrants were place specific. The Mexican cotton pickers who were recruited to the Mississippi Delta during the 1920s did not enjoy the same privileges as the Latin American population of New Orleans due to their social class position. In New Orleans, the Latin American population numbered 1,400 in 1930 and included middle-class professionals, agents for shipping companies, and refugees from the Mexican Revolution who "secured their place among European-style white immigrants."[12]

Despite the fact that Latinos have been in the Southeast since at least the early twentieth century, their presence has remained marginal in the collective memory of local populations. Many of the early migrants were largely transitory seasonal laborers who did not choose to remain in states such as Mississippi or Arkansas to form large, visible communities. Anthropologist Patricia Silver also notes the transitory nature of the earliest Puerto Rican migrants to Central Florida: "The stories we heard combine to give evidence of a diverse, and perhaps largely transient, Puerto Rican population in Central Florida in these earliest decades."[13]

However, the Puerto Rican population in Greater Orlando is no longer transient. In the 1990s, Orange and Osceola, two of the four counties in Greater Orlando, became the leading destinations for Puerto Rican migrants and Florida displaced New Jersey as the state with the second-largest concentration of Puerto Ricans.[14] The exodus of Puerto Ricans to Florida has intensified since Hurricane Maria wrought such destruction in 2017.

A History of Migration and the Puerto Ricanization of Florida

From the early sixteenth century to the late nineteenth century, Puerto Rico was a Spanish colony. The United States annexed the island in 1898, after the Spanish-American War. The Jones Act of 1917 decreed that individuals born on the island of Puerto Rico are US citizens and can move freely between the island and the states. The US occupation of Puerto Rico led to political and economic dependency and Puerto Ricans began leaving the island in the early twentieth century. Prior to the US takeover, Puerto Rico had a diverse agricultural economy that produced tobacco, coffee, and sugar for export. However, US investments increased the island's dependency on sugar. When the sugar industry declined in the 1920s, Puerto Rico experienced high unemployment and poverty and Puerto Ricans began migrating to the United States; the 1930 US census counted over 50,000 Puerto Ricans living in the United States.[15]

An identifiable Puerto Rican enclave developed in New York City during the early decades of the twentieth century. In the 1940s and 1950s, Puerto Rican migration intensified. This second wave of migration, traditionally referred to as the Puerto Rican Great Migration, coincided with Operation Bootstrap, a development strategy Puerto Rico launched in 1947, and led to the growth of the New York communities and to new settlements in New Jersey, Connecticut, Illinois, Ohio, and Pennsylvania.[16] Operation Bootstrap transformed Puerto Rico's agrarian economy into an industrial one. Thousands of Puerto Ricans left the rural areas of Puerto Rico to look for factory work in the cities. Many of these workers later migrated to the states when development programs failed to reduce unemployment.[17] During the period of rapid industrialization in the states that began in the late 1940s, almost one-third of Puerto Rico's population left for the inner-city areas of New York.[18] According to sociologist William Vélez, "The postwar economy was booming in the US mainland and there was a need for workers in the industrial and agricultural sectors, as well as in the growing service sector."[19] Thus, government and private agencies recruited Puerto Rican laborers.[20]

The last period of migration, from 1965 to the present, is marked by dispersion to other areas of the United States and greater fluctuations in net migration. During this period, which is characterized by "revolving-door migration," Puerto Ricans migrated to the mainland but also returned to the island.[21] In more recent years, the rate of growth of the Puerto Rican population in New York, New Jersey, and Illinois, the states with the largest numbers of Puerto

Ricans, decreased. By 2008, the Puerto Rican population was concentrated in Florida and the New York metropolitan area.[22] A number of factors explain the waves of Puerto Ricans from the island to the states during the various phases of migration, including overpopulation (the result of improved medical care that led to high birth rates and low death rates), displaced and surplus labor (the result of the island's economic transformations), low wages and high unemployment rates in Puerto Rico, the greater participation of Puerto Ricans in the armed forces, and the recruitment practices of US companies. The Migration Division Office of New York facilitated migration and the Puerto Rican government's communications with the Federal Aviation Administration led to the approval of low rates for air transportation.[23] Some of these same factors are connected to the influx of Puerto Ricans to Greater Orlando.

The Puerto Rican population in Osceola County grew from 417 in 1980 to 72,986 in 2010. In Orange County, the number of Puerto Ricans increased from 6,682 in 1980 to 149,457 in 2010. Tables 0.3 and 0.4 illustrate the population growth of Puerto Ricans and other Latinos in these two counties, where Puerto Ricans from both the island and the states arrived with different experiences of racialization and minoritization. According to the American Community Survey for 2006–2010, 45 percent of the migrants who arrived from outside Florida came from Puerto Rico and 55 percent came from another US state.[24] The majority of migrants from the states (68 percent) moved to Florida from the Northeast.[25]

According to anthropologists Jorge Duany and Patricia Silver, "the main points of residential agglomeration of Puerto Ricans are in the eastern section

Table 0.3. Latino and Puerto Rican population growth in Osceola County, 1980–2010

	1980	1990	2000	2010
Total population	49,287	104,836	172,493	268,685
Latino population	1,089	9,974	50,727	122,146
Puerto Rican population	417	8,122	30,728	72,986

Source: Social Explorer, "Census 1980 [Osceola County, Florida]"; Social Explorer, "Census 1990 [Osceola County, Florida]"; Social Explorer, "Census 2000 [Osceola County, Florida]"; Social Explorer, "Census 2010 [Osceola County, Florida]."

Table 0.4. Latino and Puerto Rican population growth in Orange County, 1980–2010

	1980	1990	2000	2010
Total Population	471,016	662,085	896,344	1,145,956
Latino population	19,726	49,540	168,361	308,244
Puerto Rican population	6,682	34,223	86,583	149,457

Source: "Census 1980 [Orange County, Florida]"; "Census 1990 [Orange County, Florida]"; "Census 2000 [Orange County, Florida]"; "Census 2010 [Orange County, Florida]."

of the city of Orlando, the south central area of the city, Kissimmee (in Osceola County), and Poinciana (in Polk County)."[26] They describe Buenaventura Lakes in Osceola County as the largest Puerto Rican neighborhood in Central Florida. Puerto Ricans were primarily concentrated in suburban housing subdivisions, a settlement pattern that differs from the urban enclaves Puerto Ricans migrated to in the traditional gateway cities. "They look very different from the so-called 'barrios' in the Northern cities," Duany said of Puerto Rican neighborhoods in Central Florida. "These are primarily suburban housing subdivisions. . . . Many are able to buy good houses in quality neighborhoods."[27] The settlement patterns of Puerto Ricans in the area "reflects to some degree the range of Puerto Rican socio-economic status."[28] The locally accepted reputation, according to Patricia Silver and William Vélez, "is that Osceola County, with its lower cost of living and proximity to the theme parks, is home to theme-park workers, middle-income families, and many retirees on fixed incomes. Retirees also live in Orange County, which has a somewhat higher cost of living and is home to a greater number of white-collar workers. Seminole County, the wealthiest of the Central Florida counties and known for its better schools, is also home to Puerto Rican white-collar workers."[29]

Greater Orlando, especially Osceola County, was a new destination for Puerto Rican migrants not only because of its southern location far from the traditional gateway cities of Chicago, Philadelphia, and New York but also because of the suburban spaces some members of the population occupied. The Puerto Rican migration contained both professional migrants and low-paid service sector workers, but it was much more than simply a labor migration. Over the years, multiple factors fueled and sustained the migration of

Puerto Ricans to Greater Orlando, transforming the region into an emerging gateway. Migrants were drawn to Greater Orlando by real estate marketing and the opportunities for homeownership, labor recruitment, powerful social networks or chain migration, and the perception that Florida offered a better quality of life because of its tropicality and the opportunities for upward mobility.[30] The push factors included the social consequences of Puerto Rico's economic instability, such as increasing crime rates and the fear of violence. The recession of 1973–1974 also impacted both Puerto Rico and the mainland and "helped push Puerto Ricans . . . to look for new options."[31] As the Puerto Rican economy worsened, outmigration increased.[32] Deindustrialization in the US North in the 1970s led to layoffs of Puerto Rican workers and contributed to outmigration to other regions of the country. This book focuses on the suburban locations where Puerto Ricans settled and formed communities. I examine how these communities and the real estate in them became valued and why suburbs where Puerto Ricans are concentrated developed a negative reputation because of structural factors that changed how the areas are perceived.

Methodology

This work is based on ethnographic fieldwork conducted in Greater Orlando from June 2010 to August 2012 and one month of preliminary research during the summer of 2007. During that time, I lived with several Latino migrants, both documented and undocumented, in four suburban locations. These Venezuelan, Colombian, Guatemalan, and Puerto Rican families rented out spare rooms and sometimes even couches and spaces on the floor to family members, friends, co-workers, and to unthreatening strangers—like me—to supplement their income and cover the monthly mortgage payment in an underground housing market. In addition to participant observation in houses, I collected data at local cultural, political, and business-related events and in churches, schools, and commercial establishments. Thus, the book combines traditional anthropological methods with analysis of printed and online sources. I use data gathered through participant observation, informal and semi-structured interviews, census data, newspaper archives, and Internet blogs and forums.

When I began my preliminary fieldwork in July 2007, I lived in the house of my uncle and aunt in Longwood, Florida (Seminole County), which is part of Greater Orlando. They lived in a quiet suburb where I observed very few

Latinos. Their house was about 45 minutes away from Buenaventura Lakes, the suburb where I would begin fieldwork in 2010. My uncle and aunt had moved to Seminole County in the 1980s after selling their house in the Bronx. They arranged my first interviews with people in their network of Puerto Rican friends and family living in Greater Orlando. My aunt was working as a teachers' aide in the Orange County public school system and had a large network of Latino friends and colleagues. In 2010, I resumed interviews after moving to the suburb of Buenaventura Lakes. I recruited interviewees using snowball sampling. In Buenaventura Lakes and the other suburbs where I lived, I started interviews with my roommates and then asked them to help me identify other individuals from their network of family and friends. I also recruited interviewees by emailing about and attending community events, churches, and meetings sponsored by business networking organizations that serve the Latino population.

During each of my interviews, I asked a broad range of questions. The content was shaped by who I was speaking with and what information I was looking for. For instance, when I interviewed longtime residents of Buenaventura Lakes, I asked about the character of the community and its residents, the transformations they had witnessed, and their experiences of living and working in Greater Orlando. In contrast, when I interviewed a local teacher, I was more interested in the ways students from different ethnic and racial backgrounds interacted in the classroom and how the schools have adapted to the influx of Spanish-speaking students. Of the thirty semi-structured interviews I conducted in 2007 and in 2010–2012, eleven were with Puerto Ricans who were born on the island, five were with Puerto Ricans who had moved from New York, nine were with non-Latino whites, four were with other Latinos, and one was with a person who identified as Jamaican American. Twelve of the interviews were with females and eighteen were with males. Names and identifying characteristics have been changed or withheld to protect the identity of the interviewees and informants who only agreed to participate in the study anonymously.

One of the greatest challenges was identifying African American residents who were willing to participate in an interview, since I met very few African Americans in the locations where I conducted fieldwork. The majority of the people I interacted with were Latinos or non-Latino whites. The Latino informants I was closest with identified their race as white, although I did interact with Afro-Latinos during informal interviews. I conducted no interviews with African Americans and that is a limitation of this research. This book largely focuses on the perspectives of Latinos and non-Latino whites regarding the impacts of Latinization, responses to demographic change, and the relationships between those two cultural groups.

In addition to semi-structured interviews, I gathered data through informal interviews, my preferred method of data collection.[33] Anthropologists often gather information by developing rapport with their research subjects, especially through participant observation and by engaging in personal interactions over an extended period. I often found that the most revealing information was shared during informal conversations. For instance, when I invited local residents to a restaurant for lunch, we often spent hours chatting about our lives. Since I am interested in how race- and class-based identities and distinctions surface during everyday interactions, a question-and-answer format was not always as revealing. One day as I was driving through Buenaventura Lakes with Paz, who was renting me a room in her large, luxurious Hunters Creek home in Orange County, I noticed that she was looking at the houses we passed. She commented that the Latino people who live in Buenaventura Lakes are very poor. The conversation that resulted from that comment enabled us to discuss the class-based distinctions that are manifested in homes and are evident in the community's landscape aesthetics. She was making sense of her environment and the people in it spontaneously as we drove. A formal, structured interview would not have given me access to this type of data.

To complement the data I gathered through traditional ethnographic fieldwork, I looked at newspaper articles and online commentary. I turned to newspaper articles published in the *Orlando Sentinel* in the period April 1985 to May 2010 to chronicle the increasing presence of Latinos in Greater Orlando and learn how this migration was presented to the public. I decided to stop collecting, coding, and analyzing newspaper articles so I could focus on interviews and participant observation when I relocated to Greater Orlando to begin fieldwork in May 2010. I was interested in how non-Latino whites reacted to the influx of Latinos and the region's Latinization, and the media's representation of this population provided insight into race and ethnic relations during the early days of the migration.

I also use material from *Hispanosphere*, an *Orlando Sentinel* blog that began in 2008 to report on Hispanic affairs in the region. The posts initially came from journalist Victor Manuel Ramos and later from Jeannette Rivera-Lyles. The blog was in operation for only a few years. I analyzed both the content of the blog posts and the responses to them to identify how ideologies about race, social class, language, and migration circulate on the Internet. The *Hispanosphere* blog created a public forum by providing a section where readers could comment on the story being covered. The comments section gives us a glimpse into the mind and perceptions of individual readers. While attention to blogs and Internet forums does not follow traditional ethnographic research methods, as anthropologist Tom Boellstorff points out, "to demand that ethnographic research always incorporate meeting residents in the actual world for 'context' presumes that virtual worlds [and other virtual spaces] are not themselves contexts."[34]

I also used archived transcripts from City-data.com, a website that includes statistical data and public forums about US cities and suburbs. On this website, I was able to locate archived conversations about Buenaventura Lakes, Osceola County, and other communities throughout Greater Orlando. I have not edited the text from the virtual conversations for grammar or spelling. Participants in these conversations discussed the character and desirability of communities in Greater Orlando and discussed the Latino populations in the area. Digital media are particularly important for examining the process of racialization and how racial anger is circulated since users are able to voice their ideas and feelings about Americanness, Latino migration, and belonging without revealing their identity and suffering the consequences of being labeled as a racist or politically incorrect. These sources enabled me to capture the voices of over 200 people.

The Racialization of Latinos

In this book, I use the terms Latino and Hispanic interchangeably, although there is a difference. The term Hispanic, which the United States Census Bureau created in the 1970s, refers to all people in the United States whose ancestry is from one or more Spanish-speaking countries. The term thus emphasizes language, not geographic origin, as the identifying factor. The term Latino, which originated within the community, instead focuses on geography and is "an attempt to embrace all Latin American nationalities, including those which neither have ties to Spain nor are necessarily Spanish-dominant groups," such as Brazilians and various indigenous groups living in Latin America.[35] During fieldwork, my Hispanic interviewees and informants used the term Hispanic more frequently and used the term Anglo to refer to non-Hispanic whites.

Where do Hispanics fit in the dominant US racial classification system and how have they been counted in the census and other official documents? According to federal standards mandated by the US Office of Management and Budget's 1997 *Revisions to the Standards for the Classification of Federal Data on Race and Ethnicity*, "race and ethnicity (Hispanic origin) are separate and distinct concepts."[36] Thus, the US government defines Latinos or Hispanics as an ethnic group whose members can be of any race. However, the indicators that the US Census Bureau uses to count members of the Hispanic population have evolved over time. A brief overview of the government's classification scheme is necessary to understand the complexity and ambiguity surrounding racial and ethnic identifiers. From 1850 to 1920, census takers coded Mexicans as white in the census. During that period, indicators such as country of birth, parents' birthplace, mother tongue, and Spanish surname were used to determine if someone was of "Spanish origin." In 1930, the census included a separate category in the race question for "Mexican." However, Mexican American civil rights groups, supported by the Mexican government, demanded that this designation be changed.[37] In 1940, the census bureau once again began defining Mexicans as white.

Later migrations from the Hispanic Caribbean made it necessary to begin counting Puerto Ricans and Cubans. However, the census bureau did not begin publishing information on people of Puerto Rican descent until the 1950s, when Puerto Ricans began migrating to the United States in massive numbers. In 1970, the bureau began collecting information about people of Cuban birth or parentage as a result of the exodus that followed the Cuban Revolution in 1959. During that historical moment, as Latin American and Caribbean migration was increasing and civil rights activism was on the rise, new federal legislation was introduced that required accurate statistical documentation of the disadvantages of minority groups.[38] Additionally, there was growing concern about census undercounts and organizations were demanding better data about their groups.

In 1976, Congress passed Public Law 94-311, the only law in the country's history that mandates that the government collect, analyze, and publish data about a specific ethnic group, "Americans of Spanish origin or descent," and defines the population to be enumerated.[39] The law noted that "more than twelve million Americans identify themselves as being of Spanish-speaking background and trace their origin or descent from Mexico, Puerto Rico, Cuba, Central and South America, and other Spanish-speaking countries"; that a "large number" of them "suffer from racial, social, economic, and political discrimination and are denied the basic opportunities that they deserve as American citizens"; and that an "accurate determination of the urgent and special needs of Americans of Spanish origin and descent" was needed to improve their economic and social status.[40]

As a result, the law mandated a government-wide program to collect, analyze, and publish data on people of "Hispanic origin." The Office of Management and Budget administers this work. The law considered Hispanics to be an ethnic group. "Ethnicity" can be defined as "a principle of social classification used to create groups based on selected cultural features such as language, religion, or dress."[41] In contrast, race refers to "social groupings that allegedly reflect biological differences."[42] In 1977, the US congress required the implementation of Directive 15, which required the census bureau to classify people using four racial classifications (American Indian or Alaskan Native, Asian or Pacific Islander, Black, and White) and two ethnic backgrounds ("of Hispanic origin" and "not of Hispanic origin). The data collected in the census was to be aggregated using these categories, and the Hispanic identifier that is used today emerged from these political conversations.

The term racialization, which I use throughout the book, signifies the extension of racial meanings to a previously unclassified relationship, social practice, or group.[43] In Buenaventura Lakes and the larger Osceola County area, for instance, more Latinos identified as white than any other category in the 2010 census, even though online commenters racialized Latinos as nonwhite with remarks such as, "Like I said before there are a lot of Spanish and people [of] that kind of race that live there so ur kids will feel kinda awkward being the small amount of white kids that live and go to school there. . . . I'm just basing this on if ur kids are white."[44] At the time of my fieldwork in 2010, 46.0 percent of Latinos in Buenaventura Lakes identified themselves as white in the census, 15.9 percent as some other race, 3.5 percent as two or more races, and 3.6 percent as black or African American.[45] In Osceola County, 30.6 percent of Latinos identified as white, 9.8 percent identified as some other race, 2.4 percent as two or more races, and 2.2 percent as black or African American.[46]

Sociologist Rubén Rumbaut points out that in a variety of contexts—in the media, in government publications, in academic studies, and in popular usage—the terms Hispanic and Latino are used alongside racial categories such as "Black," "Asian," or "White," resulting in a "*de facto* racialization of the former."[47] My discussion of the racialization of Puerto Ricans and other Latinos "refers to their definition as a 'racial' group and the denigration of their alleged physical and cultural characteristics such as phenotype, language, or number of children. Their racialization also entails their incorporation into a white-created and white-imposed racial hierarchy and continuum, now centuries old, with white Americans at the very top and black Americans at the very bottom."[48] In

Buenaventura Lakes, the widespread use of the Spanish language, as opposed to phenotype or number of children, is central to the racialization process. Common ideas about using Spanish reveal how linguistic practices are racialized along with other practices, physical characteristics, and signifiers of identity.

According to Elizabeth Aranda, "Race in twentieth-century America is not limited to phenotype; the social construction of race involves ethnic and global dimensions such as national origin, culture, language, religion, the historical relationship between colonial powers and their political subjects, and race."[49] She terms the racialization of ethnicity "ethnoracism." Thus, the social construction of race "consists of the interlocking effects of these ethnoracial, cultural, historical, and geopolitical factors."[50] Aranda argues that as a result, "the definition of racism must be expanded to include how ethnicity, culture, national origin, and the historical relationship between minorities' country of origin and the country of settlement . . . have been racialized."[51] I focus on both the blatant and covert ways ethnoracism manifests in response to the Latinization of Orlando in order to explore how racial and nonracial discrimination (such as anti-immigrant sentiments and xenophobia) become entangled.

Other changes have followed Directive 15 that dramatically altered how racial and ethnic data is collected in the United States. Until 1980, census takers collected data by interviewing household heads face to face.[52] During that time period, interviewers classified Puerto Ricans, Mexicans, and other Hispanics as white unless they thought differently. In 1980, for the first time ever, people had the opportunity to classify themselves because census data was collected through mail-in questionnaires. In 2000, another option was introduced: respondents could select one or more racial designations. For the first time in its history, the bureau was acknowledging that people could belong to more than one racial group, altering the "long-standing hypodescent or one-drop rule."[53]

The introduction of the Hispanic identifier and the shift to self-reporting has revealed widespread variation in racial reporting and has led to confusion, since these government-constructed designations are often inconsistent with how individuals describe themselves. For the 2010 census, a new instruction was added that immediately preceded the questions on Hispanics' origin and race. It read "For this census, Hispanic origins are not races because in the federal statistical system, Hispanic origin is considered to be a separate concept from race." However, this added instruction "did not preclude individuals from self-identifying their race as 'Latino,' 'Mexican,' 'Puerto Rican,' 'Salvadoran,' or other national origins or ethnicities; in fact, many did so."[54] People ask "why no

Hispanic/Latino category exists among the race and national origin questions" and point out that the majority of Hispanics are a mix of races.[55] Before the 2000 census, a proposal was advanced to include "Hispanic" as a category in the race question but "no Hispanic group enthusiastically endorsed this proposal" and it was abandoned.[56] In a January 26, 2018 press release, the census bureau announced that the 2020 census would continue to collect data about race and ethnicity using a two-question format.[57] The press release announced that "The Census Bureau will not include a combined question format for collecting Hispanic origin and race, or a separate Middle Eastern or North African category on the census form."[58]

Rubén Rumbaut reveals the significance of place in the formation of a white racial identity. He points out that in the 2000 census, Hispanics in Florida were far more likely to identify as white than Hispanics in New York and New Jersey. In Florida, 67 percent of Puerto Ricans reported that they were white, compared to only 45 percent in New York and New Jersey. Ninety-two percent of Cubans in Florida identified themselves as white, compared to 73 percent of Cubans elsewhere. For Dominicans, the percentages were 46 percent in Florida compared to 20 percent in other parts of the country, for Colombians it was 78 and 46 percent, and for Peruvians and Ecuadorians, it was 74 and 43 percent. This geographical influence on racial formations can be attributed to the "more rigid racial boundaries and 'racial frame' developed in the former Confederate states of Texas and Florida" that can lead to "defensive assertions of whiteness when racial status is ambiguous."[59] Patricia Silver highlights the importance of place in the formation of a white racial identity. In her research in Orlando, she points out that racial memories often differ for Puerto Ricans who arrive directly from the island and those from the diaspora.[60] Puerto Ricans who have lived in US diasporic communities "are more likely to see themselves as non-white, while Puerto Ricans from the island often use the term 'Nuyorican' as a disparaging racial and class marker for diasporic Puerto Ricans."[61] Hence, Puerto Ricans from the island and those from other states arrive in Florida with different experiences of racialization and minoritization.

Organization of the Book

In chapter 1, I document the development and marketing of the suburb of Buenaventura Lakes, which became an enclave where Puerto Ricans had concentrated by the time I began my fieldwork in 2010. My archival research dates back to the 1970s, when an international consortium of real estate developers—the so-called Mexican Millionaires—used real estate marketing strategies and images of luxurious country-club living to attract Puerto Ricans to the new suburb. The developers promised affordable prices and high-end amenities, which originally included a country club and two golf courses; in effect, they promised the American Dream. They were instrumental in fostering an awareness of Central Florida's real estate opportunities and directing the flow of mainland and island Puerto Ricans toward Greater Orlando instead of toward traditional gateway cities.

Chapter 2 traces the long-term impact of Latino—especially Puerto Rican—migration to Greater Orlando and documents the resulting Latinization to show the cultural and political influence of these newcomers on the landscape and the soundscape. The chapter identifies the various ways non-Latino whites talked about, understood, and sometimes contested demographic changes. Encounters in the public spaces of schools, supermarkets, banks, and other commercial establishments were the most contentious. The non-Latino whites I interviewed reacted strongly to the changes that altered their daily lives as the community became increasingly polarized by linguistic differences. While ethnic and racial groups did collaborate, power struggles and moments of contestation existed.

Chapter 2 connects Latinization to the formation of a white racial consciousness in Greater Orlando and explores how language ideologies get mapped onto race, ethnicity, and geographies.[62] The chapter explores dimensions of language ideologies as they relate to perceptions of the nature, identity, and character of Latino people; struggles for power; and the constructed separation between Spanish and English. Latino migration and the widespread use of Spanish led non-Latino whites to reaffirm and strategically deploy a white racial identity. They also perceived and racialized the Spanish language, Latino people, and the places Latinos occupy as nonwhite. In Greater Orlando, language ideologies and linguistic polarization impacted racial identities, the incorporation of Latinos into the area, and the non-Latino white response to Latino migrants.

In Chapter 3, I examine the recent decline of the Buenaventura Lakes suburb as a middle-class neighborhood and explore how language use and language ideologies impact residential patterns. The efforts of Landstar Homes, the developers of Buenaventura Lakes, made the suburb the epicenter of the growing Puerto Rican community and transformed Osceola County. However, as the population of Latino migrants increased, the reputation and desirability of Buenaventura Lakes decreased. The chapter describes the conversations that intertwine ideas about whether Buenaventura Lakes is "nice" with the racial and ethnic identities of its residents, their language use, and their perceived class position. Both residents and nonresidents and Latinos and non-Latinos increasingly perceived Buenaventura Lakes, once a community for country-club living and affordable luxury, as a ghetto or a slum.

Chapter 4 focuses on the upwardly mobile Latino entrepreneurs and professionals in Greater Orlando and the exclusive spaces they are creating by participating in business networking organizations. The chapter documents how Puerto Ricans and other Latinos articulate class distinctions and describe their own class identities in order to reveal the inequalities within the Latino community. Their responses highlight the significance of cultural capital for access to the resources Latino gatekeepers police. However, non-elite members of the Latino community recognize and contest the inequalities and the exclusivity of these organizations in the virtual spaces of online forums and blogs.

In chapter 5, I focus on the homes where I conducted fieldwork. The foreclosure crisis that began before my fieldwork in 2010 increasingly forced homeowners and other low-wage workers to find creative solutions to their financial instability. One of the mechanisms for paying housing costs and earning extra income is participating in the encargado system, an underground real estate economy in which homeowners rent rooms to friends, family members, and strangers. At times these rooms are unadvertised and information is conveyed verbally. In other instances, signs on a front lawn advertise available rooms, a family places an advertisement in one of the local newspapers, or the information is placed on a website such as Craigslist. In these situations, a single-family home is transformed into a multifamily dwelling. When multiple unrelated individuals live collectively under one roof, family-type bonds form, although communal living may also include infighting and disagreements over lack of privacy, the management of the home, and finances. In these settings, the tenants' rights are unclear and they are unprotected. As a result, renters move from house to house until they find an optimal environment in this housing system.

This book adds to our knowledge of the Puerto Rican and Latino experience in Greater Orlando and of the impact of migration on both the incoming and receiving populations. *Latino Orlando* reveals how demographic changes transform both the landscape and the soundscape, frequently causing tension between Latinos and non-Latinos. Language ideologies that oppose the use of Spanish lead to the racialization of Latino people and Latino-concentrated communities, which ultimately contributes to residential segregation and the growth of ethnic enclaves in suburbia. However, tensions also exist within the Latino population. Thus, the book also draws attention to a neglected segment of the Latino population, the upwardly mobile professionals and entrepreneurs who are trying to distinguish themselves based on their class position and avoid the marginalization earlier waves of migrants to gateway cities experienced.

1

Buenaventura Lakes

Acapulco Drive, Mexicali Way, Oaxaca Lane, Guadalajara Drive, Vera Cruz Avenue . . . Strange, I thought, as I passed street after street with names derived from places in Mexico. Buenaventura Lakes is a suburb in Osceola County, Florida, with a concentration of Puerto Ricans. In 2010, county officials described the county, which occupies 1,506 square miles in Greater Orlando, as the "gateway to Walt Disney World and other Central Florida attractions."[1] The northwest quadrant includes the communities of Poinciana, Buenaventura Lakes, and Celebration (a planned development the Walt Disney Company created); this is where most of the county's population lives. Ranch lands, undeveloped prairies, woods, and marshes dominate the southern and eastern quadrants of the county, although several small towns are located there also. This chapter documents the development and marketing of Buenaventura Lakes in order to understand how the suburb became an enclave with a concentration of Puerto Ricans.

In the summer of 2010, I was searching for a place to live in Buenaventura Lakes while I conducted research. I was determined to live with the residents of the Buenaventura Lakes community as I researched the mass migration of Puerto Ricans to that area. I found an advertisement on Craigslist for a room to rent in a three-bedroom, two-bathroom house in the suburb. The room was $380 per month, including utilities and Internet. Although the description expressed a preference for a male tenant, I called to inquire about the room anyway. A young man named Marco answered the phone. He said that he was the owner of the house, that the room was still available, and that I could stop by to look at it. Before I went to the house, I drove around the large subdivision to get a feel for the area. I passed a nursery school, a library, a fire station, a community center, a church, a park, a soccer field, baseball fields, basketball and tennis courts, and a track. Strip malls with supermarkets, restaurants, banks, and other commercial establishments surrounded the subdivision at the north and south entrances of Buenaventura Boulevard, the street that cuts through the development.

I then drove to a one-story pink house with a one-car garage and a pickup truck in the driveway. Marco, who was 28, had migrated from Venezuela over eleven years earlier. He answered the door and kindly invited me into the house. I noticed the tile on the immaculately clean floors. The first room I entered, the living room, was bare, but a kitchen table and chairs were in front of the sliding doors that led to a fenced-in backyard. Marco explained that he had recently divorced a Puerto Rican woman and was still in the process of "rebuilding."

At one point the house was in foreclosure, but he had been able to continue making mortgage payments by renting out two rooms. He owned another house in rural Osceola County approximately forty-five minutes away that he also rented out. "This is my business," he remarked on several occasions. The second house, he said, was just an investment that had also been in danger of being foreclosed at one point. Marco told me that he had paid around $110,000 for the house in Buenaventura Lakes and pulled out his cell phone to show me the property on Zillow, a real estate appraisal app. Because of the mortgage crisis in 2008, the worth of his house had declined. The house was now worth $80,000, but because he had refinanced, he owed around $130,000. He was under water; he owed more than the house was worth. For $500 a month, he mentioned, I could rent his master bedroom, which had a private bathroom. "Nah," I replied to the offer. "Tempting! But I'm on a budget." I chose the alternative, sharing a bathroom with Pedro, the 19-year-old undocumented hotel worker from Mexico who rented the other room. On June 10, 2010, I moved in and started preparing for what would be two years of ethnographic fieldwork in Greater Orlando.

After living in Buenaventura Lakes for several months with Pedro and Marco, I moved to Hunter's Creek in Orange County to rent a room in the house of Paz, Marco's girlfriend. I later rented a room in another house in Osceola County with Martha, one of Pedro's co-workers. I was a participant in the encargado system Sarah Mahler has written about in the context of Long Island, where Salvadorians who live in the suburbs rent or buy a house or apartment and then rent space within the home to several people.[2] This system of renting rooms is a way for workers in a low-wage economy to pay the mortgage or the rent and pocket a little extra. Through my participation in the encargado system, I built rapport with the individuals who would become my closest informants and got a glimpse into their daily lives.

Even though I had gone to Buenaventura Lakes to learn about the Puerto Rican population, I ended up living with Venezuelan, Colombian, Guatemalan, and Mexican immigrants during my two years of fieldwork. This expanded the scope of my research from Puerto Ricans to the larger Latino population, although Puerto Ricans continued to be my focus. Marco, Paz, and Martha welcomed me into their homes and helped me experience, observe, and document everyday social and cultural life in the area. Still, I wondered about the history of Buenaventura Lakes and how the community where I first lived during my fieldwork became a suburb with one of the largest concentrations of Puerto Ricans in Central Florida, a receiving community for the Puerto Rican population. I wanted to dig deeper into the community's history. I began my research with newspaper articles and interviews to learn more about Buenaventura Lakes and its residents in the hope of understanding the Latinization that was taking place in parts of Greater Orlando.

The Puerto Rican Pioneers

Many of the longtime residents of Buenaventura Lakes remember a time when orange groves dominated the landscapes and cows outnumbered people. The landscape of the area began to change in the mid-1990s, when a massive influx of Puerto Ricans took place and an ethnic enclave began to form. For the pioneers who arrived in the early 1980s, the promise of a "Landstar Lifestyle"—affordable luxury and country-club living—was enough to entice them to leave the hustle and bustle of New York or Puerto Rico for an undeveloped, secluded paradise in the South. Marco told me that "Boricuas Viven Libres [Puerto Ricans Live Free] is the nickname for Buenaventura Lakes" because of its large concentration of Puerto Ricans. In Osceola County, the Puerto Rican population grew from 0.8 percent of the total population in 1980 to 7.5 percent in 1990, 17.8 percent in 2000, and 27.2 percent in 2010.[3] The proportion of Latino residents in Osceola County, including Puerto Ricans, increased from 2.2 percent in 1980 to 11.9 percent in 1990, 29.4 percent in 2000, and 45.5 percent in 2010.[4] The growth in Buenaventura Lakes followed the same pattern. The American Community Survey 5-Year Estimates for 2012–2016 reported that 23,444, or 74.2 percent, of the 31,588 residents in Buenaventura Lakes identified as Latino and 15,592, or 49.4 percent, of the population identified as Puerto Rican.[5] Non-Latino whites numbered 4,004, or 12.7 percent, and non-Latino blacks and African Americans numbered 2,828, or 9 percent.

I knew that Puerto Ricans were the demographic majority based on the data, but I did not yet understand why so many migrants from the Northeast and Puerto Rico had ended up in this community years ago. So I turned to the *Orlando Sentinel* to identify reports about Puerto Ricans, other Latinos, and the Buenaventura Lakes community. The articles, which were published from April 1985 to May 2010, documented the experiences of the earliest residents of Buenaventura Lakes. One article was about a Puerto Rican public school teacher from the South Bronx who had moved to Buenaventura Lakes in 1984 with her husband and children. In 1991, she told a reporter why she had migrated to Greater Orlando: "'I lived in the South Bronx. . . . I needed to get [my children] out of there. Then you see ads about the sunshine, the attractions, the beach—all the wonderful things you want to hear about when you're in the inner city."[6]

When I met this teacher at a local conference and arranged an interview twenty years after the *Orlando Sentinel* article was published, she explained that "Central Florida was the right place and Disney was here." She learned about Buenaventura Lakes two years before her own move, when her mother had decided to purchase a house and relocate to the suburb from New York. Initially, her mother had considered moving to Miami, but one day in 1982 while browsing through the *New York Post*, she had spotted a Landstar Homes advertisement that promised to pay for the hotel expenses and meals of potential buyers. "Ask any of the old-timers why they picked Buenaventura Lakes and they will say it's because of that *New York Post* advertisement," she said. "They advertised in Puerto Rico as well." She recalled that when she and her mother first visited Buenaventura Lakes in 1982, there was only one house, a single entrance to the neighborhood, and a gas station. Two years later, when she relocated permanently, her family was the only Latino family on the street and there were very few Latinos elsewhere. She told me that for the first five years there was no Latino presence, although more Latinos came in the 1990s. The former Bronx schoolteacher remained in Buenaventura Lakes for nineteen years.

In 1985, a maintenance worker from New York City's East River public housing projects also discovered Buenaventura Lakes. Germán Colón was browsing through the *New York Times* when he saw an advertisement for beautiful model homes in a new community named Poinciana. The advertisement highlighted the community's proximity to Disney World, where Colón was planning a vacation. His co-workers commissioned Colón to check out the property for them. However, when he got there, he found only swampland. On the way back to his hotel he discovered a secluded area where new houses were being constructed: Buenaventura Lakes. Landstar Homes promised "a country lifestyle in a palm-tree paradise," a sales pitch that persuaded Colón to secure a $52,000 home with a $500 deposit. He later convinced some of his colleagues at the East River housing projects to do the same and the following year he and his wife retired in Buenaventura Lakes. In 2006, at the age of 76, he was still living in that same house. An *Orlando Sentinel* article recounts how he and his wife "escape[d] New York for Central Florida retirement."[7]

Like Germán, Osvaldo Berberena was on vacation in Orlando when he discovered Buenaventura Lakes. Berberena, a religious man, told an *Orlando Sentinel* reporter that he prayed for a sign that would help him decide if he and his wife should stay. That sign came, quite literally, when he passed a billboard on Interstate 4 advertising affordable homes. "We weren't desperate in Puerto Rico. We had jobs, but we felt we were not going anywhere," said Osvaldo, who was 50 years old in 1986.[8] In the mid-1980s, Berberena founded the Centro Cristiano Génesis church in his home. His congregation eventually grew so large that they needed a 20,000-square-foot hall to accommodate the hundreds of members. As I continued reading newspaper articles and began doing interviews, I recognized a pattern that existed in my own family. Individuals were following their already established friends and family to Florida, revealing the significance of chain migration in this wave of Puerto Rican migration.

Nine-year-old Eliza Rodríguez and her family were also among the Puerto Rican pioneers who arrived in Buenaventura Lakes during the early 1980s. They came from Puerto Rico and moved to Royal Palm Drive. Eliza told me that they were "looking for a better life." During our 2011 interview, she mentioned the challenges she faced. When she began attending school, she quickly realized there were no other Latinos in her classrooms. School was very challenging for her since she was still learning English. By the time she was in the eighth grade, however, "there were lots of Latinos and everything started to change. Puerto Ricans came all of a sudden! They took over!" Eliza spent many years in Buenaventura Lakes before moving to Orlando and later to the nearby city of St. Cloud. In 2003, she purchased a villa in Buenaventura Lakes that was located behind the bus stop where she caught her school bus as a child. She was renting it out. "If you ever find out the reason so many Puerto Ricans came," she asked, "please explain it to me." What follows, Eliza, is your explanation . . .

The Mexican Millionaires

One evening in June 2010, I entered the Applebee's restaurant in Buenaventura Lakes, sat at the bar, took out my computer, and started writing fieldnotes before an employee came over to take my order. At the moment, I did not realize that I was sitting next to a longtime resident of Buenaventura Lakes who would be instrumental in my research. Curious about what I was writing late in the evening, he introduced himself. Michael Smith was a non-Hispanic white retiree in his 60s. He was a former businessman and a conservative Republican who followed local politics intently. He had relocated to Buenaventura Lakes from the Midwest. After I briefly explained my research, he offered to introduce me to some of his contacts. You must speak with John Wright, a former Landstar executive, he said. He also offered to arrange interviews with the county sheriff and one of the four county commissioners. They were all his friends. I took down Michael's contact information and before the end of the week he had the interviews scheduled. What I did not realize was that he planned to be present for each interview, which was ideal since the men would often go into a more detailed conversation about the topics and questions I asked. They did so in a conversational format as they discussed everything from the development of Buenaventura Lakes to crime and local politics.

My first interview, with John Wright, provided the most history about the community. I learned about the so-called Mexican millionaires who were responsible for the Buenaventura Lakes development. According to a newspaper article from his personal archive, "An international consortium of real estate interests, headed by the leading development firms of Mexico [began] work on a new community. . . . The principals [were] Gaspar Rivera Torres, Mexico's largest land developer; Bernardo Eckstein and Manolo Stern, partners in the second largest land development firm in that country, and Juan Aja Gómez."[9] The article described Rivera Torres as one of the wealthiest men in Mexico. His net worth exceeded $100 million and he had over seventy-eight projects under way in Mexico. He and the other principal investors sold more than 5,000 homes and 5,000 home sites annually. Stanley S. Lane, the president of the marketing and management firm Diversified Property Services Inc., represented the developers. Lane, a resident of Miami who was a retired New York manufacturer, had invested in the Mexican enterprises for over twenty years.

John Wright, vice-president and project manager, had been involved from the time the group had purchased the land. He had worked on everything from

FORT LAUDERDALE NEWS
and SUN-SENTINEL

Fort Lauderdale News and Sun-Sentinel, Saturday, November 23, 1974

Mexican Millionaires Build City

Mickey Mouse Gets Neighbors

ORLANDO — An international consortium of real estate interests, headed by the leading land development firms of Mexico, has begun work on a new community near here designed for 25,000 to 30,000 residents.

The project is Buenaventura Lakes in nearby Osceola County, covering 2,350 acres with two miles of frontage along the Florida Turnpike ten miles south of Orlando. The entrance to the property is four minutes from Turnpike exit 65, the Disney World exit.

Plans provide for 6,000 single-family residents and the same number of multi-family dwellings, plus about 100 acres for commercial development. The density will be less than five units to the acre.

Preparation of the site already is well advanced, with streets and utilities going in, and a nine-hole executive-length golf course being made ready for play in the spring. A site has been set aside for a championship course to be built later.

The project received planned unit development (PUD) zoning in March 1973 from Osceola County authorities, who have established stringent regulations for land use and have strongly resisted uncontrolled growth. The site is 15 miles from Disney World.

The region is a rural one with many recreational lakes and streams. Osceola County still has less than 40,000 residents. The town of Kissimmee is three miles from the project.

Both homes and homesites are being offered, it was announced by Stanley S. Lane, a Miami resident who represents the developers, but no "sight unseen" sales of land will be permitted.

The principals are Gaspar Rivera Torres, Mexico's largest land developer; Bernardo Eckstein and Manolo Stern, partners in the second largest land development firm in that country, and Juan Aja Gomez. Together, the principals sell about 5,000 homes and the same number of homesites annually in their Mexican enterprises, with combined sales of about $100 million, Lane said.

Rivera is one of the wealthiest men in Mexico, with a personal net worth exceeding $100 million, Lane said. Currently, he has 78 projects in progress in Mexico.

Lane is a retired New York manufacturer who has been an investor in the principals' Mexican enterprises for more than 20 years. He is president of Diversified Property Services Inc., a marketing and management firm representing the landowners.

Line announced that Kenneth Schwartz of Hollywood has been appointed director of sales, and Gerald Petriccione has been named manager of real estate broker relations.

Homesite prices will begin at $7,875 for a 7,500-square-foot lot, Lane said, and homes will begin at $32,500, including the lot. Seven models are under construction on the site, along with a golf clubhouse. Total sales will amount to nearly $500 million, Lane calculated.

In the design of the community are 65 acres of lakes and streams, park sites, church and school sites. The clubhouse with its swimming pools, tennis courts, and other facilities, will represent an investment of some $900,000. Around $5,000,000 has currently been expended to begin development. The average elevation of the site is 78 feet above sea level.

Phases one and two of the development plan are being carried out simultaneously, Lane said. These encompass about 2,200 residences, both single and multi-family. The seven models range in size from two to four bedrooms, with two and three baths.

Every purchaser will be required to visit the property before contracting to buy.

"We're going to insist that he come to the project and stand on the site — on his own lot, if possible," Schwartz said.

Figure 1.1. "Mickey Mouse Gets Neighbors," *Fort Lauderdale News and Sun-Sentinel*, November 23, 1974.

sewer and water management to sales and marketing. In 1984, Landstar created, owned, and managed Osceola Utilities, Inc., a water and sewer service for more than 20,000 residents in north Osceola County.[10] Wright mentioned that he had been in Miami when he first met Stanley Lane and the group he was accompanying from Mexico. According to Wright, the Mexican land developers were trying to move their investments to the United States because they were afraid that the Mexican government would "nationalize."[11] Wright and Lane had looked at a 40,000-acre tract of land near the present-day city of Poinciana and decided it was too large. Instead, they purchased a smaller site three miles from the city of Kissimmee in 1972. The name Buenaventura Lakes, like many of the street names (Toluca Drive, Merida Drive, and Campeche Lane), is derived from a Mexican place name. During our interview, Wright recounted the day the group chose the development's name. He and his colleagues were throwing darts

at a map in the office and it landed on San Buenaventura, a city in the municipality of Buenaventura, one of the sixty-seven municipalities in the Mexican state
of Chihuahua. Since the term Buenaventura means "good adventure," "good
luck," or "fortune," they thought the name fitting for their newest project.[12]

Landstar Homes at Buenaventura Lakes Country Club

In March 1973, the Buenaventura Lakes project received planned unit development zoning from the Osceola County authorities who regulated land use.[13]
Planned unit development refers to both a type of development and a regulatory
process. For Buenaventura Lakes, it meant that the developers could use the
land they had purchased for a variety of functions, including housing, recre-
ation, and commercial centers, thereby creating a diversified subdivision. The
community was planned on 2,350 acres of land with a design that included 65
acres of lakes and streams, 100 acres of commercial development, 6,000 single-
family residences, 6,000 multifamily dwellings, park sites, church and school
sites, a clubhouse, a swimming pool, tennis courts, an executive golf course, and
a championship golf course.

According to Wright, the initial plan for Landstar was to develop and sell lots,
not homes, through the Real Estate Corporation of Florida. In 1974, the price
of home sites started at $7,875 for a 7,500-square-foot lot.[14] However, Florida
land sales dried up for three to five years and the developers needed a new sales
strategy. During the swampland scandals of the 1960s and 1970s, buyers had
purchased land sight unseen only to find that their property was under water
and thus impossible to build on. This had created skepticism among potential buyers of land in Florida. Wright met with a successful seller of retirement
homes for advice. Soon after, the Landstar developers decided to transition from
land sales under the Real Estate Corporation of Florida to home sales with the
newly created Landstar Homes Corporation.[15]

By May 1978, Landstar Homes at Buenaventura Lakes Country Club, as it
was called back then, opened its first sales outlet in the New York area and built
its first house.[16] The community opened the next month. The original models were constructed across from the Walk-N-Sticks Executive Golf Course.
Landstar hired an architect to design the homes with a Spanish influence. The
corporation's advertisements touted "affordable luxury" and "country club living." The sales office at 1184 Hempstead Turnpike in Uniondale, Long Island,
displayed photos, floor plans, and other information about the homes, which

initially started at less than $27,000 for two bedrooms and one bathroom.[17] The introductory prices included a one-year membership to the Buenaventura Lakes Country Club, which had a golf course, a swimming pool, tennis courts, a game room, and a restaurant. Membership was exclusive; only residents of Buenaventura Lakes could join the club.

Through their advertisements, the developers of Buenaventura Lakes were presenting an opportunity for upward social mobility. This appealed to and attracted buyers. The advertisements claimed that Buenaventura Lakes was "more than a place to live," but the community actually embodied a lifestyle, the "Landstar Lifestyle," that presumably was different from what could be found in the South Bronx or in the East River housing projects of New York. With their affordable prices and high-end amenities, Landstar Homes could offer the American Dream: a single-family house with a garage and a front lawn and a life filled with beauty and luxury in a landscape surrounded by golf courses, a country club, lakes, and much more, the advertisements said.

According to Lee Kingerly, who handled publicity for Landstar Homes and worked for a Chicago-based marketing firm, many of the individuals who initially moved into the development were local. However, in December 1978, Landstar began a major marketing push in Ohio, Pennsylvania, New Jersey, Boston, Chicago, and New York. Kingerly says that two groups of people were considering southern living at the time: retirees who were living on a fixed income and individuals who were trying to escape the "arctic wasteland of northern cities." However, sales in the North continued to be affected by the caution the old Florida land schemes had engendered. "'We get questions all the time about whether or not we really have all the things we say we do,'" said Kingerly.[18] To allay buyers' fears, Landstar maintained permanent reservations at a Howard Johnson Motel and offered potential buyers a free stay so they could visit the site. These offers—travel, accommodations, and sometimes Disney tickets— motivated potential buyers to travel from the Northeast to view the new development. One of my interviewees mentioned that a similar sales strategy was used in nearby Poinciana, another Latino-concentrated suburb, where developers covered the cost of hotels, flights, ground transportation, and even food for a weekend in order to sell homes.

In the late 1980s, Landstar extended its reach to a global market. The company began heavy marketing efforts in Western Europe and established brokerage offices in London and West Germany. Eduardo Stern, vice-president of marketing, said that Puerto Ricans accounted for about 7 percent of the company's total sales in 1988 and anticipated that British buyers would account for 12 percent. Additionally, German buyers were investing in commercial real estate in Buenaventura Lakes.[19] During a 1989 interview, a Landstar sales director reported that approximately 35 percent of the sales in Buenaventura Lakes and a sister development, Meadow Woods, were to people from the Northeast and that extensive sales promotions were still under way in the Midwest and overseas.[20]

The suburb's population reflected the success of Landstar's national and international marketing efforts. In May 1991, the *Orlando Sentinel* described a street in Buenaventura Lakes that housed "New Yoricans, Italians, Cubans, Filipinos, Indians, Jamaicans, Colombians, Brits, Anglos, and Puerto Ricans."[21] Until the 1990s, former Landstar employee Wright lived on Bit Court, a street in Buenaventura Lakes that contains large, luxurious homes on lots with a minimum of one acre. The neighbor on his left was from Holland, a neighbor on the right was from Venezuela, and a Cuban family and a British family occupied the other houses on the cul-de-sac. In 1994, the *Orlando Sentinel* reported that "Landstar retains sales representatives as far away as England, Germany, France and Kuwait."[22] In the early 1990s, Landstar continued to appeal to a global market. However, that eventually changed; in 2006, Buenaventura Lakes was described as "a former British enclave."[23]

What sparked Landstar's interest in Puerto Rico's real estate market and how did Puerto Ricans get introduced to Buenaventura Lakes? Fortunately, I stumbled upon a former Landstar employee one afternoon in 2007 while I was scouting the area before deciding on a research field site. As I drove down East Osceola Parkway on the outskirts of the subdivision, I noticed a new gated community of town homes with a for-sale sign outside the gate that indicated that several units were available. The gate was unlocked because the sales office was open, so I entered and was greeted by a young woman. When I told her I was researching Buenaventura Lakes and the surrounding community, she pointed me in the direction of María García, a former Landstar employee who was willing to be interviewed.

According to María, who began working with Landstar's water and sewer systems in 1979 before the company transitioned to sales, Landstar did not begin selling homes to Puerto Ricans on the island until the mid-1980s. However, I caught a glimpse of a 1976 newsletter written in Spanish at a time when the first house was not yet built. More than one of my informants who were longtime residents of Buenaventura Lakes purchased their house from a Latin American national who was using their property as a vacation home. María also mentioned earlier marketing efforts in Venezuela, Mexico, and Colombia. Thus, there was a class transition as the community shifted from people who owned Buenaventura Lakes properties as vacation homes to people who owned a home as their primary residence. During our interview, María briefly mentioned a social network that fostered Landstar's initial interest in Puerto Rico's real estate market but did not say more.[24]

However, a 1993 article in the *San Juan Star* described the connection in detail. The partnership began when Gloria Berman, president and cofounder of the Trans Indies Realty and Investment Corporation (TIRI), one of Puerto Rico's largest and most prestigious real estate firms, had a meeting with "a representative of Landstar Homes" and Carlos Romero-Barceló Jr. The article reported that "Romero was more than just another real estate lawyer. Besides being a friend of Berman's, he is the son of the former Puerto Rico governor who is now the island's resident commissioner and delegate to Congress."[25] Before agreeing to work with Landstar to market the homes to Puerto Rican buyers, however, Berman, aware of previous Florida land scandals, visited the project site. According to journalist María Picó, "Florida property scams are not new to Puerto Rico . . . and during the 1970s, Puerto Rico residents were major buyers of worthless Florida land."[26] Unlike some developers, Landstar Homes made good on their promises. "I really loved Orlando," Berman said. "I felt it was the perfect place for families from Puerto Rico to buy. . . . The way of life was the way of life we had had in Puerto Rico 25 years ago and had lost because of crime."[27]

Soon after Berman's visit, TIRI began marketing Buenaventura Lakes to Puerto Ricans on the island. TIRI assumed complete responsibility for the sale of Buenaventura Lakes properties, which included finding financing for prospective buyers and developing advertising campaigns. TIRI held seminars, showed videos of the property and surrounding area, and sponsored trips to Central Florida for prospective buyers. María García told me that as part of TIRI's recruitment strategy on the island, the company offered $500 toward a plane ticket and three nights in a hotel. A bus or van would pick up the prospective buyers at the airport and transport them to the site. For its efforts, TIRI was entitled to a 3.5 percent commission, which was later decreased to 2.5 percent. Berman claimed that TIRI created an awareness of the Greater Orlando real estate market among Puerto Ricans, "'and Puerto Rico being a small island and a family-oriented community, once you begin to get the word out, it ripples through the community.'"[28] The initial response was enthusiastic and reached a critical mass in 1988, when TIRI sold more than 200 homes.[29]

At the same time, Landstar was successfully marketing homes in Puerto Rican communities in New York City and Chicago. Landstar's success was clear: annual Orlando-area home sales grew from $2 million in 1986 to more than $11 million in 1988. One article attributes the influx of Puerto Ricans in the 1990s to Landstar's marketing strategy and its conversion of cow pastures and sod farms to a city-sized subdivision.[30] According to Estrella Schoene, Landstar's regional sales and marketing director in the 1990s, the San Juan office sold 200 single-family homes in 1993, which constituted one-third of the company's Orlando-area business that year.[31] Then, in September 1993, Landstar decided to open its own offices on the island and eliminated TIRI as its exclusive broker.

Landstar continued to dominate real estate sales in Puerto Rico of property in Greater Orlando and by the end of 1993 it had sold almost all of the Buenaventura Lakes properties. The company began focusing its marketing efforts on Meadow Woods, its newest development in Orange County. Sales eventually slowed down in the international market and by 1994 Landstar's only full sales office outside Florida was in San Juan. Landstar was extremely successful in Puerto Rico and became the "island market's dominant player for Central Florida real estate."[32]

Landstar's successful marketing efforts transformed Osceola County and encouraged other Central Florida developers to target prospective buyers in Puerto Rico. Before Landstar's arrival in the area, other real estate companies had sold property in Greater Orlando and had targeted Puerto Rican buyers, albeit on a smaller scale. Through an oral history project, anthropologist Patricia Silver learned that "Puerto Ricans have been present in Central Florida for at least sixty years as migrant agricultural workers, as military personnel or family of military personnel, as real estate investors, as engineers recruited to the Kennedy Space Center, and as visitors or workers in the tourism industry."[33] Silver's oral history interviews document the experiences of Puerto Ricans who served in the US armed forces, especially at the McCoy Air Base (now Orlando International Airport), and moved to the Orlando area in the 1940s and 1950s.[34] In the 1950s and 1960s, Florida land developers targeted military populations. In 1952, for example, when construction of the Monterey subdivision began in Orange County, the first residents, who included Puerto Ricans, were members of the US Air Force. Street names in the Monterey development were Spanish: Hermosa Street, San Juan Boulevard, Santiago Avenue, and Coquina Court.[35]

Silver documents the history of developers who targeted Puerto Ricans for settlement in the South.[36] In 1954, the Mackle brothers founded the General Development Corporation, which targeted middle-class buyers.[37] As part of their marketing strategy, the brothers sent sales agents to various locations around the world. In 1962, the company's Latin American director traveled to Puerto Rico to recruit a local representative. In the 1960s, "hundreds of islanders acquired properties near the Orlando area, particularly in the city of Deltona in Volusia County."[38] The opening of Walt Disney World in 1971 intensified real estate development in Greater Orlando. However, the vast surge in migration that transformed Greater Orlando from a new destination into a gateway for thousands of Puerto Ricans did not begin until the mid-1980s.[39]

From 1985 to 1993, more than 200 brokers obtained licenses in Puerto Rico to sell Florida property.[40] The focus of real estate marketing in Puerto Rico shifted from Tampa and Miami to Greater Orlando.[41] In 1991, for instance, Lizette Pagán "traded the Caribbean breezes of Ponce, a city on Puerto Rico's southern coast, for the wider opportunities of what was then the mostly rural, wooded area of Osceola County called Buenaventura Lakes." She had no idea how many other Latinos would soon follow: "It has changed drastically. . . . I didn't know so many other Puerto Ricans would come. This is like back in the years after [World War II] when everyone went to New York."[42]

It became common for the Sunday edition of *El Nuevo Día*, San Juan's main Spanish-language newspaper, to contain a dozen ads for Central Florida properties and only two or three ads that mentioned Miami or Tampa. In the fall of 2003, one developer, Pulte Homes, sponsored a free seminar in San Juan in order to sell homes in an area that stretched from Hunter's Creek and Metro West to Casselberry, Tuscawilla, and Lake Mary, a distance of about thirty miles. Lilian Castaneda, a Puerto Rican broker who operated out of Isla Verde, east of San Juan, sold ninety refurbished condominium villas priced from $55,000 to $70,000 in Las Palmas at Sand Lake, about twelve miles from Buenaventura Lakes. According to Castaneda, most of the Puerto Ricans who purchased the properties were not yet ready to move and wanted to purchase vacation homes they could rent to other Puerto Ricans. Smaller developers held similar seminars for various types of properties, including town houses and reconditioned apartments that sold for as low as $22,000. The shifting of the location where Puerto Ricans were concentrated from Miami to Greater Orlando continued. In 1990, 44 percent of Florida-based Puerto Ricans lived in the Miami Metropolitan Statistical Area, but by 2008, that percentage had decreased to 27 percent.[43]

Throughout the years, Puerto Ricans were drawn to Buenaventura Lakes by the hope of finding a better quality of life for an affordable price. Landstar Homes, according to employee Alonso, gave sales pitches to family members that emphasized the better education and health care that was available in Central Florida.[44] For many, Orlando was a promised land and a good place to raise children and find some peace and quiet. According to Tom Martínez, former president of the Asociación Borinqueña de Florida Central, Orlando has a lot of appeal for Puerto Ricans who hope to leave behind a crowded island with high levels of unemployment and enjoy the undeveloped landscape: "It's like a promised land here. . . . We've got all this wide-open space."[45]

According to Estrella Schoene, Puerto Rican home buyers found the Greater Orlando market attractive because of the price: "You don't get anything for your money in Puerto Rico—that's the problem."[46] Furthermore, while home prices throughout Greater Orlando increased dramatically during the housing bubble of the millennium—the median home price in Buenaventura Lakes increased 67 percent from 2004 to 2006—home prices in Buenaventura Lakes remained far lower than in most parts of Orange, Seminole, and Lake Counties. When Daniel Ortiz, a 53-year-old auto technician from Puerto Rico, started looking

Figure 1.2. Buenaventura Lakes home, 2010. Photograph by Simone Delerme.

for a new home in Osceola County that would accommodate his wheelchair-bound daughter and teenage son, the houses on the market were too expensive or too far from his Orlando workplace. "Prices have gone crazy here," Ortiz told a reporter.[47] However, he was able to purchase a four-bedroom, lakeside home for less than $250,000 in Buenaventura Lakes. Ortiz told a journalist that his home was close to his mother, his aunt, and two cousins who also lived in Buenaventura Lakes.

Buenaventura Lakes remained attractive to potential home buyers because of its affordability, it proximity to shopping, the nearby tourist attractions, and jobs in the hospitality industry. Real estate agents such as Jorge Moreno, the sales associate for Coldwell Bank who helped Ortiz find his home, reminded potential buyers that "you can get to Disney in less than 20 minutes."[48] According to Norman Quintero, a realtor who markets homes to Puerto Ricans, Buenaventura Lakes is a "Puerto Rican Levittown . . . one of the first places to which Puerto Ricans come before exploring the rest of Orlando."[49] In the years that followed the development of the Buenaventura Lakes suburb, an ethnic enclave formed, expanded, and contributed to the Latinization and globalization of Greater Orlando. In 2006, an *Orlando Sentinel* journalist wrote that "in the New Orlando of 2020, nearly one in every three residents will be Hispanic—with a new generation on the rise. In Buenaventura Lakes and the surrounding neighborhoods, a slice of that New Orlando already exists."[50]

Although some of the people I interviewed remembered a time when the landscape was dominated by cattle and orange groves, an international consortium of real estate interests fostered global connections to develop a suburban subdivision with a concentration of Latinos, primarily Puerto Rican. The "Mexican millionaires" who developed Buenaventura Lakes are partly responsible for the globalization of Osceola County because of the connections they fostered between Mexico, Puerto Rico, Florida, and a number of other countries. Despite previous swampland scandals, the promise of a "Landstar lifestyle" lured Puerto Ricans from the island and from diasporic communities to Buenaventura Lakes. For some Puerto Ricans from the historic gateway cities, this was an opportunity to become homeowners and embrace a new suburban lifestyle in what was described as "the most identifiable core of the Central Florida Puerto Rican community."[51]

2

Latinization, Landscapes, and Soundscapes

On June 28, 2007, I sat in the audience of the Orlando Hispanic Summit at the Hyatt hotel at Orlando International Airport. As the mayor of Orlando, Buddy Dyer, addressed the audience, he used the term "melting pot" to describe the region. Although he was not sure about the actual number of Puerto Ricans in Central Florida ("400,000, 500,000 or 600,000"), he was quite certain that the number was larger than it was in San Juan, Puerto Rico. When Henry Cisneros (the former mayor of San Antonio and the secretary of housing and urban development during the Clinton administration) took the stage, he reminded the audience that "it is easy to overlook the Hispanic community with the tourism in the region, but the Hispanicization of the country cannot be overlooked!" Of all the things we see as changes, he remarked (naming globalization, biotechnology, and other large trends), the Latinization of US society will be one of the influences.

This chapter documents the cultural, political, and economic transformations that resulted from Puerto Ricans' migration to Greater Orlando. The growth of Latino-owned businesses created a distinct cultural landscape and political victories put Puerto Rican leaders in a position of power. Some non-Latino whites reacted negatively to the linguistic changes that resulted from the presence of so many Spanish speakers. In this chapter, I examine how linguistic practices are racialized along with other practices, physical characteristics, and signifiers of identity. The Latinization of the region made some of my non-Latino white informants increasingly aware of their white racial identity and led to the development of a stronger white racial consciousness as they became a "minority" for the first time in their lives. This led to claims of reverse discrimination and white victimization and to the articulation of ideologies that purported to be color blind.

The process of the Latinization of Orlando began long before I arrived in Buenaventura Lakes in 2010. Latinization is "a power process of social differentiation and cultural production" based on the notions of a shared Latino/a or Hispanic identity and latinidad, "an analytical concept that signifies a category of identification, familiarity, and affinity . . . [and] identifies a subject position (the state of being Latino/a in a given discursive space)."[1] Thus, Latinization refers to specific social practices and particular sites where discourses of latinidad are produced and performed over time and in space.

As early as 1986, the *Orlando Sentinel* was reporting on the surge in the Puerto Rican population, describing the change as more of a "trickle than a downpour."[2] The article explained that because of poor economic conditions in Puerto Rico in the 1980s, the ratio of Puerto Ricans to Cubans in Orlando had changed. In 1987, journalist Peter Francese asked his readers, "Habla usted Español?" and advised "you might want to think about taking some lessons," pointing out that the number of Hispanics in the United States was increasing rapidly. In Osceola County, these demographic changes were most visible in the public school system, where the number of Hispanic students had grown exponentially since 1975.[3] Some Osceola County schools were sending report cards home in Spanish and English, a foreshadowing of the linguistic changes to come. By 1989, the *Orlando Sentinel* was using the term Latinization to describe how businesses and schools were adapting to the "quiet" migration of Latinos:

> Evidence of the increased Latinization is staggering. Five years ago, there were no interstate moving companies serving only Hispanics. Today there are five Hispanic-owned companies that bring several thousand Latins every year from Puerto Rico, New York and Chicago. Hispanics can do business in Spanish at 24-hour, bilingual teller machines. School-age children can attend classes taught in Spanish. Last year, a Puerto Rican opened the area's first store to sell only Spanish-language books.[4]

In 1989, Renee Mitchell reported that 180 Hispanic doctors and 40 Hispanic lawyers were operating in the region, which had 56 Spanish-language churches.[5] There was talk of opening a Hispanic bank and in August that year, a group of Hispanic businessmen started a low-power television station that aired programs in Spanish. That same month, in an article entitled "They Are Citizens," the paper noted that the demographic changes could affect all Orlando residents and that the flow of migrants would increase in the coming years:

They are popping up everywhere, and we can expect thousands more to migrate to Central Florida in the next year. In one way or another, all of us will be affected by the sudden change in our community's ethnic and social makeup. Our public schools already are experiencing the onslaught of so many new non-English speaking students. Surprisingly, most teachers (including university professors), journalists, civil servants, the clergy, politicians and other taxpayers know little about them.[6]

The economic power of Puerto Rican newcomers did not go unnoticed. In February 1989, journalist Oscar Suris reported that "advertisers and marketers are focusing on a niche market they feel can no longer be ignored—Hispanics—and Central Florida is a target." The "buzz in Orlando" was that "Puerto Ricans are setting their sights on the city beautiful, and the market was poised to respond."[7]

Some business owners made a conscious effort to appeal to the growing population of Latino consumers. For example, Pueblo International Inc., a Puerto Rican company, had brought an Xtra Super grocery store to Winter Park and was making plans to open another in Seminole County later that year. Although Pueblo's executives were targeting "the general population" in their marketing campaign, they acknowledged that that would change as the demographics changed. By 1989, Florsheim Shoe Company was embracing the demographic changes by adding Spanish-language capabilities to its Florsheim Express shops, video terminals that enabled customers to select and purchase their shoes electronically.

By 1991, Osceola County had experienced one of the nation's largest Hispanic population surges since 1980: the Hispanic population had increased by an astounding 815 percent. Jorge Del Pinal, ethnic and Hispanic statistics chief for the US Census Bureau, commented, "I can't think of any place where I've seen that. . . . That's an amazing figure."[8] That year, Greg Grafal told the *Orlando Sentinel* that the adjustment from Puerto Rico had not been difficult when he, his wife Isabel, and their two children had followed family members to Osceola County in 1985. He explained that Osceola offered many familiar conveniences: "You can buy Spanish products here. . . . We can go to the stores and buy seasonings we need."[9] The Blockbuster Video store in Buenaventura Lakes, for instance, was the only one of twenty-seven Central Florida stores that offered American-made movies dubbed or subtitled in Spanish. "Almost everything we get in English, we get in Spanish. . . . We felt it was something we needed," said store manager Scott Koob.[10]

In 1994, journalist Michael McLeod visited Gateway High School, five miles outside Buenaventura Lakes. When the school had first opened in 1986, non-Hispanic whites made up the vast majority of students. However, as school enrollment grew, the percentages shifted. By 1993, Hispanics were the new majority. McLeod wrote that "the Latin influence at the school is obvious from homeroom to homecoming" and described a typical day at Gateway:

When the morning papers carried news of a South American drug czar death, a Nicaraguan student gave her class an impromptu lecture about cartels. When Miss Vasquez' English literature class decided to perform scenes from Shakespeare this year, Lady Macbeth had a Spanish accent. When the students in a Spanish literature class had a discussion about the macho image in Hispanic cultures, the macho image made a personal appearance: Some of the more tradition-bound Hispanic boys loudly disagreed with some of the more progressive, independent-thinking Hispanic girls in the class.[11]

That year, journalist Nancy Feigenbaum wrote that Central Florida "is a more festive place than it used to be—to a Hispanic beat."[12] Six Hispanic festivals were planned for that year. "The growth of festivals hints at the vitality of the Puerto Rican community in Central Florida. . . . Festivals are a strong Puerto Rican tradition commemorating anything from historic anniversaries to patron saints' days and the opening of a new park on the Caribbean U.S. commonwealth." Sprint/United Telephone-Florida used these festivals in its strategy for targeting the growing Hispanic market through its support and presence.

In 1995, Puerto Rican businessman Benito Fernandez and a group of investors bought the Orlando Vacation Resort on US Highway 27 south of Clermont, in the Disney area. Fernández, the husband of New York state senator Nellie Santiago, was the operator of a resort in Puerto Rico and had experience in the tourism industry. He and his investors paid $3.5 million for a 233-room motel and planned to change the country theme in the resort's restaurant to an island theme. Fernández planned to target Puerto Rican tourists. By 2007, Hispanic-owned businesses accounted for 37.6 percent of all businesses in Osceola County and 20.9 percent in neighboring Orange County. Spanish names, Spanish-language signage, national flags, and tropical colors contributed to the transformation of the commercial landscape. Clearly, Puerto Ricans and other Hispanics were important consumers.

Latinos were also valuable business owners. In 1996, Banco Popular, Puerto

Figure 2.1. Tropico restaurant, 2010. Photograph by Simone Delerme.

Figure 2.2. Tropico restaurant mural, 2010. Photograph by Simone Delerme.

Rico's largest bank, announced plans to build as many as five branches in Greater Orlando the following year. The company was targeting Orlando's "burgeoning Hispanic population."[13] Banco Popular planned to buy Seminole National, a small community bank, and build branches in communities where Hispanic residents were concentrated. Journalist Barry Flynn claimed that Banco Popular, the first Hispanic-owned bank in Central Florida, "has gotten other banks' attention."[14] Sun Trust Banks Inc. said it would be focusing more on the Hispanic community by launching a Latin Banking Group. Barnett Banks of Orlando claimed to have six Hispanic branch managers to accommodate the growing Hispanic population. By 2003, "from Sun Trust to Southern Community Bank, everyone [was] targeting the Hispanic market now, with varying degrees of success," said Alex Sánchez, the executive director of the Florida Bankers Association.[15]

In 2006, the *Orlando Sentinel* reported that "signs of the Puerto Rican community's vibrancy are everywhere," including real estate offices, auto repair shops, banks, supermarkets, dance clubs, churches, and funeral homes that catered to Latinos.[16] The increasing number of Latino-owned businesses altered the commercial landscape. When a number of individuals of the same ethnic background in a particular geographic area collectively use a shared set of "fixed-feature" or "semi-fixed feature elements," a distinctive cultural landscape emerges.[17] In Osceola County, the most common features were displays of a national-origin flag or symbol and Spanish-language advertising and storefront signs. Semi-fixed feature elements such as these cost little to alter and are therefore accessible to individuals of all socioeconomic levels. Fixed-feature elements such as architectural style and building interiors and exteriors change rarely and slowly, but in Osceola and Orange Counties there was evidence of both types of features in the residential and commercial landscapes. Latino-owned restaurants, grocery stores, supermarkets, and other small businesses served as symbolic markers, sending the message that the population had reached a critical mass. As the Latino population grew, Puerto Ricans became increasingly visible and their economic, political, and cultural influence intensified. By 2002, for instance, Puerto Ricans owned 4,963 businesses in the Orlando metropolitan area and Cubans owned 4,537.[18]

According to the 2010 US Census, Puerto Ricans numbered 11,618 in Buenaventura Lakes and 72,986 in Osceola County.[19] Puerto Rican flags hung in garages and windows and as insignias on cars. On weekends, garage sales, yard sales, and posters in front yards advertised the sale of alcapurrias (meat fritters),

Figure 2.3. La Caribeña Grocery, 2010. Photograph by Simone Delerme.

empanadas (stuffed pastries), or pinchos (shish kebab) cooked on a grill set up on the front lawn or in a nearby commercial parking lot. The concession stand at the Archie Gordon Memorial Park in Buenaventura Lakes sold empanadas and pernil sandwiches, while the gentleman behind the counter blasted salsa music on a radio. I could even purchase pasteles from the Walmart parking lot, where a daring vendor sold food from his van. Then there were the auto body shops with lawn chairs and grills set up out front during the weekend with signs advertising pinchos to attract customers. This ever-present form of entrepreneurship, the selling of food in the suburban streets of Osceola County, was striking to me. The advertising that accompanied these enterprises were powerful visual signs of the region's Puerto Ricanization. I wrote about this in my field notes:

> What I always find interesting are the many signs that contribute to the Latinization of space and the food trucks that help the process! For example, on Semoran Boulevard today I was surprised to see the airport parking garage (off-site) with a flashing sign that alternated between the

price of parking and an advertisement for alcapurrias and other Spanish food available from a mobile truck in front of the parking lot. I have seen those mobile trucks with benches (picnic table style) in a few locations.[20]

I often experienced the Latinization of parts of Osceola County during my everyday activities. Residents of rural Osceola County who chose to remain struggled to dissent against the increasing Latinization of the region. The contrast between the two cultures was evident to me on March 14, 2011, when I began my day at the annual Kowtown Festival in downtown Kissimmee. I observed a hot dog-eating contest and a meatloaf-tasting competition before stopping at a booth sponsored by the Women Cattle Ranchers Association, all the while acutely aware that I was one of only a few people of color at the event. The only others were a group of West Indians who had set up a booth where they sold baked goods. After the Kowtown Festival, I drove a few miles to a church in Buenaventura Lakes for a car show. Car shows were a staple of the community and were regularly held at churches, at the Old Town theme park, in downtown Kissimmee, and as part of festivals or fairs. At the church, Latin music was playing and modified cars lined the parking lot displaying license plates from different parts of Puerto Rico. The piraguas (shaved ice) and fritters people were selling at this event were a sharp contrast to the cuisine at the Kowtown Festival.

Later that evening, when I went bowling, the jukebox alternated between reggaeton and country music as Hispanics and non-Hispanics took turns putting coins in the machine and choosing songs. When I visited a flea market on Interstate 192 the following day, I entered a dirt road and passed the Cracker House Saloon on my left on my way to the parking lot for the flea market. While many Hispanics attend the flea market, bikers were the customers for the saloon on certain nights. At the flea market, a booth sold both the Confederate flag and the Mexican flag. Less than ten miles down the road from the flea market is the Silver Spurs Arena, where a rodeo takes place and the county fair is held. But you could also attend the King de La Calle Car Show or hear reggaeton and bachata artists Don Omar and Prince Royce in the same arena. Then there is the Chinese restaurant in Old Town with its grill out front where an Asian employee yells out "pinchos, pinchos!" Meanwhile, I saw signs on State Road 535 that advertised gator jerky, boiled peanuts, and oranges.

Indeed, while Latinization was evident in the landscape, so were the remnants of rural, small-town Florida, particularly in parts of Osceola County where cattle ranching still dominated. In the rural parts of the county, I was told, "real cowboys can still be found, in Kenansville and Yeehaw Junction." Others told me that although some Hispanics had moved into the neighboring city of St. Cloud, it remained a redneck stronghold. However, Johnny, a resident of St. Cloud, felt that Hispanics were taking over that city: "There was a battle between the rednecks and the Hispanics, and the Hispanics won. But, you don't want to mess with the cops in St. Cloud," he warned. "Hispanics can't drive through St. Cloud without their car getting searched completely." However, when Johnny went to the Applebee's in Buenaventura Lakes, it felt to him like the restaurant was "like Puerto Rico." People often made a distinction between the "Puerto Rican spaces" of Buenaventura Lakes and Kissimmee and the neighboring "non-Hispanic white spaces" of St. Cloud. However, the population estimates in the 2017 US census revealed that the Hispanic population of St. Cloud was growing. Of the 51,282 residents of the city, 35.7 percent were Hispanic and 52.0 percent were non-Hispanic white.[21]

Political Representation

The growing political power of the Latino community and the presence of Puerto Rican elected officials further contributed to Greater Orlando's Latinization. Puerto Ricans such as former county commissioner John "Q" Quiñones were able to bring resources to the Hispanic community and awareness of the needs of Latino residents. In his campaign message, he pledged "to give Buenaventura Lakes, where the bulk of Puerto Rican voters reside, more attention, to have office hours in the community, and to work with the community to build a bigger community center with after-school programs."[22] Places such as Buenaventura Lakes were no longer monopolized by dominant US norms, social practices, and styles. Instead, competition had increased for cultural and linguistic space in the residential and commercial landscape.[23]

A federal voting lawsuit involving residents of Buenaventura Lakes, Osceola County, and the US Department of Justice led the county to create the Hispanic-concentrated district that Quiñones represented. This increased the political power and representation of Hispanics. Previously, the Board of Commissioners of Osceola County was elected through at-large elections to four-year staggered terms. Candidates sought election for numbered seats that corresponded to the district where they lived. Although candidates were required to live in a particular district, all the voters in the county elected them at large. As the Hispanic population grew, Hispanic leaders began expressing an interest in achieving political representation at the county level. In 1991, the Osceola County Hispanic American Association formally requested that the Board of Commissioners change the election system and threatened to pursue legal action if it did not. Hispanic leaders felt that a single-member-district system, by which voters living in a particular district could elect that district's commissioner, would be more fair to minority voters. No Hispanic candidate had ever been elected to the Board of Commissioners in an at-large election. Hispanics were not the only ones that faced this obstacle; it was a problem for all minority groups.[24] "The political science literature is extensive and very clear about the impact of at-large electoral systems on minority representation, including Hispanics," José Cruz writes, "whenever voting patterns are racially polarized, at-large elections dilute minority voting and impede descriptive representation."[25]

In 1996, a Hispanic candidate, Robert Guevara, was elected as a county commissioner in a single-member-district election that was racially polarized. While Robert Guevara was elected to the Board of Commissioners to represent a district that included Buenaventura Lakes, his campaign generated racial hostility from non-Hispanics. His opponent sent a campaign mailer that depicted himself as day and Guevara, who had darker skin, as night. While he admitted that the flyer was in poor taste and apologized privately to Guevara, he did not denounce it publicly.[26] Other remarks were made such as "we do not want Osceola to turn into another Miami," a reference to the Cuban population's political influence there.[27] The return to an at-large system prompted activists and Osceola County resident Armando Ramírez to file a complaint with the US Department of Justice in 2000. These individuals demanded that the county enforce their right to representation and political participation. They wanted to make sure that Hispanics participated in county-level decisions that would affect their district. Political scientist José Cruz documented the polarization in the political culture of Osceola County:

> Former County Commissioner Chuck Dunnick, in discussing how Puerto Rican leader Robert Guevara acted as a bridge between the Hispanic and Anglo communities in Osceola during Guevara's term on the board of county commissioners, stated that there was 'an almost hostility or outright frustration' within the Anglo community regarding things they did not understand about the Hispanic community.[28]

In 2005, Bill Hunt, a member of the local Democratic Party executive committee, "publicly complained to a fellow party member that there was too much Spanish spoken in the county, too many Puerto Rican flags, and not enough interest by Hispanics to truly 'become Americans and assimilate into society.' 'This is America,' he further stated, and 'I further resent ballots being printed in any language other than English.'"[29] The Spanish-language ballots were connected to a 2002 agreement. On May 21, 2002, the Justice Department threatened to sue Osceola County "after investigators concluded that election officials failed to adequately help those who didn't speak English." Osceola County averted a federal voting-rights lawsuit that time by "promising the U.S. Justice Department that Spanish speakers won't be turned away from the polls and that they'll get help casting ballots in their own language."[30]

In 2002, the county signed a consent decree with the US Department of Justice that required it to provide voter registration information and voter registration cards in Spanish.[31] The terms of the consent decree required the county to

> translate all of its material into Spanish, conduct outreach to Spanish-speaking voters through Spanish language coordinators, insure that half of the poll workers were bilingual in areas where Hispanics were 40 percent or more of registered voters, and have at least one bilingual poll worker in areas where Hispanics were 5 percent or more. Of the estimated 650 poll workers needed, at least 103 were supposed to be bilingual.[32]

That same year, "the government of Puerto Rico mounted a massive, $6 million voter registration campaign in the United States, and in particular in Osceola, Orange, Seminole, and Volusia Counties in Florida, to encourage the political participation of stateside Puerto Ricans."[33] However, the at-large election system was still impacting political representation for Latinos in Buenaventura Lakes. In 2005, US Attorney General Alberto Gonzales filed an action pursuant to sections 2 and 12(d) of the Voting Rights Act of 1965 against Osceola County, supervisor of elections Donna Bryant, and the Board of Commissioners of Osceola County. Once again Armando Ramírez and other community activists helped bring attention to the inequalities. A US district court heard the case on September 18–20, 2006. The following month, the court issued a memorandum opinion stating that Osceola County's voting system diluted Hispanic votes, in violation of the Voting Rights Act. José Cruz describes the court's findings:

> Hispanics in Osceola County were a sufficiently large and geographically compact community to constitute a majority in a single-member district; that they were politically cohesive; and that the county's white majority voted consistently as a bloc to prevent the election of Hispanic candidates.

For these reasons, the court ordered an end to the at-large system of election at the county level. Once again, the county was *forced* to act in favor of Hispanics.[34]

After spending more than $2 million to defend its at-large voting system, the county complied with the judge's orders and created five single-member districts, including a newly drawn Hispanic-majority district that includes Buenaventura Lakes, Lakeside, Remington, Kissimmee Bay, and parts of Mill Run and Oak Run. The five single-member districts were "designed to give Hispanics more influence at the polls and make it easier for candidates without connections or money to get elected."[35]

Since the voting rights lawsuit, several Hispanics have been elected or appointed to positions in the governing bodies of Osceola County and the city of Kissimmee. The Voting Rights Act lawsuit set a precedent in its ruling against discriminatory political practices in Osceola County. According to Morton Winsberg, a Florida State University professor who studies Hispanic growth, "The good old boys will have to make an appeal to the Hispanics or not get voted in."[36] Luis Román, president of the Hispanic American Association, commented, "It won't be long before the candidates for office will be relative newcomers instead of the old-line representatives who have dominated Osceola politics."[37] Although Latinos in Osceola County still faced obstacles such as linguistic barriers, open hostility, and racist comments, legal victories meant that the political landscape was marked by a Puerto Rican presence.

The 65th Infantry Veterans Park

In February 2011, Michael Smith, a retiree who had helped me schedule several interviews, phoned to inform me that District 2 commissioner John Q had called him a racist and stupid in a public meeting. His call caught me off guard and I wasn't sure how to respond. I apologized sympathetically. I immediately went online to stream the footage of the weekly Osceola County commission meeting to see what had happened. Michael and I have different political ideologies; in our conversations he had revealed his anti-immigrant sentiments. In the footage, County Commissioner John Quiñones, a native of Puerto Rico, introduced a proposal to rename 33.6 acres of county property in Buenaventura Lakes that used to be the Walk-N-Stick Executive Golf Course as the 65th Infantry Veterans Park. Michael, a Vietnam veteran, objected to the park's name.

The 65th Infantry, known as "the Borinqueneers," was an all-volunteer US

Army regiment of Puerto Ricans who fought in World War I, World War II, and the Korean War. Congress had created the regiment in 1899. The segregated unit is the only all-Latino regiment in the army's history. The members of the regiment are heroes in the Puerto Rican imagination, particularly since some of the Borinqueneers lived in Buenaventura Lakes and other parts of Central Florida. In addition to renaming the park and making improvements with a budget of approximately $400,000, Quiñones wanted to erect a permanent memorial in honor of the 65th. When the general public was invited to comment on the proposal, Michael was the first to address the five county commissioners:

> The Infantry Unit 65 is stationed or headquartered in Puerto Rico. As a Vietnam veteran, and one that spent a year in country, I take that as a personal affront! You're gonna name a park after a company in the military that's headquartered out of another country!

Retired US army colonel Dennis Freytes interrupted Michael, shouting, "It's not another country!" The commissioners called for order so Michael could continue. He said:

> I think if you want to honor the service people there are more appropriate names. . . . Yes, there were a lot of Puerto Ricans that died . . . but after that it was changed to where they basically are non-combat support role troops, so I think it's time that somebody take a different view of this and pull it off and rename the park.

Colonel Freytes spoke next:

> I've commanded infantry. I've commanded Special Forces. I've commanded airborne units, and I've commanded ROTC. . . . And our veterans, they don't fight for just one county. They fight for all Americans no matter what county they are, and Osceola County is part of America. Puerto Rico is not a separate country. Puerto Rico is a US territory under the American flag! My father fought in the 65th infantry regiment. My uncle Erasto Freytes fought in the 65th. . . . I'm an American patriot, and I believe that this segment that hasn't been duly recognized should be recognized by this honorable commission.

After scattered applause, Commissioner Quiñones thanked the colonel for his service and mentioned the names of two Buenaventura Lakes residents who served in the infantry. He pointed out that the golf course had closed down years ago.

And how interesting that now we can bring not only the culture of Americans born in the United States and unfortunately who cannot vote for the president of the US, but who can defend the country of the US and Osceola County and so now they are being commemorated. . . . And I will tell you, those of you who continue to be ignorant about their involvement I encourage you to go to the PBS website and look at the documentary called *The Borinqueneers* and it will tell you more about the history of these brave men.

Another commissioner asked if the 65th was recognized in another state or on the island and awkwardly tried to find the phrasing to connote Puerto Rico's territorial status: "Is this the first or only national recognition inside, outside of Puerto Rico? I'm trying to think of the proper way to say it. Within the continental territory of the US, is there any other place that nationally recognized the 65th?" Quiñones responded, "Yes, Colorado." Then he made a motion to approve the resolution. The public hearing concluded with a unanimous vote and the commissioner invited everyone to the ribbon-cutting ceremony. In the weeks that followed, a memorial was constructed and the park was renamed. However, two months later, a group of Buenaventura Lakes residents, including Michael, formed a group of about thirty people to protest these actions.

The park is an important symbol of Osceola County's Puerto Ricanization. This was a significant political victory for the Puerto Ricans of Greater Orlando. Commissioner Quiñones's resolution named a communal, public park after Puerto Rican people, reaffirming the Puerto Rican presence in Buenaventura Lakes. The park memorializes veterans whose worthiness was being contested, who were denied full citizenship, and whose belonging was challenged by a "recall group." According to spokesperson Jennifer Robertson, the group was particularly bothered about the renaming of the park, which took place without consulting the residents or the county's Parks Advisory Committee. The group wanted the name of the park changed and they wanted Commissioner Quiñones to be removed from office. Group leader Kathy Sperling told the press that the name of the park was "inappropriate" because close to 100 members of the infantry had been court-martialed for disobeying orders to fight during the Korean War.[38] The charges varied from willful disobedience of a superior officer to cowardice before the enemy, since some refused to fight. Historian Harry Franqui-Rivera points out that a high casualty rate, shortages of ammunition, poor leadership, and linguistic barriers were factors that contributed to the men's behavior.[39] Additionally, the replacement of highly trained troops with poorly trained recruits who spoke little English, a dearth of bilingual sergeants, and new "continental officers" from the mainland who did not speak Spanish and openly showed their prejudice toward the Puerto Rican soldiers led to declining morale.[40] While the recall group was planning its offensive, another group was meeting six miles away from Buenaventura Lakes in the Puerto Rican Cultural Center to plan the first Puerto Rican parade in Osceola County. The event was dedicated to the Borinqueneers.

On April 21, 2011, Quiñones held a press conference at the park to defend the bravery and valor of the Borinqueneers and his initiative to rename the park. Accompanied by Latino commissioners from the city of Kissimmee, Quiñones argued that the recall group's efforts were "100% motivated by bigotry and racism." He cited a 2007 newspaper article that revealed an email from one of the leaders of the group that said "An Anglo needs to win this [county] seat and not a Hispanic." To their attack on diversity, the commissioner proclaimed, "¡Basta Ya! [Enough already!] Over 300,000 Americans of Hispanic descent . . . live in Central Florida, and they're here to stay, they're not going anywhere. They're here to pay taxes, to denounce this group's racist motives. ¡Basta Ya!"[41]

For the next nine days, the Internet lit up with commentary about the historical events surrounding the court-martial, the Puerto Rican community's defensiveness, the racism against Osceola County's Puerto Rican newcomers, and control of the landscape and soundscape of Buenaventura Lakes. Anonymous Internet users, vocal community activists and politicians, the Puerto Rican son-in-law of a recall group member, and the producer of *The Borinqueneers* documentary posted comments on the *Orlando Sentinel's Hispanosphere* blog. Respondents highlighted the "racist" motives of the recall group, defended the heroism of the 65th, debated the facts surrounding the largest court-martial of the Korean War, and questioned the validity of the pardon. In defense of the Borinqueneers, a person with the username "Ernest Acosta" asked the public to remember "that the 65th soldiers were not able to vote for President of the United States or for voting representation in the U.S. Congress. Yet, they went to war for America."[42] Another respondent wrote: "Puerto Rico had more servicemen killed per capita than just about every state in the USA during the Korean War. That's worth an 'American' memorial."[43]

The attack on the memorialization of the 65th Infantry led to allegations of racism:

This is beyond any Latino political. The issue is about an act of racism as well calling these military heroes traitors. The racism needs to be confronted head on. This is an insult to every Puerto Rican/Latino who has served in the military. Ms Robertson needs to do a better job researching since the Puerto Rican 65th Infantry Regiment are genuine heroes.[44]

In response, Internet user "luis Martinez" wrote:

All I got to say is that my Mother in Law Jennifer Robertson is not a racist. Im her son in law 100% Puertorican born in Rio Piedras PR. She has a beautiful granddaughter that's half PUERTO RICAN that she watches for my wife and I everyday. The reason for her speaking was why is Quinones naming a park all by himself, when the park is a public park for all races. To each its own but this was not about racism.[45]

Other respondents articulated an all-too-common attitude about the social and linguistic transformations taking place in the region:

They fought—they were soldiers, let the park be named in their honor. My only gripe is that for the current Puerto Ricans who live in the United States—learn and speak ENGLISH! If I moved to Puerto Rico, I would learn the language. And don't try to turn Florida into Puerto Rico West. If you miss Puerto Rico so much, stay there. Don't fly your flag here—fly the American flag.[46]

These comments reflected the larger struggles over the Latinization of Greater Orlando. Another individual wrote, "Let the ricans keep their park name they own the rest of bvl anyways."[47]

Anthropologists Ana Y. Ramos-Zayas and Nicholas De Genova refer to a "politics of worthiness" that asks Puerto Ricans to prove that they are deserving of US citizenship and are entitled to civil rights and social benefits that other populations assume are inalienable. Puerto Ricans engage in this politics of worthiness as a way of "circumventing their own racialization" and avoiding negative stereotypes "by following prescriptive rules of patriotism, social mobility, and national acceptability."[48] Military service connotes belonging, patriotism, and worthiness of citizenship. By labeling the entire infantry as traitors and calling into question whether they deserved a memorial on Florida soil, opponents of the park challenged the patriotism, Americanness, and citizenship of Puerto Ricans.

For my Puerto Rican informants, the military service of the Borinqueneers signaled worthiness and belonging in the United States and thus merited memorialization in the park. My informants never interpreted the name of the park or the memorial as a way to exclude non-Puerto Ricans. Instead, for them, the memorial was a signal that Puerto Ricans were equally entitled to recognition. When the recall group leader called the Borinqueneers traitors, the Puerto Rican community immediately interpreted the comments as racism. The contestations over place-making and over who has the right to be represented and memorialized in public spaces point to larger questions about race relations and the full incorporation of immigrants in new destinations of migration. In this case, non-Latino whites viewed spaces they considered to be white spaces as race neutral and spaces marked by Hispanic culture as exclusionary. The discourses surrounding the 65th Infantry Veteran's Park controversy revealed the growing fear of non-Latino whites as they continued to lose power and political representation and were silenced by allegations of racism. Soon after the April 2011 press conference, the recall group went silent. However, the Latinization of places in Greater Orlando continues to ignite controversy regarding demographic, linguistic, and spatial transformations.

Linguistic Transformations

When I decided to do research in Buenaventura Lakes, the last thing I intended to study was language. But one day as I was reviewing my fieldnotes after five months of research, a theme I had not noticed before emerged: the tensions the dominance of the Spanish language in public spaces was creating between ethnic and racial groups. This tension was caused by language ideologies—ideas, perceptions, and beliefs about the nature and use of languages. Ideas about language become naturalized, shared, commonsense understandings that connect language to identities, values, and morals.[49] In Greater Orlando, language frequently becomes an index of ethnic identity, status, character, and personhood.[50] Language ideologies are closely connected to the acquisition and maintenance of power and other political, economic, or individualized interests. Thus, the expression of language ideologies I documented point to the power struggles that result from the demographic shifts and increasing economic and political power of the Latino community.

The massive influx of Latinos has transformed the soundscape of Greater Orlando. Bilingualism was an asset in the business community and Spanish could be heard as frequently as (if not more frequently than) English in many public places. In residential enclaves such as Buenaventura Lakes, Spanish was increasingly present in public and private life. It did not take long for me to become desensitized to the use of Spanish everywhere I went in the community. The local media highlighted the growing presence and influence of Hispanics with headlines that accentuate the changing soundscape: "Orlando Develops Hispanic Accent," "Latinos at the Helm of Orlando's Public Broadcasting," "Seminole to offer ballots in Spanish," "A New Home—One of Every Three Puerto Ricans in the State Calls Central Florida Home, Giving the Region A Bilingual Flair," and "Ever Wonder why ATMs in Central Florida Speak Spanish?"[51] Some Latinos defended these changes by highlighting the "multicultural" demographics of the United States and the inevitable results of globalization. Other residents objected to the growing presence of Spanish in public spaces.

Linguistic Polarization

When I arrived in Buenaventura Lakes in 2010, the process of integrating Spanish into public life had long been under way. Chris Williams, a 75-year-old retiree who had lived in Buenaventura Lakes for twenty-four years, told me in an interview that "there are basically two separate communities, the English speaking and Spanish speaking. This results in mistrust, it's difficult with the language barrier." Longtime residents of the area recall how things were before the large influx of Latinos in the 1990s. During our interview, Chris pointed out the neighboring houses that were once occupied by "white, English-speaking people." He said, "I used to interact with the people, but there has been a gradual change. They are all gone now, for various reasons: relocated, died, normal transitions."[52]

When Hilda Berríos first moved to Osceola County, "it was really a nice small town. But it grew too fast." She decided to move to Lake County to escape the congestion, but she often returns to Osceola County to shop and visit family. According to Berríos, a native of Puerto Rico, "there's so many Puerto Ricans, it's a Spanish country over there."[53] In 2005, historian Félix Matos-Rodríguez commented that "this surge is an interesting development, because Puerto Ricans are really the first group that comes to Central Florida in numbers that are sizable enough to challenge the homogenous culture."[54]

When I was reading through my fieldnotes, I saw that multiple encounters and incidents highlighted the linguistic polarization between English and

Spanish speakers. In a 2005 article entitled "Orlando Develops Hispanic Accent," Luis Martínez-Fernández mentioned the opening of the first Publix Sabor supermarket in Buenaventura Lakes as evidence of the influence of the growing Latino population.[55] At the time of my fieldwork, the Publix Sabor in Buenaventura Lakes was one of four supermarkets the Publix supermarket chain had introduced in Florida to cater to the Latino population. Publix Sabor makes all product information and signs bilingual and offers a wider variety of Caribbean and Latin American products than other Publix stores. On July 13, 2010, that supermarket emerged as an important site of contention. As I stood outside the Robert Guevara Community Center (named after the first Puerto Rican elected to the Osceola County Commission) with a group of non-Latino white Buenaventura Lakes residents after a poorly attended community meeting, I listened to them vent their frustrations with the local supermarkets and retail chains that cater to the Latino population. The residents were especially frustrated by the plethora of products that catered to the Latino market that had replaced the products they once purchased. Additionally, they were astounded by the lack of English-speaking employees. Michael Smith expressed his frustration about the fact that the local Publix Sabor had stopped carrying his brand of cheese and had introduced several Latin American brands in its place. He had gone so far as to make a formal written complaint to the manager, but the manager had not responded. Michael had begun traveling to supermarkets outside the area.

Brett Rogers, a Buenaventura Lakes resident, described his experiences at the Bank of America and Publix Sabor, where several store associates had to search for an English-speaking worker to assist him as he waited patiently in disbelief. Other group members spoke about their frustrating experiences at the local Bank of America, emphasizing that it is the Bank of A-M-E-R-I-C-A and that it is therefore unacceptable to be greeted and spoken to in Spanish. "Can't they tell we are not Hispanic?" Brett joked, pointing out his blond hair and blue eyes. Another woman complained about the Sedano's supermarket that had replaced her former market and expressed a hope that it would not succeed financially.

In 2010, Sedano's, a Miami-based Cuban-owned supermarket chain, entered the Central Florida market. Sedano's purchased three Albertson's markets and planned to keep them open while the conversion took place. In the Sedano's stores, customers hear salsa music, buy pastelitos in a café, and are greeted in Spanish, although signs are in English. When the Sedano's in Orlando opened, a person by the supermarket entrance was selling churros and piraguas from a

Figure 2.4. Publix Sabor, 2010. Photograph by Simone Delerme.

cart. The store owners were proud of the wide variety of products they were able to offer their customers. Shoppers were not limited to Goya brand products but also had access to brands such as Iberia, Conchita, and Norteño. Sedano's was planning to offer different products than those in the South Florida markets. Instead of catering to a Cuban market, the company planned to stock more items that could appeal to the Puerto Rican population. According to Augusto Sanabria, president and chief executive officer of the Hispanic Business Initiative Fund, "'Anytime that a big Hispanic company comes into town, it just reemphasizes the power of the Hispanic community here in Central Florida. . . . That's recognizing that in Central Florida, the Hispanic community is growing and it is powerful. It's music to my ears.'"[56]

After the *Orlando Sentinel* published an article December 28, 2009 about the new Sedano's chain, many Internet responses were quite critical. On January 8, 2010, "tim" posted the following two responses:

Hispanics need their own supermarkets . . . wow! . . . the regular supermarkets are not good enough for them??

You people continue to divide the community, next will be Hispanic only
churches and in a few years will be segregated again and the cycle will begin for another round. Again, the Cubans who came fleeing Fidel brought
to the US a lot of money, which has been used to purchase influence and
power in Florida. This is the beginning of the cubanization of Orlando.

In an interview, Sandra López recalled having to drive to downtown Orlando,
to an area close to Church Street and Orange Avenue, to find Hispanic products
in the late 1980s: "It took between forty-five minutes to an hour to get plátanos
or pernil. As time progressed, the food changed." Food, she said, was a measure
of the demographic transitions: "Eventually the supermarket created an 'international' food aisle and you knew that was your section." Eventually, entire supermarkets that catered to Hispanic consumers replaced the single international
food aisle.[57]

Another day when I was having lunch with Michael Smith, he expressed
the language ideology that links speaking English with being American as
he described how he reprimands Spanish speakers. Michael admitted that he
finds it incredibly disrespectful when Spanish is spoken in front of him. He
claimed that "about 95% of [Latinos] understand English but choose to speak
in Spanish." When people speak to Michael or in front of him in Spanish, he
responds, "This is America, speak English!" He does this partly to generate a
reaction, to force a startled Spanish speaker to utter a response in English, but
he admits he also responds this way because he feels he is being talked about
in a previously "white" public space. According to Setha Low, "white public
space is linguistically constructed by the monitoring of racialized populations
for signs of linguistic disorder" in the same way that non-Latino whites police
elite suburbs to ensure racial purity.[58] Michael associated speaking Spanish
with resistance to assimilation and drew a distinction between Puerto Ricans,
who do not assimilate, and South and Central Americans in the area, whom he
believes assimilate faster. He chose not to elaborate on the particular experiences that had led him to distinguish Puerto Ricans from South and Central
Americans.

Instead, he told me a story about an Italian friend he had in childhood. When
he visited his friend's house for dinner, the mother would instruct everyone to
speak only English so Michael could understand what was being said. On one

occasion the father forgot and started speaking in Italian. The mother reprimanded him and insisted that he speak in English. In Michael's experience, the disciplining and self-monitoring of language usage was a conscious attempt to assimilate to American culture and he commended that mother for aiding the process by making her family speak English around a non-Italian speaker.

On another occasion, as Michael and I were chatting about the local churches in the Buenaventura Lakes area, I asked him if he attended any of the services. He told me about his experience at an event held in a church located behind his house. At one point, the pastor told the audience, "let's make English the second language here." Michael described this incident as "unwelcoming" and expressed his resentment, since he interpreted the pastor's message as one intended to divide Latinos and non-Latinos and replace the language of the nation's majority. The language ideology that connects being American with speaking English was expressed time and time again when non-Latino white residents challenged the use of Spanish in public spaces or in their presence.

On November 18, 2010, I participated in a voluntary teach-in sponsored by the Osceola County school district. I visited two classrooms in a local high school to discuss Hispanic migration in the region and the racial and ethnic tensions I had observed during my fieldwork. In the first class, Sean, who claimed to have some Cuban ancestry, although the teacher later described him as a self-identifying "redneck," was in constant debate with the Latino students sitting on the other side of the room. Latinos constituted a clear majority and, as the teacher pointed out, African American and Haitian students were the smallest minority. Once the conversation began, the students unapologetically verbalized the language ideologies my adult informants had expressed. Sean insisted that there are appropriate places for English and declared, "You are in America, speak English!" He argued that if he went to Bravo, a Latino-owned supermarket chain, he expected to hear Spanish, but he did not want to hear it in Walmart. In response to Sean, José raised his hand and mentioned freedom of speech, Martin Luther King, and the "I Have A Dream" speech. Christina defensively declared, "They just don't like us!" But one thing was certain: the Spanish-speaking students did not apologize for speaking Spanish in public spaces. Miguel asked, "Why don't they just learn Spanish? After all, it's the second most spoken language." Juan agreed, pointing out that in the Dominican Republic they have to learn Creole, Spanish, and English. Sean's classmates, however, frowned at the idea of an additional language requirement. As our conversation continued, two students shared experiences of discrimination. One student described an encounter with police officers who demanded that he show them his documentation. The second student described the experience of a family member who did not speak any English whose teacher "wrote him up" every time he spoke Spanish in school. Another student said that three derogatory terms are used in the area: redneck, Mexican, and the "n" word.

Some established residents expressed resentment toward Latino students. When I interviewed an administrator from the Osceola County public school system, I asked if any racial tensions existed in the schools. She explained that language rather than skin color was what caused tensions. The students who were bilingual were not a problem; people from Puerto Rico, whose first and only language was Spanish, caused tension. She often heard the comment, "This is America, you have to speak English!" and teachers would ask why they had to accommodate the Spanish-speaking students. "When you go East to St. Cloud [in Osceola County] you still see this type of opposition," she said. When the META consent decree was introduced, which requires English speakers of other languages (ESOL) courses and other student services for Spanish speakers, the teachers in St. Cloud were most resistant to taking classes that certified them to teach English to speakers of other languages, while others realized the need for and importance of certification classes.[59] The St. Cloud teachers would say, "we don't need to take these classes," but as the Latino population began settling farther and farther east, moving from Kissimmee to St. Cloud, everyone had to take the classes.

Because of the increase in Latino students, school districts recruited and hired bilingual teachers. Some teachers were recruited directly from Puerto Rico. During our interview, the administrator recalled some of the responses to the presence of Latinos in the school system. Some parents complained about teachers with an accent. They would claim that their child could not understand what the teacher was saying because of the Spanish accent and demand that their child be moved to another class. "Spanish-speaking children would be made fun of and the teachers would think [that] the Spanish-speaking kids are not smart or have a type of disability. But these monolingual children are in fact smart in their own language, they just don't know English," she said.

The influx of Latino migrants has also impacted other public spaces. In the summer of 2010, I observed an exchange between two English-speaking men and a Spanish-speaking woman in a bodega owned by a couple from the Dominican Republic that was quite revealing of the everyday encounters between Spanish speakers and monolingual English speakers. I was sitting at a table in the back of the store when two workers walked up to the lunch counter. Their shirts said "Smith's Septic Service." One of the men attempted to ask the woman behind the counter if a particular stew was oxtail. She responded to him in Spanish, but he did not understand and once again asked if the stew was oxtail. Several customers sitting at the tables surrounding me turned their attention to the interaction. The customers and the employee went back and forth in their respective languages until a man sitting at one of the nearby tables spoke up to translate. Then both men placed their orders with the assistance of a third party. When the female worker asked if the food was para aquí o para llevar (for here or to go), the male worker got agitated and shouted "no hablo espanol!" (I don't speak Spanish!). The woman behind the counter repeated the question in Spanish and the male worker responded in frustration, "she just keeps talking away!"

In this instance, the two men were encroaching on a Spanish-dominated space, so the employee made no effort to speak English or communicate with

Figure 2.5. Lunch counter at La Caribeña Grocery. Photograph by Simone Delerme.

them in any way except through the Spanish language. Perhaps the employee could not communicate in English and repeated herself in the hope that the two men would be able to decipher what she was saying. Another possibility is that the employee could in fact say a few words in English but chose not to accommodate the English speakers since she was in a Latino-owned store, where the majority of the clientele can communicate in Spanish if necessary.

The hostile response to the use of Spanish also seeped into the workforce. In October 2011, a post appeared on the *Hispanosphere* blog titled, "Workforce Central Florida Had an English-Only Policy." It posted an April 2009 memo from the management of Workforce Central Florida that reminded Spanish-speaking employees that using a language other than English was not allowed, even during breaks or during lunch hours, unless a customer was unable to speak English.[60] The text of the memo said:

Hey Team!

We have had some recent complaints about staff speaking in Spanish [in] the offices in lieu of speaking in English.

All staff are being advised that while in WCF offices, *all staff must speak English*. This includes break time, lunch time and/or if you are on the phone at the WCF office. Spanish speaking will only be allowed in the office if a customer is unable to speak English.

Please adhere to this policy as this is important that we do not offend and/or exclude non-Spanish speaking customers and/or staff[.] No exception to this policy.

Thanks.[61]

The blog reported that when questioned by local journalist Jim Stratton, a spokeswoman for Workforce Central Florida claimed that the English-only policy had been in place for two to six weeks and that no employee had been reprimanded while the policy was in effect. However, former employees told Stratton that some workers had received warnings that had been placed in their personnel files. According to the agency spokeswoman, the company had put the policy in place after it received several complaints from job seekers and non-bilingual employees who felt uncomfortable with staff members speaking Spanish to one another. Although Workforce Central Florida's policy was later amended to allow bilingual staff to speak the language they chose during breaks, the company encouraged them to be sensitive to those around them and to avoid excluding their monolingual peers by speaking Spanish in their presence.

Three comments in response to the *Hispanosphere* post commended Work-force Central Florida and three defended the use of Spanish. "Ruffus" empha-sized that English is the language of this country and that Latinos will never fit in if they don't adapt. "Then if you don't fit in don't complain that you are be-ing discriminated [against] because you did not work to improve your English communication skills," he wrote. "In summary, learn English, assimilate and survive."[62] The next respondent agreed and described their discomfort around individuals who speak a foreign language:

> I have been around some foreigners that communicate in their mother tongue and make all kinds of facial gestures, including body language, and the act gives the impression they are mocking me when they have to switch to their secret language because they are afraid of telling me in the face. . . . Workforce employees should not be seen promoting segregation and/or discrimination . . . the fact remains that in the USA people speak English.[63]

Another commenter felt that speaking Spanish hindered assimilation:

> You said it, American don't need another language to survive but Eng-lish. . . . You don't want discrimination but you want to keep alive that element that separates the Americans from those who apparently are not. English is the native language of this land, and the people at WorkForce were in the right track when they required an "English only" policy.[64]

While Workforce Central Florida executives communicated the English-only policy virtually, via email, other employers subjected bilingual employees to the same mandates verbally and unofficially. At times, these mandates contradicted the employers' involvement with the Latino community and their increased interest in hiring bilingual staff to service the Spanish-speaking clientele. The ideologies about the spaces where speaking Spanish is acceptable reveal how discrimination regarding language use is publicly acceptable and often goes un-challenged. Because of the dominance of the black-white racial binary, other forms of exclusion and discrimination based on language use, national origins, or other cultural factors are often invisible to non-Hispanic whites.

In June 2011, I interviewed Miranda Otero at the Seminole County bank where she worked. During our conversation she explained the increasing need for a Hispanic presence in the staff. "Before, [the bank was] catering only to the Anglo population, and Hispanics would be looking for a Hispanic presence or a Hispanic bank." When Hispanic clients approached her, they would comment, "Oh, finally a Hispanic." "Why did they want another Hispanic?" I asked. "Because they like to do business in their language," she replied. Other branches of her bank would call and ask her to translate for a client or would ask her to be present at their branch for an appointment with a Spanish-speaking client. Miranda approached her regional manager and explained that they need to hire bilingual speakers since Hispanics were an "untapped market."

Miranda has since witnessed increased involvement with the Hispanic community and managers at branches of the bank have hired bilingual staff. Her branch joined the Hispanic Chamber of Commerce and began sponsoring events for the Hispanic community. "They know the strength of the Hispanic community," said Miranda, "and the Hispanic community is close, tight-knit. If you do something right we will give you referrals, but if you do something wrong we will tell everyone not to go there." Despite the bank's increased engagement with the Hispanic community and its practice of hiring bilingual speakers, management controlled the use of Spanish in the branch. According to Miranda, her employers wanted bank employees to speak English unless they were communicating with a Spanish-speaking client. She said that the unofficial policy of the bank was that "if you have a Spanish-speaking co-worker you can speak in Spanish at lunch or if there are no clients. But if there is someone in the lobby there should be no Spanish because it can offend someone. There is a lot of resentment from the true Floridians." She told me that someone had said to her that "Florida is not the same since you Hispanics moved here." Miranda felt the resentment mostly at her job and believed that the remarks and hostility were conscious and intentional: "They just want it to be known." While these unofficial rules infringe on individual, constitutional rights, company policing of the use of Spanish is not contested at Miranda's bank.

Political scientist José Cruz has documented the linguistic polarization and discrimination Latinos experienced. In 2006, Cruz traveled to Osceola County to research Puerto Rican and Hispanic political participation and to document the attitudes of the majority population toward Latino newcomers. Initially, non-Hispanic white people treated Latinos with indifference because of their small numbers, Cruz notes. However, this "began to change as their number increased; of particular concern was their speaking of Spanish."[65] Prejudice was sometimes subtle and sometimes overt. For example, in 1988, the executive director of the Kissimmee/St. Cloud visitors' and conventions bureau ordered that Hispanic employees were not to speak Spanish in front of their co-workers "because this made the latter uncomfortable."[66] A school bus driver told Hispanic students that they would not be allowed to ride the bus if they spoke Spanish. In the early 1990s, the concerns of non-Latino whites increased. According to Jose Cruz:

> In 1992, Osceola's Hispanic population was "growing at breakneck speed, faster than almost anywhere else in the nation. That's worrisome to segments of the non-Hispanic population, who simply aren't sure how to react when it seems most of the people in K-mart are speaking Spanish. They don't like bilingual instructions on automatic teller machines or the fact that grocery store clerks wear pins announcing *Se Habla Español* or that a Hispanic column appears in this newspaper each Thursday." Employees at a McDonald's restaurant in Osceola have been told by the manager not to speak Spanish at work. José Hoyos, a former vice-chair of the 2001 Osceola redistricting advisory committee, reported that he himself had witnessed language-based discrimination. He felt that it stemmed from a fear among the Anglo community that Hispanics may "take over and are not willing to learn English."[67]

Other messages Cruz documented include the statements "that 'God speaks English' or that 'Here, we are lying down and becoming Puerto Rican, Dominican, South American. . . . I am not against Hispanics. I am against giving up America for anyone' as well as characterizations of Hispanics as a 'lazy, side-stepping, minority who refuses to allow the American way to continue.'"[68] Cruz concluded that at the time of his fieldwork, there was evidence "of a disconnect between the Anglo and Hispanic communities and also a stark reminder of the lower social status some in the Anglo community attribute to Hispanics."[69] Ethnoracism and xenophobia were part of the everyday culture of Osceola county for decades.

On several occasions bilingual informants admitted that they sometimes speak Spanish in front of monolingual English speakers intentionally, just to give them a hard time. However, other Hispanic informants instructed their children and reminded their Spanish-speaking peers to be sensitive and to avoid speaking Spanish in a setting where people who did not speak Spanish were present. While there are practical challenges for non-Spanish speakers who are trying to carry out their daily life activities, the discourses surrounding language usage represent much larger concerns and ideologies surrounding language, Hispanic migration, and belonging in the United States. Hence, as Bonnie Urciuoli argues, "what seems at first glance a simple classification of language turns out to be fundamentally a classification of people."[70] In Greater Orlando, Spanish speakers were classified as nonwhite and un-American because of linguistic differences and anti-Hispanic nativism sparked by Latinization, while non-Hispanic whites defended the privileges they once experienced as the majority.

Race, Language, and Virtual Dissent

Throughout my fieldwork, I found that purchasing food and doing other everyday activities such as banking, shopping, pumping gas, or eating at a restaurant were the most contentious for non-Latino whites because they were constantly reminded of their minority status in some quarters. As a result, there was a backlash against Latinos and there was evidence of tensions between Latinos and non-Latinos based on linguistic differences more than on perceived physical differences. Linguistic polarization led to allegations of reverse discrimination, the expression of color-blind or race-neutral ideologies, and the development of a stronger white racial consciousness among non-Latino whites.

The development of a white racial consciousness was a direct response to demographic shifts, Latinization, and perceptions that Latinos threatened non-Hispanic whites in some way. In Buenaventura Lakes, for example, many non-Hispanic whites believed that the presence of Latino-owned businesses and Spanish-speaking employees gave workers who speak both Spanish and English an advantage in the labor market. I frequently observed job advertisements in newspapers or on billboards that noted a preference for bilingual speakers. Latino-owned companies constituted 37.6 percent of all businesses in Osceola County in 2007, an increase from 22.4 percent in 2002, and the county's 122,252 Latino consumers constituted 45.4 percent of the total population. Spanish-speaking employees are a necessity.

While bilingual speakers are needed in industries in the low-paid service sector, they are also needed in the professional settings of insurance companies, real estate offices, and banks. This increases competition for jobs throughout the Central Florida labor market. However, whether or not non-Latino whites considered bilingualism to be an asset was often contingent on perceptions of whether the bilingual employee spoke "good" English. Bilingual people were also careful about when they speak Spanish at work. The growing size of the Latino population in this area of the state made bilingualism a clear asset in Greater Orlando.

Figure 2.6. Century 21 advertisement for realtors, Osceola County, Florida, 2010. Photograph by Simone Delerme.

Some non-Latino whites interpreted the widespread presence of Spanish speakers and employers' preference for bilingual speakers as reverse discrimination and white victimization. In the summer of 2010, the US Justice Department sponsored a forum on hate crimes and cultural sensitivity at the Robert Guevara Community Center in Buenaventura Lakes. The *Osceola News-Gazette* documented the stories forum panelists told about how biases had been directed toward them in the July 24, 2010, issue of the paper. In my fieldnotes, I documented what happened next. On July 31, 2010, a resident of Osceola County responded in the opinion section of the *Osceola News-Gazette*: "I have a gripe. . . . The editor failed to mention all the Latino businesses and restaurants that only employ other Hispanics to work there. If that is not job discrimination, then I don't know what is. People should clean up their own back yards."[71] This opinion was consistent with some of the online commentary on *Hispanosphere*, where non-Latino whites focused on the "discriminatory practices" of Latinos. Non-Latino whites challenged a changing American South that made them feel like outsiders in a community they thought they dominated.

In her book *The Everyday Language of White Racism*, anthropologist Jane Hill examined a "folk theory" of racism that many white middle-class Americans share. The premises of this theory are that racism is entirely a matter of individual beliefs, intentions, and actions; that prejudice is natural for the human condition; and that all people prefer to be with their own kind. According to this set of beliefs, anyone—not just whites—can be a racist and the behavior of whites and blacks, for instance, can be judged using the same moral standards. Thus, some whites speak of blacks who choose to sit together at a lunch table as engaging in "black racism" as if it were exactly like white racism. This is the basis for allegations of reverse discrimination. However, as Hill points out, these discourses of white victimization ignore the privileges whites have because of de facto segregation and persisting inequalities. She also notes that the ramifications of discrimination are more serious for blacks and other minorities than they are for whites because of disparities in access to housing, the labor market, health, and wealth, among other things.

For some whites, the presence of Spanish in places that they believed to be "race-neutral" generated a great deal of anger and hostility and a defense of whiteness that they linked with Americanness. Proponents of race neutrality advocated for "color-blind" social policies. They believe that racial equality requires laws treat people equally or similarly instead of creating ethnic or race-conscious solutions. Because of such beliefs, some whites criticized Latinos in Greater Orlando for participating in identity politics when they defended their citizenship rights, advocated for the Latino population, or made allegations of discrimination. When Latinos claimed rights or demanded resources on the basis of their ethnic identity, a history of discrimination, or the need to protect their rights, non-Latino whites interpreted these actions as "playing the race card."

Online commentary in response to funding for Latino-focused projects reveals the color-blind ideologies and hostility. On December 21, 2009, a story entitled "Congressman Grayson Gets Funding for Latino Projects" was posted to the *Hispanosphere* blog. Representative Alan Grayson had secured $700,000 from a $13 million package of federal appropriations for two Orlando-area Latino projects: Spanish-language materials for the public library and expanded programming for the Hispanic Chamber of Commerce. From December 21, 2009, to February 2, 2010, forty-six people wrote comments in response to the article. The conversation immediately turned into a heated debate and some individuals began to challenge both Grayson's action and the need for Spanish-language books:

> Why does any one race require their own projects paid for by American Tax payers.[72]

> This is ridiculous. If they want to live the "American Dream," they need to be American, Americans speak English. If we keep catering to these people they will have no reason to learn english. If they don't want to learn english they need to go back to Puerto Rico or the spanish speaking country of their choice. . . . It's true, the Anglo community has gotten some benefit from the directed spending in the past, but that is precisely as it should be. The descendants of those that sacrificed the most to develop this nation are the ones that should be first in line to receive all benefits available.[73]

> Why are they spending American money on books in Spanish?[74]

> Where is the funding for Caucasian projects? Grayson is a racist nut job![75]

In these examples, respondents were displaying the color-blind ideology that correlated resources for Latinos with reverse discrimination and the language ideology that connected being American with speaking English. This commentary also revealed a nativist critique that rejects Latinos' rights to resources. Commenters made it clear that they saw this ethnic group as a separate, non-white race of people who were unable to assimilate. They also positioned Latinos as non-American and thus as a subclass of citizens who were not as entitled as the "real" Americans. According to "Barton," these programs created "separation and animosity. . . . All this money does is reinforce to Spanish speakers that they don't have to make any effort at all to learn English."[76]

The anti-Spanish commentary of online respondents and of some of my interviewees revealed two additional concepts about language usage. First, these individuals revealed their investment in the existence of a "proper," standardized English, ignoring the many dialects and many Englishes that exist.[77] Such people construct standard English as natural, patriotic, and necessary for the unity and identity of the nation. This is what anthropologist Michael Silverstein refers to as "monoglot standardization." Online commenters connected the ability to speak "proper" English to personal value, worth, Americanness, and personal and professional success.[78] These norms and ideas about "proper" English usage are maintained through institutions, and as Silverstein notes, "these [linguistic] practices acquire an explicitly-recognized hegemony" over other linguistic forms.[79] Second, these individuals also mistakenly presume that one language must be lost in order to gain proficiency in another; one language exists "at the expense of the other." This is a zero-sum language ideology.[80]

In November 23, 2009, *Hispanosphere* announced that an Orlando radio station was switching to Spanish-language sports. Some individuals responded with anger, anti-Spanish hostility, and nativism. They perceived speaking or writing in Spanish as an encroachment on spaces that should be "race neutral," by which they meant white. Sociologist Amanda Lewis summarizes how white people construct the idea of race neutrality: "Blacks and other racial minorities are thought to bring race into situations that previously were understood, in their all white formation, as nonracial or as racially neutral."[81] Thus, non-Latino whites in Osceola County interpreted the designation of resources for a particular ethnic group as an exclusive, race-based decision; although they believed that resources that favored their own group were race neutral. They believed that the public libraries, radio airwaves, supermarkets, and even Latino-focused blogs were spaces that should be treated as "race neutral," "American," and dominated by English. In other words, these spaces were the domain of white hegemony.

So when is it permissible to speak Spanish? Anthropologist Bonnie Urciuoli writes that "languages other than English become safe and acceptable when used in carefully scripted contexts . . . where language is part of a commodity that is familiar and comfortable to most Americans."[82] Such contexts include print and electronic media, festivals and parades, and ethnic restaurants where the waitstaff speaks English with an accent. In Greater Orlando, however, language difference and displays of ethnic group membership were constantly challenged in spaces that Urciuoli defined as safe spaces for speakers of languages other than English. For example, in September 2009, *Hispanosphere* posted an article about a Puerto Rican Roundtable that was forming in Orlando. The idea was that several Puerto Rican organizations would form an umbrella group and represent a common agenda that would foster unity among Puerto Ricans in Central Florida. The first person to respond posted, "My question; how is racism ever going to disappear when we keep being exposed to examples of it? Instead of a Puerto Rican Roundtable, how about a Central Florida Roundtable?"[83] This is an example of Jane Hill's folk theory of racism, whereby a population that is racialized as nonwhite faces accusations of reverse discrimination or racism.

The discussion became a heated debate about the appropriate places for the use of Spanish when "Hector Ivan Rodriguez" wrote a response in Spanish. "Ed" responded angrily to Hector:

Ok now will someone please translate this into English so we all can understand it. Hector it is the height of arrogance to write in Spanish on an English speaking blog in an English speaking newspaper. . . . If you wonder why non-Hispanic people hold Hispanics with contempt it is because of the arrogance displayed by some Hispanics such as Hector. Speak Spanish at home. Speak Spanish with your friends and family. Speak English in public and when dealing with non-Spanish speaking people of all races. That alone will go a long way towards easing the backlash against Hispanics that comes from both white and black non-Hispanics.

Ed pointed to another post in which the commenter had switched from English to Spanish:

Here is another one. Luis R Pastrana began posting in English but mid sentence changed to Spanish. Why? It is obvious that you can speak and write in English yet you choose to be arrogant and post part of your comments in Spanish. Is it an inside joke? Are you laughing at the gringos who don't speak Spanish and can't understand what you are saying?[84]

Latinos have not remained quiet when non-Hispanic whites challenge the use of Spanish. A segment of the Latino population defended using Spanish, advocated for the end of white hegemony, and highlighted the growth of Latino power in the United States due to demographic shifts, noting that the Latino population was increasing and the non-Latino white population was decreasing. Most often these people put using Spanish in the context of the greater access to job opportunities bilingual people had. In online conversations, people emphasized the labor market advantage and rarely mentioned the significance of language for maintaining a Puerto Rican ethnic identity, although cultural preservation is indeed important to many Hispanics. Thus, Hispanics openly suggested that non-Hispanic whites should learn Spanish if they did not want to be at a disadvantage in Greater Orlando's increasingly competitive labor market. They also defended bilingualism as freedom of speech and thus a constitutional right. These were the most defensive responses to the attack on the Spanish language. But other Hispanics agreed with the attacks on the use of Spanish and the privileging of bilingualism, advocated for assimilation, and prioritized knowing English as a route to success in the United States.

Opposition to using Spanish has continued. It circulates not only among adults but also among young people. In the contact zones of Greater Orlando, where non-Hispanic whites encounter Puerto Ricans and other Hispanics and the Latinization of the region, some non-Hispanic whites produce racialized subjects and circulate and refine ideologies about language use, migration, and belonging in the United States. During everyday conversations and encounters, non-Hispanic whites responded to the use of Spanish by referring to deeply embedded language ideologies that fostered a white racial consciousness and revealed the color-blind, race-neutral beliefs that led to allegations of reverse discrimination and white victimization. This was the response of some, though not all, non-Latino whites to the Latinization of the region.

The non-Latino whites I interacted with justified their strong reactions to the use of Spanish as a response to a disruption of the social norms they were familiar with now that an English-dominated soundscape was no longer guaranteed. My interviewees viewed Latinos as the newcomers who were transforming a place they felt entitled to dominate because of their longevity in the region. Additionally, some non-Spanish speakers felt that encountering Spanish in everyday life was uncomfortable and inconvenient. The disruption of everyday tasks that could not be avoided created the most hostile reactions, particularly when the burden of communication and adaptation was placed on non-Latino white residents who felt like victims or minorities in a space they considered home.

While I was visiting a high school classroom near Buenaventura Lakes to share my initial data, a male student who had remained quiet throughout the discussion timidly raised his hand and said, "It is not that we are afraid of Spanish, we are afraid of change." Because Latinos are at the forefront of demographic shifts in the United States, the resulting social, cultural, and political changes continue to cause tensions. Non-Latino whites no longer perceived the Buenaventura Lakes suburb and the other Latino-concentrated areas in Osceola County as desirable communities and saw the Spanish soundscape as partly responsible for their discomfort.

3

The Fractured American Dream

In June 2007, a city-data.com user who goes by the name of Indiana-to-Florida posted a question in the website's online forum: "I've been researching places to live within a 30-minutes drive from the Orlando International Airport. Does anyone live in the Buena Venture Lakes area?? If so, is it a nice, clean, affordable area?" The first response came less than an hour later. "AJ67" wrote, "BVL is HORRID the Crime is outta hand in that area, there are some nice homes there but I would not move to that area if you gave me a house." Nineteen other users joined the conversation thread and continued to post comments until May 2008.

"Blueoktober" responded next. "I have to completely agree with AJ67 on this. BVL was a nice place even up until 3 years ago but now it's pretty bad." "Cmj_fla" wrote, "I have lived in Kissimmee my entire life and do have to agree with the other 2 posters and I am generally a positive person on this board. BVL is overcrowded and the county has ignored this and allowed it [to] become 'run-down.' . . . I think it would be irresponsible to tell anyone to live there at this moment." Of the nineteen respondents, twelve said negative things about Buenaventura Lakes, mentioning crime and gangs or landscape aesthetics. Only two respondents defended the suburb's reputation and place-identity. Four recommended other places to live without mentioning Buenaventura Lakes and one comment was unrelated.

The ethnic and class identities of BVL's residents were not mentioned until ten days after the initial post. Stugots32837 described Buenaventura Lakes as "a working class, predominately Hispanic neighborhood for at least the past 20 years. . . . The crime rate is above average, but not out of control." Another individual who had lived in Buenaventura Lakes for eighteen years before moving in late 1998 described some of the origins of the community's problems: "The problem as I see it is that the builder/developer did not come thru on the promises like happens so often in Florida and elsewhere. There was to be a homeowner's association, that never happened, there were to be restrictions, those were never enforced so the HUGE development became completely rundown. . . . I'd steer clear of BVL and look in other areas." Another person wrote, "I would not recommend Kissimmee, Poinciana, or BVL. Looks nice on the outside but locals know that it is trashy." All three locations this person mentioned have a high concentration of Latinos—specifically Puerto Ricans.

Even current residents hinted at the undesirable conditions. "CJC2008," a new homeowner in Buenaventura Lakes from out of state reached out to the group writing, "I would be interested in getting a homeowner's association going to bring the level up there. . . . i.e. parking cars in driveway instead of on yards☺." "Meinbvl," a resident for twenty-three years, admitted that the community was a bit rundown but added, "if you are afraid of diversity then don't live here. But if you can be tolerant of others then BVL is fine." "**NoodLes**" defended Buenaventura Lakes: "Be careful of what other posters say, most of them live secluded and afraid to come out of their caves."

By the time I moved to Osceola County in 2010, the two golf courses in Buenaventura Lakes had closed, the country club had been demolished, and local newspapers were reporting that the suburb had the second-highest foreclosure rate in the county. Latinos and non-Latinos and residents and non-residents used the terms poor, ghetto, slum, horrid, bad, trashy, overcrowded, rundown, horrible, the pits, drug and gang infested, and working class to describe the suburb. Additionally, online commenters said that the Spanish-language soundscape was a deterrent for monolingual English speakers. In 2010, when I mentioned that I was living in Buenaventura Lakes, I was warned about danger, crime, and gangs. The data I collected from various sources suggested that these were more than just perceptions.

The Decline of Buenaventura Lakes

One July day in 2010, I interviewed a retired police officer who lived in Buenaventura Lakes. I hoped to learn more about BVL's reputation from an insider. Daniel Miller, a non-Latino white who was 75 years old, had moved to Buenaventura Lakes twenty-four years earlier. He had purchased his house from South Americans who were using it as a part-time vacation home. When I asked him why he chose to move to Buenaventura Lakes, he said that it was close to the Interstate 4, Disney World, and the airport. Additionally, he liked the appearance of the suburb, particularly the golf courses and lakes. He also mentioned the country club he used to patronize. But then he said that all of that was gone now. "What would you tell someone who wanted to move here?" I asked. "Go someplace else! This is not a good place to invest!" he responded without hesitating. "Crime is a problem, it is unsafe, and the community [has] deteriorated from the appearance of a good place to the appearance of a poor place." He also mentioned that properties were rapidly deteriorating and that property values have decreased.

We spoke about crime and the absence of a homeowners' association (HOA). Residents felt they had no way to voice their complaints in the absence of a HOA, he said. There had been a self-appointed HOA when Landstar, the company that developed the neighborhood, was still in business. Daniel used to go to packed meetings. However, the meetings had ended ten to fifteen years before our interview. Daniel also noted that code enforcement was very relaxed and deed restrictions were not enforced. "It caused the community to go down. People lose interest when there is no light at the end of the tunnel." One group, the Concerned Citizens of Buenaventura Lakes, still held meetings, but fewer than twelve people were active in 2010. Daniel felt there was a lack of leadership and a lack of representation at both the community and county levels. He had heard that the money the county collected in taxes and fees from Buenaventura Lakes got used elsewhere.

"Do you know about the broken windows theory?" Daniel asked. This criminology theory argues that preventing minor crimes, maintaining the landscape, and maintaining social order can prevent more serious crimes. Miller, who had been a state trooper in Pennsylvania and then worked as a security officer in Greater Orlando, claimed that he could recognize "the symptoms" leading to the decline in Buenaventura Lakes and the resulting increase in gangs, drugs, and the number of robberies, assaults, and home burglaries. Because the major employer in Osceola County was in the low-paying hospitality sector, Daniel felt that the economic situation had a lot to do with the increase in crime. He believed that low-paying jobs lead to social problems because they attract people who are less fortunate, uneducated, or undereducated.[1]

The other problem Daniel mentioned was a breakdown in community spirit. In the past, the big attraction was the country club, which had tennis courts, a pool, a restaurant, a golf course, and a Christmas party. Now there was nothing to pull the community together. "There is nothing for the adults," Michael said. When I asked about the social class of the residents of Buenaventura Lakes, he replied, "Lower-middle class or maybe lower than that."

Newspaper articles corroborated Daniel's descriptions of the decline of Buenaventura Lakes. In 2009, an article quoted Buenaventura Lakes resident John Sidley, a retired hotel employee who explained that he and his family had moved to Florida from Massachusetts twenty years earlier because they had fallen in love with the weather, the Epcot Center, and their home on the edge of a golf course in Buenaventura Lakes. "'The area was beautiful,' said Sidley. 'My backyard was a lush, green golf course in a thriving community.'"[2] However, Sidley was disillusioned with the current state of Buenaventura Lakes because it was nothing like the luxurious country-club community he had bought into years ago:

> The golf course is now deserted, shut down about 10 years ago. A smaller executive golf course in the neighborhood is no longer operating. BVL Boulevard, the community's main artery, is riddled with potholes. The neighborhood streets lack sidewalks. Drainage ditches cut through people's yards. And the problem is compounded by unkempt yards and facades—some of them boarded up—of hundreds of homes facing foreclosure or already in the process.[3]

The article noted that Buenaventura Lakes, which was thirty years old at the time, had not aged gracefully. "No one likes to talk this way about the place where one lives," Sidley said, "but BVL has turned into the slums."

John Quiñones, the county commissioner for Buenaventura Lakes, feels that many of the problems can be traced back to the late 1970s, when the community was built:

> "BVL was not properly planned," he said, faulting the county and the developer. "It was done in a rush. There isn't enough parkland. The small community center is not big enough for so many residents to have a place where they can hold meetings and activities." On many streets, the county did not retain easements—a slice of land between the road and front yards—for future utilities, sidewalks or drainage ditches.[4]

In a 2009 editorial, Buenaventura Lakes resident Larry Steirer wrote, "Several years ago, we had a home built in a beautiful subdivision known as Buenaventura Lakes. We joined the country club for the golf, swimming pool and clubhouse activities. There was a good school, and plans for another in the area. This was an ideal location for my family."[5] He continued, "As of today, there are no clubhouse activities, no swimming pool, no major golf course and fewer activities at the community center. We have lost at least three businesses, and now we have even lost our grocery store." He suggested that Buenaventura Lakes residents start by cleaning up the debris in the community and said that the county needed to enforce codes to "bring our neighborhood back to standards set in my legal papers when I purchased the home. NO one wants to live in a dump." Steirer wrote that "you could start a trend in your neighborhood by being a good citizen."[6]

One of the community's Puerto Rican pioneers, Sandra López, described the transformations she had witnessed during the nineteen years she had lived in Buenaventura Lakes. "When I first moved to BVL," she said, "I had a community of neighbors. It was a neighborhood." Her kids played with and had sleepovers with the other children in the community. But in the second half of the 1990s, white residents had started to move out and new people had started to come in. The neighborhood became more "Hispanic." Sandra said that 75 percent of the people in Buenaventura Lakes were now Hispanic and that Buenaventura Lakes had become "less of a community. People [stay] to themselves." Before, if you needed an aspirin you could ask several neighbors. But as time went on it wasn't like that anymore and that's when it was time to move, Sandra explained. She did not know what the catalyst was, just that things had started to change: "There were fewer Hispanics before, but it was more tight-knit."[7]

I asked Sandra about the changes to the landscape she had observed. First, she mentioned the growing presence of gates and bars on homes "like you see in [Puerto Rico]." "Why do people need gates and bars on their homes?" she asked before mentioning the "cultural change" that had taken place, subtly drawing a distinction between Puerto Ricans from the island and those from the states. Sandra was blaming the gates and bars on Puerto Ricans from the island. She also mentioned the way people cared for their property and described the visual changes to front lawns, which were not taken care of or were, in her opinion, excessively ornate.

Sandra, like so many others, decided to leave when the community began to change. She sold her home to a single Puerto Rican mother with three children. The woman had been looking for a house for six months and fell in love with the home. Sandra said that the woman who bought her home did not have much furniture when she was moving in: "She was buying a shell, but she was proud to buy a home." When Sandra drove by the house several months after the sale, she was shocked at the condition of the home:

> The garage was dented because one of the kids had backed into the garage. Out front were collapsed tents. They had been set up for the kids to play, but had been left there in disarray for some time and remained in front of

the home. The moving boxes were still out front and the grass was growing tall. Maybe it was a result of there being no man in the family. The new resident had two sons, but they aren't doing much, obviously.

Such negative responses to Buenaventura Lakes were not unique. Interviewees rarely drew interethnic distinctions between Puerto Ricans and other Latinos; they primarily referred to the socioeconomic status of Puerto Ricans and to island or mainland status. María Santos, a county worker and a native of Puerto Rico with a BA from the University of Puerto Rico, told me that although her mother lives in Buenaventura Lakes, she would not want to live there. She mentioned the positive things about living in the community. "There is a lot of freedom there," she explained. "We don't like people to tell us what to do so there are no restrictions." Buenaventura Lakes used to have drug-trafficking problems, María said, but it is much better now. She attributed the improvements to John Q, the Puerto Rican county commissioner. Yet she said that "it's almost, you can call it the ghetto."

In June 2010, I met with Martin, a Jamaican American in his early 20s who worked in the insurance industry. He had moved from New York to the Lakeside

Figure 3.1. Defaced white picket fence on a property in Buenaventura Lakes, 2010. Photograph by Simone Delerme.

subdivision next to Buenaventura Lakes fourteen years earlier with his family. When I asked him about the reputation of Buenaventura Lakes, he responded, "good question," and began telling me a story about a girl he had met. In the process of getting to know her he asked if she lived in Buenaventura Lakes, to which she responded defensively: "I'm not poor! I live in Hunters Creek." "BVL isn't poor," he said, "but people don't say positive things about it." He said that it used to be nice but has changed a lot, particularly as Latinos have moved in and non-Latinos have moved out. "Do you know about white flight?" he asked, a term that came into use during the mid-twentieth century to describe the large-scale migration of non-Hispanic whites from racially mixed urban regions to racially homogenous suburbs. He used the term to explain what had happened in Buenaventura Lakes. "The houses are getting older now," he explained, "and they are not being maintained." He mentioned people fixing their old cars in front of their houses, parking on the grass, and the February 1998 tornado that had caused a lot of damage. He also talked about the economy and the lack of good jobs.

We talked about everything from crime and the police presence to suburban sprawl and revolving businesses in strip malls. He mentioned that his subdivision had one of the highest rates of forced entry in the county and recalled an incident when a young person broke into a house with a bat and beat up a resident and their dog. He also described the time he saw a dead body, when an incident involving one of his neighbors turned tragic. Several other individuals I spoke with mentioned crime and/or gangs in Buenaventura Lakes during our conversations. One woman said she avoided the area because it was "a bad place with thugs." A teacher told me that while parents move from New York and New Jersey to get away from gangs, they bring the gangs with them. Both residents and nonresidents mentioned vandalized property, graffiti, break-ins, and other criminal incidents.

In July 2008, journalist Alsy Acevedo noted that "Buenaventura Lakes residents say crime is still one of their main concerns."[8] This view was expressed during a meeting State Representative Darren Soto held in the Robert Guevara Community Center. As I searched through the newspaper archives for evidence of criminal activity, several incidents caught my attention. Operation Zero Tolerance, which targeted criminal and gang activity, took place in Buenaventura Lakes, west Osceola County, and Poinciana on October 29–31, 2007.[9] It resulted in 83 arrests, 239 citations, and 21 warnings. At the time, it was the fifth large-scale operation in the county since January 2006. In December 2007, police discovered a drug and cash stash in a Buenaventura Lakes home that they connected to a Mexico-to-Florida drug ring.[10] In July 2008, police charged a Buenaventura Lakes resident with second-degree murder after he beat a man to death.[11]

The list of criminal activity went on and on. In August of 2008, two men were arrested for attempted murder in Buenaventura Lakes after shooting at two Osceola County deputy sheriffs inside an unmarked law enforcement vehicle.[12] In July of 2009, a trio of convicted felons were arrested in Buenaventura Lakes for their ties to a series of crimes across Central Florida.[13] In October of 2009, a teenager was stabbed to death after attending a house party in Buenaventura Lakes.[14] In April of 2010, gang members were blamed for a fatal brawl at another Buenaventura Lakes house party. According to the sheriff's office, Osceola County was home to about twenty street gangs with more than 400 members.[15] In 2009, residents of Buenaventura Lakes and the Osceola County Sheriff's Office organized a Neighborhood Crime Watch group to patrol the streets daily. However, the group was not in operation when I lived in the suburb. Crime Watch is a crime-prevention program where law-enforcement personnel train people "to be their eyes and ears in the community."[16] One resident mentioned the required training as a deterrent for some residents.

On July 15, 2010, Michael Smith accompanied me for an interview with the county sheriff. The sheriff, who is originally from Osceola County, talked about how the county has changed in waves since the early 1970s. He had been with law enforcement for thirty-four years and had been elected sheriff in Osceola County in 2004. He attributed the growth in volume to the relative population growth. When I asked him about areas that have high call rates, he mentioned Poinciana, Buenaventura Lakes, and an area on "192 near the turnpike exit." He confirmed that gang members live in Buenaventura Lakes and Poinciana. While there have been gang-related murders in Buenaventura Lakes, he noted that a gang unit monitors things constantly. He wouldn't confirm the number of gangs in Buenaventura Lakes but he mentioned Latin Kings, Bloods, Crips, and motorcycle gangs. He did not draw a link between Latinos and crime.

The sheriff also mentioned an increase in violent crimes and property crimes but said that statistics can be deceptive: "There might be a drop in crime this year but it fluctuates and it doesn't take much, many incidents to cause the fluctuation." He also said that foreclosures have an impact on the community: "The signs get posted and the place becomes a rat hole." The banks can't handle all the houses and that detracts from the value. He and Michael speculated about how long it would take for property values to get back to normal. Michael cited a source that estimated ten to fifteen years. Foreclosures were also affecting the county budget, they added. Fewer tax dollars were coming in but the county still needed to provide the same level of services.

In June 2010, three Puerto Ricans who were originally from the Northeast and who did not live in Buenaventura Lakes drove through the subdivision with me and commented on their perceptions while I took fieldnotes. They focused on the landscape and the social class position of its population. One was female and the other two were male. Although none of them had been born in Puerto Rico, they traveled to the island regularly to visit family. One of the distinctions the three made was between Puerto Ricans from the island and Puerto Ricans from the mainland. Many of their comments drew distinctions about social class based on their judgments about the cultural and economic capital of Buenaventura Lakes residents. The group mentioned "junk" in people's garages, uncut grass, clotheslines hanging in garages, flower beds with plastic flowers in front yards, minimal landscaping, and a general lack of maintenance. They also talked about individuals drinking beer in front of the house or in a garage decorated like a living room with a couch, chairs, and tables; cars parked on the front lawns; Christmas lights on a house in the summertime; bright, multicolored houses; and a hammock in front of one person's home. "A hammock is supposed to go in the back of the house," one interviewee said. "Beautification is not important to these people and there must not be a HOA," someone else said.

Then the group discussed the "Puerto Rico mentality" of the residents, who they assumed were from the island. "They put no money into their homes, that's what happens in Puerto Rico too. It's like Levittown [a suburb in Puerto Rico]. It kills me. It looks like a birdcage with all those gates and fences, like in Puerto Rico," one interviewee proclaimed. She went on, "No blanco [white] would come here and put up their house." They all agreed. Tensions between Puerto Ricans who are from or were born in Puerto Rico and those who were born in the mainland states are well documented.[17] Puerto Ricans from the mainland are frequently stereotyped as "Nuyorican," a term that implies a lack of cultural capital, ignorance of island life, and a lower social class. The term "Nuyorican" is "an epithet applied by island-born Puerto Ricans to all U.S.-born residents of Puerto Rican ancestry, regardless of their place of residence."[18] All three of my interviewees might be identified as Nuyorican because they had been born in New York City and lived there for a long time before moving to Florida. However, these middle- to upper-middle-class Nuyoricans were putting down island-born Puerto Ricans instead of the other way around.

Are distinctions between mainlanders and islanders prevalent in Orlando, Florida? The island-born Puerto Ricans of Jorge Duany's Orlando study "were at pains to distinguish themselves from Nuyoricans."[19] Duany's study is based on interviews with well-known leaders of Orlando's Puerto Rican community. The interviewees were highly educated people who worked in upper-class occupational sectors; most had been born and raised on the island of Puerto Rico. Duany's informants describe Nuyoricans as "brass," "assimilated," and "in your face." They described Puerto Ricans from the mainland as behaving differently, having a different way of dressing, and speaking in an aggressive way. As a result, the informants identified Nuyoricans as "a very different community" despite their shared culture, language, and experiences. Duany's interviewees described Puerto Ricans from Chicago as having a "certain idiosyncrasy." One informant said that "you have to be careful" with Puerto Ricans from Chicago, implying

Table 3.1. Household income, Buenaventura Lakes, 2014

Household income	Households	%
Less than $10,000	488	5.8
$10,000 to $14,999	486	5.8
$15,000 to $19,999	630	7.5
$20,000 to $24,999	471	5.6
$25,000 to $29,999	672	8.0
$30,000 to $34,999	811	9.6
$35,000 to $39,999	564	6.7
$40,000 to $44,999	423	5.0
$45,000 to $49,999	365	4.3
$50,000 to $59,999	786	9.3
$60,000 to $74,999	1,316	15.6
$75,000 to $99,999	832	9.9
$100,00 to $124,999	262	3.1
$125,000 to $149,999	156	1.9
$150,000 to $199,999	111	1.3
$200,000 or More	42	0.5
Totals	8,415	99.9
Median household income	$41,155	

Source: Social Explorer, "ACS 2014 (5-Year Estimates) [Household Income: Buenaventura Lakes]."

that they were more dangerous and more prone to crime than Puerto Ricans from the island. Duany's interviewees portrayed Puerto Ricans who migrated to Orlando from New York and Chicago as lower class.

As I continued to ride around the suburb with my three companions, they debated the class position of Buenaventura Lakes residents. One person claimed that the real estate market was bringing in lower-income people. But another person claimed that owning a home does not make you lower class or low income. Homeownership means middle- or possibly lower-middle-class status. Another person called out, "Income is the real test." The two women agreed that this area was low income. For the period 2010–2014, the American Community Survey estimated a median household income of $41,155 for residents of Buenaventura Lakes (see tables 3.1 and 3.2).[20] Are the residents of Buenaventura Lakes low- or middle-income residents? It wasn't clear.

Table 3.2. Household income, Buenaventura Lakes, 2017

Household income	Households	%
Less than $10,000	633	7.20
$10,000 to $14,999	308	3.50
$15,000 to $19,999	651	7.40
$20,000 to $24,999	444	5.10
$25,000 to $29,999	761	8.70
$30,000 to $34,999	633	7.20
$35,000 to $39,999	535	6.10
$40,000 to $44,999	398	4.50
$45,000 to $49,999	483	5.50
$50,000 to $59,999	830	9.50
$60,000 to $74,999	1,049	12.00
$75,000 to $99,999	1,147	13.10
$100,000 to $124,999	578	6.60
$125,000 to $149,999	213	2.40
$150,000 to $199,999	39	0.05
$200,000 or more	57	0.07
Totals	8,759	98.92
Median Household Income	$45,194	

Source: Social Explorer, "ACS 2017 (5-Year Estimates) [Household Income, Buenaventura Lakes, Florida]."

Figure 3.2. For-sale sign, Buenaventura Lakes, 2010. Photograph by Simone Delerme.

"If you want to know about an area you need to look at the cars. These are all simple cars," one of the women said. She feels that a house worth around $100,000 is low income, a middle-class home is worth $200,000 to $400,000, and an upper-class home is worth more than that. "You also need to look at the property taxes."

According to the 2009 American Community Survey 5-Year Estimate, the majority of the 6,544 owner-occupied units in Buenaventura Lakes (71.4 percent or 4,671) were valued at $150,000 to $299,999 (see table 3.3). The second-highest category was $100,000 to $149,999; 11.7 percent (765) of the residents owned units in that range. Two years later, American Community Survey data showed that 53.5 percent (3,328) of the 6,219 owner-occupied housing units were valued at $150,000 to $299,999 (see table 3.4). The second-highest category was $50,000 to $99,999; 18.4 percent (1,141) of housing units were in that range. By 2016, there were only 5,448 owner-occupied housing units and the percent of units valued at

Table 3.3. Value of owner-occupied units, Buenaventura Lakes, 2009

Value	Units	%
Less than $20,000	119	1.8
$20,000 to $49,999	94	1.4
$50,000 to $99,999	295	4.5
$100,000 to $149,999	765	11.7
$150,000 to $299,999	4,671	71.4
$300,000 to $499,999	546	8.3
$500,000 to $749,999	0	0.0
$750,000 to $999,999	15	0.2
$1,000,000 or more	39	0.6
	6,544	99.9

Source: Social Explorer, "ACS 2009 (5-Year Estimates) [House Value for All Owner-Occupied Housing Units, Buenaventura Lakes, Florida]."

Table 3.4. Value of owner-occupied units, Buenaventura Lakes, 2011

Value	Units	%
Less than $20,000	82	1.3
$20,000 to $49,999	239	3.8
$50,000 to $99,999	1,141	18.4
$100,000 to $149,999	1,127	18.1
$150,000 to $299,999	3,328	53.5
$300,000 to $499,999	250	4.0
$500,000 to $749,999	0	0.0
$750,000 to $999,999	16	0.3
$1,000,000 or more	36	0.6
	6,219	100.0

Source: Social Explorer, "ACS 2011 (5-Year Estimates) [House Value for All Owner-Occupied Housing Units, Buenaventura Lakes, Florida]."

Table 3.5. Value of owner-occupied units, Buenaventura Lakes, 2016

Value	Units	%
Less than $20,000	80	1.5
$20,000 to $49,999	139	2.6
$50,000 to $99,999	1,676	30.8
$100,000 to $149,999	1,464	26.9
$150,000 to $299,999	2,034	37.3
$300,000 to $499,999	33	0.6
$500,000 to $749,999	0	0.0
$750,000 to $999,999	12	0.2
$1,000,000 or more	10	0.2
	5,448	100.1

Source: Social Explorer, "ACS 2016 (5-Year Estimates) [House Value for All Owner-Occupied Housing Units, Buenaventura Lakes, Florida]."

Table 3.6. Value of owner-occupied units, Buenaventura Lakes, 2017

Value	Units	%
Less than $20,000	110	1.9
$20,000 to $49,999	67	1.2
$50,000 to $99,999	1,134	19.7
$100,000 to $149,999	1,494	25.9
$150,000 to $299,999	2,836	49.2
$300,000 to $499,999	45	0.8
$500,000 to $749,999	54	0.9
$750,000 to $999,999	10	0.2
$1,000,000 or more	11	0.2
	5,761	100.0

Source: Social Explorer, "ACS 2017 (5-Year Estimates) [House Value for All Owner-Occupied Housing Units, Buenaventura Lakes, Florida]."

$150,000 to $299,999 had decreased to 37.3 (2,034; see table 3.5). The 2016 survey also revealed that 30.8 percent (2,034) of housing units were valued at $50,000 to $99,999. In 2010, Michael Smith told me that the value of his house in Buenaventura Lakes had depreciated from $95,000 to $57,000. A Puerto Rican doctor who practiced and lived in Buenaventura Lakes told me that the value of his house had decreased from $300,000 to $150,000.[21]

The Foreclosure Crisis

When I moved to Buenaventura Lakes, I could see that the 2008 mortgage and foreclosure crisis had greatly impacted the suburban subdivision. For-sale signs could be found on street after street, lawns were unmowed, and newspapers were piling up in driveways. Some homes had graffiti on the exterior and broken windows that were not fixed for weeks. In 2009, the *Orlando Sentinel* reported that Osceola County had the highest foreclosure rates in Central Florida. The majority of foreclosed homes in Osceola County were in Buenaventura Lakes and Poinciana, both suburbs with concentrations of Latino populations.[22] In February 2010, county property appraisers in Central Florida identified the communities where values had fallen the most. Buenaventura Lakes made the list for Osceola County. In 2009, sales in the area had ranged from $65,000 to $239,000; most properties sold for "a little more than $150,000."[23] Just one year later, homes were selling for $40,000 to $170,000 and most were selling for a little more than $75,000.

While the 2008 foreclosure crisis spread across broad segments of the US population, a 2009 study by the National Community Reinvestment Coalition (NCRC) found that minorities experienced disproportionately high rates of foreclosure as a result of disparities in the types of loans they had received. A subprime or high-cost loan has a higher interest rate than loans with competitive rates in order to compensate for the added risk of lending to a borrower with imperfect credit. The NCRC defines a predatory loan as an "unsuitable loan designed to exploit vulnerable and unsophisticated borrowers."[24] Predatory loans, a subset of subprime loans, have one or more of the following features: 1) they charge more in interest and fees than is required to cover the added risk of lending to borrowers with imperfect credit; 2) they have abusive terms and conditions that trap borrowers and lead to increased indebtedness; 3) they do not take into account a borrower's ability to repay the loan; and 4) they violate fair lending laws by targeting women, minorities, and communities of color.[25]

Studies that control for income levels, gender, creditworthiness, and other housing market factors show that in the first decade of this century, ethnic and racial minorities were receiving a disproportionately large amount of high-cost loans.[26] The NCRC study notes that minority communities in inner cities were at the epicenter of the foreclosure crisis, but the crisis spread from those neighborhoods into suburban communities. The NCRC suggests "that as the crisis spreads towards suburban areas, suburban minority communities, including middle- and upper-income ones, appear to be the next in line for rising rates of mortgage default and foreclosure."[27] *Orlando Sentinel* journalists Vicki McClure and Mary Shanklin noted a shift in 2008, when banks began issuing subprime loans to people in the region's suburbs: "In a historic shift that continues to fuel the housing crisis here, high-priced mortgages known as 'subprime' loans broke out of Central Florida's mostly poor and urban neighborhoods in recent years and multiplied by the thousands in the region's suburbs, according to an *Orlando Sentinel* analysis of federal lending data."[28]

In Central Florida, only 8 of the 100 US census tracts with the highest numbers of subprime loans were in low-income urban areas. The remainder were in suburban communities. In 2008, the Central Florida census tracts with the highest concentration of subprime loans included Buenaventura Lakes, Meadow Woods, Poinciana, and Celebration. Table 3.7, taken from the *Orlando Sentinel* article, reveals the number of subprime loans and defaults in the subprime hot spots in Orange and Osceola Counties.[29]

One of the most important findings of the NCRC study is that middle-class or upper-class status does not shield minorities from problematic, high-cost loans. The NCRC observed that ethnic and racial differences in lending actually increase as income levels increase.[30] Table 3.8 reveals this trend in the Orlando-Kissimmee Metropolitan Statistical Area. Middle- to upper-income Hispanic fe-

Table 3.7. Subprime hotspots, Florida, 2004–2007

Community	County	Subprime loans, 2004–2006	Defaults, 2007
Buenaventura Lakes	Osceola	1,789	136
Poinciana	Osceola	2,926	275
Meadow Woods	Orange	3,191	297
Celebration	Osceola	2,654	393

Source: McClure and Shanklin, "The Subprime Mess."

Table 3.8. Prime loans and high-cost loans in the Orlando-Kissimmee
Metropolitan Statistical Area by race, ethnicity, gender, and income category, 2007

	Total loans	Prime loans	High-cost loans	% High-cost loans
Middle- to upper-income Hispanic female	2,974	1,873	1,101	37.02
Middle- to upper-income white female	5,302	4,430	872	16.45
Middle- to upper-income Hispanic male	4,345	2,735	1,610	37.05
Middle- to upper-income white male	8,608	7,138	1,470	17.08
Low- to moderate-income Hispanic female	1,074	826	248	23.09
Low- to moderate-income white female	2,254	1,914	340	15.08
Low- to moderate-income Hispanic male	980	755	225	22.96
Low- to moderate-income white male	1,719	1,399	320	18.62

Source: National Council of Negro Women, "Assessing the Double Burden."

males and males received a higher percentage of high-cost loans than their white
female and male counterparts. There is less disparity in the types of loans banks
offered to low- to moderate-income Hispanic females and males compared to
low- to moderate-income white females and males (see table 3.8).

In Buenaventura Lakes, there was visible damage to the exterior of bank-
owned properties and some homes were structurally damaged and had been
stripped. Magna, an employee in one of the chambers of commerce and a native
of Puerto Rico, spoke with me in an interview about the anger and resentment
those who lost their homes to foreclosure felt. She told me about her Latino
neighbor who stripped the house before being evicted and poured cement down
the kitchen sink, destroying the plumbing of the house. An Osceola County
teacher and several other interviewees also mentioned that evictees often strip
homes to recover any money they can by selling doors, doorknobs, stoves, re-
frigerators, ceiling fans, and anything else of value. Additionally, squatters or
youth have been known to enter foreclosed homes and damage them.

Katharine Newman and colleagues identified several factors that explain the
US foreclosure crisis, including an increase in subprime originations, borrower
and lender exuberance, poor underwriting, aggressive marketing, unscrupulous
mortgage brokers, fraud, naïve borrowers, a declining housing market, tight-
ened credit, servicer accounting errors, and a lack of regulation.[31] Yet my in-

formants and interviewees emphasized the greed of buyers, predatory lending, loan qualification standards, job loss, and the county's economic dependency on tourism. The opinions of the people who spoke with me were formed by their personal experiences, the experiences of others, and the information that circulated in the media.

When they placed blame for the mortgage and foreclosure crisis, they most often highlighted and condemned the greed of prospective buyers. My informants argued that homebuyers knew their financial situations and what they were capable of paying but they had been greedy and purchased beyond their means. This led outside observers to speculate about the personal responsibility of the buyers rather than the mistakes lenders and the government had made. When I asked a high-ranking county official about the county's large number of foreclosures, he immediately responded, "That's what happens when you give people who make $30,000 a $300,000 home."

John López, a licensed broker in Osceola County's real estate industry, claimed that it used to be easy to get a mortgage for a house because credit was not tight. John, who is Puerto Rican, works in a real estate franchise less than a mile away from Buenaventura Lakes that employs fourteen realtors and has a clientele that is almost 99 percent Latino. He claimed that Latinos are not educated and would think, "Oh, my buddy can get me a mortgage, so let's do it." John characterizes this as impulse buying. In the past, he argued, there had been limited opportunities for Hispanics to own homes and then suddenly people could obtain loans.

However, John mentioned job loss and unemployment as the primary reasons his clients have defaulted on their mortgages. He said, "Osceola County does not have a good pool of professional jobs, they are all low to middle income, and as a result it is difficult for the area to prosper." He felt that Osceola County is not bringing in the "good" jobs and that when tourism is down the entire county struggles. In his analysis, the people who come into Osceola County have trouble with credit and can spend only $120,000 to $125,000 for a house. He described his Latino clientele as "regular people"; they are not doctors, lawyers, or people with PhDs. "It's just not the area." He also wanted me to realize that housing lenders target Latino consumers, at times under predatory conditions.

According to Buenaventura Lakes homeowner Michael Smith, there was fraud and greed on the part of both parties, the realtors who changed the numbers to get the loans approved and the buyers who doctored their numbers to get a mortgage. He noted that "the law did not require employment or income verification" and blamed the government and financial institutions for being careless. He claimed that "Clinton's 1996 Bill, which didn't let people's income be verified" was to blame. Thus, Michael blamed government policies and greedy people for the mortgage crisis, including the lenders who lied on the paperwork to make it appear like a family's income was higher and the buyers who sought loans beyond their means.

Similarly, Sarah, a housing specialist for Osceola County who works with first-time home buyers, emphasized lending practices and the willingness of financial institutions to lend more than what customers could afford. "The income-to-debt ratio should be at 30 percent to be considered affordable," she explained, "including principal, taxes, insurance, homeowner association fees, and interest." Nonetheless, some banks were willing to accept a higher income-to-debt ratio. "That's what got people into trouble," Sarah said.

The strong connection between suburban living and prosperity is weakening. Two trends have been noted in suburban communities across the nation: an increase in poverty rates and an increase in the foreign-born population. Suburbs are more than a physical or geographic location; they "have become physical manifestations for American values and cultural ideas."[32] The neighborhood-scout.com website uses neighborhood statistics to build a profile and provide information in the categories of neighbors and demographics, real estate, public schools, and crime rates. In 2016, the site claimed to provide information about a neighborhood's "character" and "personality," the "feeling one gets when experiencing the neighborhood as a true resident."[33] In 2016, in the neighbors and demographics category, the site described Buenaventura Lakes as "lower-middle income, making it a below average income neighborhood." It noted that the average income of residents of Buenaventura Lakes is lower than that of 61.1 percent of US neighborhoods and that 26.2 percent of the children live below the federal poverty line, a higher rate than 66.9 percent of neighborhoods in the United States.

Until the 2010s, downward mobility and poverty were not the dominant images of suburban life. As sociologist Alexandra Murphy points out,

Stories of downward mobility in America's suburbs have not exactly cluttered the headlines over the past decade. Gated communities of dream homes, mansions ringed by man-made lakes and glass-cube office parks: These are the images typically evoked by the posh, supersized subdivisions built during the 1990s technology boom. Low-wage jobs, houses under foreclosure, families unable to afford food and medical care are not.[34]

However, in the 1990s many of the deteriorating conditions associated with inner cities were found in the American suburbs as poverty rates increased.[35] From 1990 to 2000, the number of people living below the poverty line in American suburbs rose 21 percent, compared to an increase of 8 percent in cities. Murphy writes that by 2000, "49 percent of all people living below the poverty line resided in the suburbs, making the suburbs home to the greatest share of the American poor."[36] In 2008, the Brookings Institution reported that the largest and fastest-growing poor population in the United States lived in the nation's suburbs.[37]

Several things account for the growing poverty in and the declining conditions of American suburbs. First, new subdivisions sprang up as the overall population increased. Thus, poverty rates increased in suburbs since more people were living in these areas. Other reasons include the decline in income of long-term residents, the migration of low-income households from cities to suburbs, and the outmigration of middle- and upper-middle-class families from first- and second-ring suburbs to exurbs farther from cities. Additionally, low-income households have been driven to the suburbs by urban renewal projects, urban gentrification, and the decentralization of low-wage employment. The classic migration story has been reversed and the white flight that was first documented in the 1960s has taken a new form. The jobs and housing that once attracted migrants to inner cities are now leading them to the suburbs and non-Hispanic whites who once fled inner cities are returning from the suburbs or leaving their suburban residence for a "nicer" exurb community. One of the consequences has been economic and political disinvestment in aging suburbs, as is the case in Buenaventura Lakes. The 2008 housing crisis and recession that devastated some Florida communities made conditions worse.

An increase in the immigrant population is also changing demographics in the suburbs. According to the Brookings Institution, more immigrants (52 percent) now live in suburbs than in central cities (48 percent).[38] However, suburban poverty is not an immigrant problem; Suro and colleagues found that while immigrants accounted for almost 30 percent of population growth in the suburbs in the period 2000 to 2009, they accounted for less than 17 percent of the increase in the poor population. Suburban poverty increased the most among the US-born population, who accounted for 83 percent of the growth in suburban poverty in the first decade of the twenty-first century.[39] However, these numbers vary from place to place. Tables 3.9, 3.10, and 3.11 show the foreign-born and native-born poverty rates in the Orlando-Kissimmee Metropolitan Statistical Area and the

Table 3.9. Percent living in poverty in the Orlando-Kissimmee Metropolitan Statistical Area by place of birth, 2000 and 2009

	Born outside US			Born in US	
2000	2009	Percent Change	2000	2009	Percent Change
15.1	15.1	0.0	10.1	13.1	+3.0

Source: Suro, Wilson, and Singer, "Immigration and Poverty in America's Suburbs."

Table 3.10. Poor population born in the United States living in the suburbs of Orlando-Kissimmee, 2000 and 2009

2000	2009	% Change	Native-born share of poor, 2009	Native-born share of poor population growth, 2000–2009
119,010	193,257	62.4	82.1%	80.8%

Source: Suro, Wilson, and Singer, "Immigration and Poverty in America's Suburbs."

Table 3.11. Poor population born outside the United States living in the suburbs of Orlando-Kissimmee, 2000 and 2009

2000	2009	% Change	Foreign-born share of poor, 2009	Foreign-born share of poor population growth, 2000–2009
24,437	42,037	72	17.9%	19.2%

Source: Suro, Wilson, and Singer, "Immigration and Poverty in America's Suburbs."

surrounding suburbs. Consistent with national trends, in the suburbs, the native-born population constitutes the majority of the suburban poor.

Virtual Discourses and the Racialization of Latinos

City-data.com forums conveyed the reputations and place-identities of Buenaventura Lakes, Kissimmee, and the surrounding communities in Osceola County to a wider local, regional, and national audience. On November 4,

2009, "nberry7" posted a question on the city-data.com site. She and her husband were thinking about moving from "middle of nowhere" Kansas to Osceola County and wanted to know the pros and cons of such a move. They had two daughters who were in elementary school and nberry7 was planning to open a daycare like the one she owned in Kansas. The couple had found "some very nice houses for cheap" on the Internet but wondered if there was a catch: "Why . . . so cheap?" "annerk" replied almost immediately: "I wouldn't put my kids into Osceola schools. If you don't speak Spanish you'll have a hard time opening a day care in Kissimmee. Houses are cheap for a reason. The majority of Kissimmee and Poinciana are NOT a desirable place to live."[40]

Respondent "don macauley" echoed annerk's comment about speaking Spanish: "Forget Kissimmee, I have been living here 25 years and if you don't speak Spanish, forget it. . . . kissimmee is a 'no go' on my list, its going down hill."[41] Another user, "ComSense," quoted don macauley and wrote, "I agree too, especially about the Spanish speaking part. I'd stay away from Kissimmee. It looks like a big carnival lining the streets."[42] Eighteen city-data.com users participated in this thread. Eleven comments were negative, one was positive, three recommended other locations without commenting on Osceola County or Kissimmee, and three were unrelated. "lifelongMOgal" wrote, "Have to agree with the 'don't move to Kissimmee' crowd. . . . The area has run its course from good to bad. No area that is largely populated with migrants and illegals will see property values or the quality of schools increase. Areas that were once just average affordable 'old Florida' neighborhoods in Kissimmee now have the appearance of 'barrios.'"[43] The thread continued into 2010. "hxrguitar" warned nberry7 about the presence of Spanish-speaking Latinos:

Well First thing is first there are. TONS of Spanish, Mexican's, Latin Americans puerto ricans u name it Barely any white people not being racist but that's all you will see or Hillbilly's/Rednecks but that is more saint cloud area that's one thing u might not be to happy about and all of them speak Spanish mostly. They "Can" speak english but per-fer Spanish. And people there especially Spanish tend to be rude, But there are cool ones. . . . Like I said before there are alot of Spanish and people that kind of race that live there so ur kids will feel kinda awkward being the small amount of white kids that live and go to school here. Not being racist i have many Mexican and Spanish friends I'm just basing it on what i see EVERYDAY. I'm just basing this on if ur kids are white.[44]

This commenter classified Latinos as a separate, nonwhite race of people based on cultural characteristics like the use of the Spanish language. Another respondent referred to Latinos as neither black nor white:

> Kissimmee is a city in transition. . . . WIKIpedia says the Latino pop in Kissimmee is only 40%, I beg to differ. I work in the ER, and I am always startled when I see a White person or a Black person, because its almost a rarity. . . . Spanish is spoken as frequently, if not more frequently, than English. . . . I love that Kissimmee is diverse, but its loosing that now too, as it becomes completely Caribbean Hispanic. . . . Its mainly people form the Northeast and PR.[45]

Through these discourses, respondents carved out a third space in Greater Orlando for Latinos and contributed to the formation of a Latino-concentrated enclave by discouraging "whites" from living in Kissimmee. They also contributed to the social construction of a "Hispanic race" that challenges the historic black-white racial binary.

In June 2008, city-data.com user "poodlestix" asked about the place-identity of Buenaventura Lakes.

> I was looking at homes with the realtor and found a house at the corner of Lakeside and Anhinga that I really liked. I heard some loud music playing a couple of doors down that evening, and it kind of got me concerned about the neighborhood. I also noticed a broken window on the side that faces Lakeside which looked like could possibly have been made by a bullet. Is that possible? I'm not familiar with whether this is a good neighborhood, but I loved the house.

The first response, from "Wilshire81182," came less than an hour later:

> Buena Ventura Lakes is a lower income neighborhood in general. I would not recommend the area, but I know it is not the worst area to move to overall. I am sure it has some safety concerns and people may not take the best care of their property or yours given the nature of the area. The area is synonymous with the posts about Kissimmee and the reasons why people advise to avoid it.

The next commenter suggested that poodlestix trust her instinct and said that the area has problems with overcrowding and a lack of community spirit. When "NowInGreenville" responded, the conversation turned to the ethnic makeup of the community, the "lack of diversity" (meaning a majority of Hispanics rather than non-Hispanic whites), and the use of Spanish:

> You're coming from Texas so maybe you speak Spanish. If not than you may want to take lessons. If I'm not mistaken, BVL is about 80–85% Hispanic. That doesn't mean it is a bad area, it just means that area of central florida is not as diverse as others. In most other area of CF, the racial make up is much more evenly distributed.

poodlestix received responses from only three users, but their negative comments was enough to convince her to purchase elsewhere:

> Nah, I'm just a white girl with a limited Spanish repertoire. The house was lovely, but I was leery about the neighborhood for sure. Too bad you can't pick up your ideal house and set it down on a lot in a better neighborhood! We're going to go with the other house we had our eye on in what seems to be a better part of Kissimmee. Thanks for the input!

The soundscape in Buenaventura Lakes, where Spanish could be heard as frequently if not more frequently than English, fostered a stronger white racial consciousness among non-Latino whites. The Internet sites with comments about Buenaventura Lakes, Kissimmee, and Osceola County revealed many of the reasons why Buenaventura Lakes was no longer a "nice" place to live: crime, drugs, and gangs; overdevelopment and overcrowding; the "run down" appearance of the houses; the age of the community; the absence of a HOA to enforce restrictions; the absence of amenities like the golf course and country club; and the increase of foreclosed homes. Additionally, the concentration of Latinos and the presence of the Spanish language were cited as reasons to live elsewhere, thereby hurting the reputation of Buenaventura Lakes and perceived "niceness" of the area.

Commenters in the online forums racialized the community of Buenaventura Lakes as a nonwhite space that was unsuitable and uncomfortable for "white people." In the US census, however, the largest share of residents in Buenaventura Lakes and Osceola County identify themselves as white. At the time of my fieldwork in 2010, 46 percent of Latinos in Buenaventura Lakes identified themselves as white in the census, 15.9 percent identified as some other race, 3.5 percent identified as two or more races, and 3.6 percent identified as black or African American.[46] In Osceola County, 30.6 percent of Latinos identified as white, 9.8 percent identified as some other race, 2.4 percent identified as two or more races, and 2.2 percent identified as black or African American alone.[47] In Buenaventura Lakes, the widespread use of Spanish is central to the racialization process. Dominant language ideologies racialized speaking Spanish along with other practices, physical characteristics, and signifiers of identity. The discourses that circulate on the Internet impact residential patterns and can lead to segregation on the basis of cultural characteristics, what Elizabeth Aranda and Guillermo Rebollo-Gil refer to as ethnoracism.[48] One city-data.com commenter said: "be aware that people here seem to segregate themselves more here than out west, I've found . . . and generally the areas that are nicest here are very un-diverse (read: VERY white)."[49]

In July 2010, "GinnyFavers" posted a question on the city-data.com forum: "I heard from someone that the Buena Ventura Lakes subdivision was a majority to all Hispanic area. Just curious if that's really true? No negative implication intended! ~Amanda."[50] "Metrowester" responded. "Yes, BVL is a primarily Hispanic area. Landstar homes was heavily marketed in Puerto Rico several years ago."[51] Metrowester spoke favorably about the Publix Sabor supermarket in the area, noting that its deli served Cuban coffee, pastries, and roasted pork. He identified himself as "a gringo with a Puerto Rican girlfriend."

Eleven people joined the conversation. Some provided recommendations about where to live, opinions about the "niceness" of the community, descriptions of the area, and references to race, ethnicity, and the Spanish language. "itsajourney" wrote "also would agree that BVL is an overwhelming majority of Hispanics. . . . If you are not Hispanic and would find living in such a community would make you feel uncomfortable in any way, I would suggest you look in other areas. . . . However, do not get me wrong—it is not a bad area. Most of it is pretty decent. Not upscale & not ghetto—but decent." Warnings that some people might feel uncomfortable in such a neighborhood if they were white stigmatized the Latino population, the community of Buenaventura Lakes, and the Spanish language. Some respondents rejected the community outright. "I'm Hispanic, I personally wouldn't live there," said "Ir5497."[52] "Infinite loop" wrote, "I would not recommend BVL."[53] Others commented on the widespread use of Spanish in Buenaventura Lakes and other parts of Greater Orlando. "Watchdaride" wrote, "I work in the SE Orlando and I have noticed some latin restaurant/store don't even speak english and just ignores you if you don't speak Spanish. . . . Miami is little Havanna. Orlando is little puerto rico."[54] "DavieJ89," a Buenaventura Lakes resident from 1995 to 1997, suggested that GinnyFavers "look carefully" because "some of the areas aren't that good."[55] He claimed that in the supermarkets in the area "neither the cashier or the bagger, or anybody in the store spoke english."

Niceness and a Fear of Others

Anthropologist Setha Low's theoretical discussion of niceness, fear of others, and white privilege can be used to analyze these comments about Buenaventura Lakes, Kissimmee, and Osceola County residents. She defines niceness as "keeping things clean, orderly, homogenous, and controlled so that housing values remain stable," noting that it is also "a coded way to talk about and take action against racial differences and a loss of white privilege."[56] Low argued that while niceness and a fear of others are "discursive means for justifying and rationalizing" residential choices, they "[inscribe] racist assumptions on the landscape."[57] Discussions about the niceness of a community like Buenaventura Lakes reflect people's moral and aesthetic judgments. Low argues that discussions about a desire for niceness and the fear of others are covert ways of talking about racial differences, ethnic changes, changing socioeconomic environments, and a loss of white privilege.[58]

According to Genevieve Carpio, Clara Iraz Abal, and Laura Pulido, the "possessive investment in whiteness" and the assumptions, privileges, and benefits that accompany being a non-Latino white or living in a community where this group is the majority can take various forms, including "higher property values, better schools, or the ability to exclude people of color from the workplace."[59] However, "whites do not necessarily *intend* to hurt people of color, but because they are unaware of their white-skin privilege, and because they accrue social and economic benefits by maintaining the status quo, they inevitably do."[60] Non-Latino whites' responses to the transformations of Buenaventura Lakes draw attention to the subtler strategies they use to maintain whiteness and niceness by controlling the social and physical environment. For many decades, it was realtors, redlining practices, mortgage lenders, and zoning ordinances that influenced neighborhood composition. Today in Buenaventura Lakes, neighborhood composition is influenced by online forums where strangers can warn someone from another state about a Latino-concentrated community by circulating information that brands a place such as Buenaventura Lakes as poor, crime-ridden, aesthetically undesirable, or as a Spanish-speaking "Puerto Rican," "Hispanic," or "Latino" place. Such characterizations conflate the identity of the residents with the niceness of the suburb. Non-Latino whites use talk about the built environment to reproduce and circulate racial meanings and class distinctions.

The online comments about the place-identity of Buenaventura Lakes also reveals how white privilege is expressed and protected in the spatial arrangements of suburban neighborhoods. At its inception, suburbanization was a primary form of white privilege; it enabled "whites to live in inexpensive, clean, residential environments."[61] For much of the twentieth century, people of color were denied the opportunity to live in US suburbs because of redlining and other discriminatory practices, yet they subsidized white suburbia through their tax dollars and suffered from the declining conditions in inner cities that white flight and disinvestment caused.[62] Today, white privilege involves the production of communities with a very high proportion of "white" people. Carpio, Abal, and Pulido note that one component of white privilege is the fear that "'too many' people of color might reduce a neighborhood's status, property value, or general level of comfort for white people."[63] Hence, online commenters often told potential homebuyers in Buenaventura Lakes to look elsewhere if they were "white" and did not speak Spanish. These discourses contribute to the concentration of Latinos and other Puerto Ricans in particular locations such as Buenaventura Lakes.

Patricia Silver and William Vélez note that in the first decade of the twenty-first century, the degree to which Puerto Ricans were exposed to non-Hispanic whites decreased. This change was most pronounced in Osceola County. This research "points to a shift from dispersed settlement crossing the metropolitan area to increasing concentrations in specific locations, especially in Orange and Osceola counties."[64]

A county commissioner in Osceola County used the term "rocky road" to describe the challenges of transitioning from an "old school rural service provider" to an urban space that attracts international tourists and a Latino population that continues to grow. He also used the term "desperate" to describe the current condition of Buenaventura Lakes and Osceola County, referring to the increasing unemployment rates; the preponderance of low-skilled, low-wage jobs; low occupancy rates in the hotels; poverty; homelessness; and the high rates of foreclosure the county was facing in the late 2000s. Landstar's successful marketing efforts in the 1980s and 1990s made Buenaventura Lakes the epicenter of a growing Puerto Rican community, transformed Osceola County, and encouraged other developers to target prospective buyers in Puerto Rico. But as the population of Latino migrants increased, the reputation and desirability of Buenaventura Lakes decreased. The comments that circulated online, that were published in newspapers, and that people made to me during interviews helped explain why the place-identity of the community had changed over time. Those changing perceptions were sometimes connected to racial, ethnic, and social class identities. The data sources suggest that several factors were responsible for change such as the foreclosure crisis or the closing of the country club and golf courses. Buenaventura Lakes, once a community for country-club living and affordable luxury, has turned into a ghetto or a slum in the eyes of many residents and nonresidents, Latino and non-Latino alike.

Individuals drew more explicit connections between the perceived racial identity of residents, language use, and the "niceness" of Buenaventura Lakes when they were protected by anonymous usernames in the virtual spaces of the Internet. Some peoples' responses to inquiries about the suburb racialized Puerto Ricans and other Latinos as a separate, nonwhite "Hispanic" or "Latino" racial category. Therefore, the online posts are articulations that lead to the "de facto racialization" of Latinos in popular usage that Rumbaut discusses.[65] In this case, commenters also racialized a place and a language. These individuals did not intend to do any harm or have an impact on the community's demographics. Instead, they were looking for advice before making a substantial financial investment or were attempting to provide assistance to someone from Kansas or Mississippi who was unfamiliar with the area. Still, discussions about the place-identity and desirability of Buenaventura Lakes contribute to residential segregation in the suburbs and the formation of "new ethnic enclaves" on the basis of language, race, and ethnicity.

When I moved to Buenaventura Lakes, I expected to find a middle-class suburb, but the community was perceived differently. José Cruz used data from the US census to demonstrate that "Hispanics in Osceola County are a predominantly working-class population."[66] Census data reveals that "a full 56 percent of the population 16 years and over are employed in service, construction, and production occupations. Another 28 percent work in sales and office occupations. A smaller proportion—15 percent—work as managers, professionals, and in related occupations."[67]

However, while representations and perceptions of the Buenaventura Lakes suburb emphasized working-class and low-income Puerto Ricans and other Latinos, the migration to Greater Orlando included individuals from a variety of social class positions. While I lived in Greater Orlando, I encountered business networking organizations where upwardly mobile Latino homeowners, professionals, and entrepreneurs came together to ensure that they would be successful in Greater Orlando. These individuals were dispersed in suburban communities throughout the region. For example, Jerry, who described himself as Puerto Rican and Spanish, emphasized the connections he has with people based on class rather than on ethnicity. When I asked him where he lives and why he chose not to live in a Hispanic-concentrated community like Buenaventura Lakes, he laughed and said that in the past people might have moved near the bodegas (grocery stores) to be around one another and feel at home. A bodega, he said, "was a guarantee of a [Hispanic] community developing in the area." However, living in close proximity to other Hispanics was not important to him: "Now it is more about being identified as a professional, as a success. You want to live where other middle class people live. Go to the nice restaurants and nice places that other middle class people go to." Jerry told me that his social circle was not exclusively Hispanic. His networks and group affiliations are related to business. He said that he did not involve himself in the associations that focused on culture.

The strong connection between suburban living and prosperity is weakening, and as a declining suburb, Buenaventura Lakes is representative of the changing social and economic conditions and demographics in suburbs across the United States. The widespread perception that Buenaventura Lakes had become a slum led me to explore other Latino groups in Greater Orlando to document the class diversity of the incoming migrant population.

4

Social Class Distinctions and the Latino Elite

In June 2010, I learned about a networking event that catered to Latino professionals in Greater Orlando. I was attending a college graduation ceremony at a hotel on International Drive, a popular tourist destination. Sistema Universitario Ana G. Méndez, which was founded in Puerto Rico, had established a campus in Orlando in 2003. The keynote speaker was an immigrant from Venezuela who was president of the Hispanic Chamber of Commerce. While there, I learned that Amigos Profesionales and HYPE (Hispanic Young Professionals and Entrepreneurs) of Orlando were co-sponsoring an event in another part of the hotel. For a $15 fee I was granted admission to the venue.

At the event, two attorneys, two magazines, and a BMW representative were advertising their services and products at a series of tables. People stood in clusters chatting with one another, among them Carlos Irizarry, commissioner of the city of Kissimmee; John Quiñones, an Osceola County commissioner; and several candidates who were running for office in the upcoming elections. Sissy, a Cuban model featured on the cover of *Epiko*, one of the magazines represented at the event, took the stage to welcome the attendees. She mentioned Disney World and spoke of her surprise at the dynamic growth in the Latino population. A pianist who had migrated from Puerto Rico years earlier performed for the audience. Then the founder of Amigos Profesionales, who had migrated from Puerto Rico in the late 1980s, introduced the board of directors, which included both Latino and non-Latino white professionals. As I glanced around the room, I observed the demeanor and attire of the well-dressed crowd. I had come to Orlando hoping to encounter a solidly middle- to upper-middle-class population of Puerto Ricans, the well-educated professionals and managers Jorge Duany and Felix Matos-Rodriguez wrote about.[1] My intention was to learn about the migration experiences of a population that is not well represented in the literature about the Puerto Rican diaspora.[2]

Myriam Marquez, a journalist who was present at the installation banquet of the Hispanic Chamber of Commerce of Central Florida in February 1995, documented the event. She wrote, "If you weren't at Church Street Station's Presidential Ballroom last Friday night you wouldn't know it, but what happened there was awesome. The Hispanic business and professional community of Central Florida arrived that evening—and boy, what a party!"[3] In another article, published a year earlier, a journalist wrote about the status of the attendees: "Everyone at the cocktail party in downtown Orlando had a business card and a formal title. There was the vice president for something important at a local bank and the assistant to the Puerto Rican head of something else. Then there was Titi Chagua, a celebrity guest who needed no introduction to this Puerto Rican crowd."[4]

Although the region's tourism industry attracted low-wage, service sector workers, the wave of Puerto Rican migrants to Greater Orlando also included college-educated professionals and entrepreneurs.[5] As early as 1986, newspaper accounts reported that Puerto Rican entrepreneurs were coming together in the area. In October of that year, Puerto Rican entrepreneurs announced the creation of a new agency to help Hispanics to establish businesses in the Orlando area.[6] The agency planned to link entrepreneurs in Orlando, Miami, and Puerto Rico to make it easier for new migrant entrepreneurs. "Let's say that I am a businessman in Puerto Rico who wants to relocate in Orlando," said José Gomez, a member of the chapter board. "All that I will need to do is contact the chamber there and avoid spending two or three months looking for the information here."[7] There were also plans to create an Orlando Chapter of the Puerto Rican Chamber of Commerce. One member explained, "We decided to go ahead and form the group . . . when we saw that there are a lot of Puerto Rican professionals coming here from the island who needed information and advice about how to start their own business."[8] The new chapter planned to conduct a marketing study that members or large corporations interested in exploring the local Hispanic market could use. The Puerto Rican Chamber continued to exist into the early 1990s, then merged with the Latino Chamber of Commerce to form the Hispanic Chamber of Commerce. In 2005, a group of business owners revived the Puerto Rican Chamber of Commerce. It was still active when I did my fieldwork.

The media attempted to differentiate middle-class members of the Puerto

Rican migration to Florida from the working-class migrants who had settled in New York in the middle decades of the twentieth century. On April 7, 1988, for instance, a respondent told journalist Dora Delgado that "low- and middle-income Puerto Ricans move to New York because they want a decent paying job, while professionals such as lawyers and doctors are coming to Central Florida."[9]

In 1989, an *Orlando Sentinel* article emphasized the upper-class segment of the Puerto Rican population that was attracted to Orlando: "Orlando is getting one of the best immigrant groups ever available anywhere. The Puerto Ricans who have come here during the last five years are businessmen, entrepreneurs, professionals and wealthy retired people who are contributing to our economy." The journalist acknowledged the presence of "some poor and unskilled workers" but was careful to add that "they're not looking for welfare, They're looking for jobs and opportunities."[10] Similarly, in 1993, journalist Sean Holton wrote that "unlike the waves of destitute farmers who left for New York and Chicago in the 1950s, most of these Puerto Ricans have money and education. The Puerto Rican migrants of the 1980s and 1990s are looking for a place to buy homes, find jobs, raise families and enjoy weather and an overall pace that makes them feel closer to home."[11]

In 2002, the Puerto Rican Professional Association (PROFESA), a Miami group, began launching a Central Florida chapter. According to José Fernández, a Puerto Rican community activist and lawyer, "our goal is to unite all Puerto Rican professionals so we can share our ideas to further develop our community into a more professional and diverse place."[12] Puerto Rican professionals emphasized that "there is a void of professional organizations." Aside from the Puerto Rican Chamber of Commerce, which caters to entrepreneurs, no other group dealt directly with Puerto Rican professionals, claimed Pedro Vázquez, a Puerto Rican accountant.[13]

A 2004 article in the *Orlando Sentinel* drew a sharp distinction between the unskilled poor migrants who had settled in the Northeast and the middle-class migrants who were settling in Orlando:

> Puerto Rican migratory waves during the middle decades of the 20th century were mostly composed of poor, unskilled, rural migrants displaced by the island's fast-paced processes of industrialization and urbanization. They mostly migrated to New York City and other Northern urban centers. In contrast, the more recent migration of Puerto Ricans to the Orlando region reflect a wide representation of the island's population, with a large percentage of professionals and members of the middle class."[14]

Miguel López, former president of the Puerto Rican Chamber of Commerce of Central Florida, emphasized the professional and skilled occupations of Orlando's Puerto Rican migrants: "There is a stereotype that Puerto Rican immigrants are poor and uneducated. . . . To the contrary . . . many are college-educated, professional business people, such as accountants and medical personnel. Most immigrants are skilled workers, such as mechanics. They're not coming here to pick up vegetables."[15] In 2002, journalist Gary Taylor wrote that "Hispanic lifestyles are no longer dominated by jobs in the service industry. There are growing numbers of Hispanic professionals, and Hispanics are moving into technology fields at a record pace."[16] While some articles highlighted the low-skilled, low-paid service sector workers who were attracted to the tourism industry or the criminality of the incoming Puerto Rican population, reports like these emphasized that the majority of Greater Orlando's Puerto Rican migrants were entrepreneurs, property owners, professionals, and well-educated people.

Anthropologist Patricia Silver points out that "the field of Puerto Rican Studies includes a dominant narrative about a largely working-class migration from Puerto Rico to northern US cities between the 1940s and 1960s."[17] However, her ethnographic research and the oral history interviews in her project provide evidence of a "cross-class group of individuals who decided to 'do something different' and head to Florida" during that time period. Silver used data from the American Community Survey and the US census to compare socioeconomic indicators for Puerto Rican and Latino populations in the Northeast and the South and in Florida and the Orlando-Kissimmee Metropolitan Statistical Area (see table 4.1). In 2015, Puerto Ricans constituted 14 percent (318,101) of the total population in the Orlando-Kissimmee Metropolitan Statistical Area. Latinos constituted 27 percent (642,282) of that population. The data show that Puerto Ricans who were coming to the South were "faring better than their counterparts in the Northeast" in terms of median household income, educational attainment, civilian unemployment, and number of families below the poverty level.[18] For instance, the median household income for Puerto Ricans in Orlando was $40,000; for Puerto Ricans in the Northeast, it was $36,000.

The class diversity of the Puerto Rican population is also evident in data about household income and employment sectors (see table 4.2). Thirty-one percent of employed Puerto Ricans in Orlando were working in sales and office jobs, 24 percent had jobs in the service sector, and 22 percent were managers, businesspeople, scientists, and artists.[19] Employers in the Southeast are increasingly recruiting Puerto Ricans with "professional credentials and bilingual

Table 4.1. Median household income, education, civilian unemployment, and percent of families with incomes below the poverty line, Puerto Ricans and Latinos in Florida, the US South, and the US Northeast

	Orlando	Florida	South	Northeast
MEDIAN HOUSEHOLD INCOME				
Puerto Rican	$40,000	$41,000	$45,000	$36,000
Latino	$41,500	$42,000	$43,000	$42,000
PERCENT WITH BA OR HIGHER				
Puerto Rican	18	20	23	14
Latino	21	23	17	17
PERCENT UNEMPLOYED				
Puerto Rican	6	8	7	11
Latino	7	7	6	9
PERCENT LIVING BELOW POVERTY LINE				
Puerto Rican	17	16	16	26
Latino	19	18	20	23

Source: Silver, "Sunshine Politics."

Table 4.2. Income in Puerto Rican households in Orlando-Kissimmee Metropolitan Statistical Area by percent

Income category	%
Under $15,000	14
$15,000–$24,999	14
$25,000–$34,999	15
$35,000–$49,999	18
$50,000–$74,999	21
$75,000–$99,999	9
$100,000–$149,999	5
Over $150,000	2

Source: Silver, "Sunshine Politics."

skills."[20] Professionals and managers and the organizations that support their professional ambitions are the focus of this chapter.

Scholars have noted the significant role that class identity plays in the life of migrants. Elenga Sabogal found that middle-class Peruvian professionals in South Florida "classify themselves and others on the basis of socio-economic and cultural factors" such as level of education, lifestyle, family name, manners and social poise.[21] These migrants did not abandon class ideologies and class divisions when they migrated; they reproduced them in the new location. These distinctions are significant in social life. Helen Marrow points out that scholars who have observed a triracial divide in the United States among Hispanics, blacks, and whites point to growing "material, subjective, and behavioral gaps both between and within contemporary racial groups, driven primarily by class and skin color."[22] Social relations among Hispanics in Greater Orlando are characterized by such internal divisions; "elite" Hispanics collaborate with non-Hispanic whites and alienate poor and working-class Hispanics.

Laura López-Sanders's study of Mexican, Colombian, and Guatemalan migration to the Bible Belt found that distinctions based on ethnicity and class were the two main forces that shaped the relationships and rising tensions among Hispanic groups in the churches in the communities they had migrated to. Colombian immigrants in this study, who were better off than Guatemalan and Mexican migrants, "carefully guarded their privileged class and racial standing by managing the affairs of all Hispanics and by creating social distance between groups."[23] These Colombians maintained class boundaries by preventing Mexican and Guatemalan newcomers from becoming leaders or decision makers in local churches. This hindered the development of solidarity based on ethnicity among the new Hispanic population. Such divisions are also evident within the Puerto Rican migrant community in Orlando.

During the period of my fieldwork, a community of upwardly mobile professionals and entrepreneurs was solidifying in Greater Orlando at networking events, leads meetings, award ceremonies, galas, golf courses, and ribbon-cutting ceremonies. For some Latinos, participation in membership-based business organizations generated social, symbolic, and economic capital. These individuals were members of a visible cohort of Latino entrepreneurs and professionals who were working in the finance, insurance, and real estate sectors. I was interested in the social class identities of the members of Latino-focused business networking organizations. How did they make sense of their class position and articulate class distinctions?

I began attending events and meetings sponsored by the Hispanic Chamber of Commerce, Amigos Profesionales, Hispanic Young Professionals and Entrepreneurs of Orlando, the Hispanic Area Council of the Osceola County Chamber of Commerce, and the Puerto Rican Chamber of Commerce. These events took me into Seminole County, Orange County, and the city of Orlando. I asked members of these organizations to describe their class position and the factors that shaped how they saw themselves and perceived others. I wanted to know if members were creating class boundaries, exclusive social spaces, or a visible cohort of elite professionals and entrepreneurs through participation in these organizations. I was also interested in how they articulated class distinctions and how their attitudes might be creating or reinforcing inequalities.

Theorizing Social Class Distinctions

Four criteria are commonly used to gauge class position: education, income, occupation, and wealth. Literature from several disciplines reveals that behavior, taste, status, lifestyle, consumption patterns, cultural capital, and power also influence social class identities and positionality.[24] While source of income and conditions of employment undoubtedly influence class formation, I am interested in a different dimension of class: the things that appear to be superficial (such as playing golf versus playing dominoes) but have a social meaning and thus influence and reinforce class identities and social inequalities. Sociologist Celia Ridgeway argues that all too often, studies of stratification focus on power and economic resources and neglect other forms of social inequality.[25] She maintains that social status is an independent mechanism that creates and sustains inequalities. During my fieldwork, it became increasingly evident that members of the Puerto Rican community in Greater Orlando often understood class distinctions in terms of lifestyle differences, tastes, status, and other forms of cultural and symbolic capital. Thus, I focused on how people articulate, perform, defend, and contest social class identities and positions.

Pierre Bourdieu theorized that four types of capital—economic, symbolic, social, and cultural—contribute to class formation, reinforce one another, and cannot be easily disentangled.[26] This was evident in interviews and conversations with Puerto Ricans in Greater Orlando. Many people referred to multiple forms of capital that intersected. Economic capital usually refers to an individual's income, which is directly related to their position in the labor market and their assets and investments. Symbolic capital refers to the resources that are available to an individual based on honor, prestige, or recognition. Social capital is based on the value of networks.

Cultural capital consists of things such as social skills, habits, linguistic styles, and the tastes a person acquires. Bourdieu discusses three types of cultural capital. Objectified cultural capital consists of the material goods that are associated with economic capital. Institutionalized cultural capital refers to the certifications that officially acknowledge our knowledge and abilities. Embodied cultural capital, the most significant for Bourdieu's discussion of tastes, is the cultural capital that lives in us and is expressed through the body and manifests as tastes. Bourdieu argues that cultural capital is embodied in our habitus, or how we present our body to the world. Habitus is the result of how we are socialized and functions as a marker of our social class position. It is internalized and it becomes part of our identity. Cultural capital is evident in our thoughts, our feelings, our actions, our postures, and our language. In other words, it is not only what a person does for a living and how much they make that is important for class formation. What a person does with their income and how they behave, act, and perform in society also matter. Thus, as cultural anthropologist Sherry Ortner argues, "we may think of class as something people are or have or possess, or as a place in which people find themselves or are assigned, but we may also think of it as a project, as something that is always being made or kept or defended, feared or desired."[27]

Sociologists Michele Lamont and Annette Lareau have introduced a definition of cultural capital that emphasizes social and cultural exclusion on the basis of particular "institutionalized, i.e., widely shared, high status cultural signals (attitudes, preferences, formal knowledge, behaviors, goods and credentials)."[28] They followed this several years later with a broader definition of cultural capital that stresses "micro interactional processes." They argue that the most important aspect of cultural capital is that it enables people to use culture "as a resource that provides access to scarce rewards." Other aspects of cultural capital are that it can be monopolized and that it can be passed from one generation to another. Lamont and Lareau emphasize that cultural capital is socially constructed.[29]

The work of these theorists can be used to examine how cultural capital functions as a mechanism of power in business networking organizations that create and maintain socially exclusive spaces for Latino professionals and entrepreneurs. Membership in such organizations creates social ties that foster solidarity and provide access to valuable resources for building capital. Belonging to such groups gives people access to the power, control, and privileges of the dominant social class. For Puerto Ricans in Greater Orlando, access to cultural capital contributes to the formation of social class identities, the construction of class boundaries, and the creation of a visible Latino elite.

Latino Networking Organizations

Martín Rodríguez

In 2010, Martín Rodríguez, the founder of a for-profit business networking organization, met me at a café in Hunters Creek in Orange County for an interview.[30] In 1980, Martín migrated from Puerto Rico to Central Florida, where he spent several years working as a fire protection engineer. In 1997, he started a media production business. In 2001, he shifted to finance. However, when he first migrated to Orlando at the age of 18, he worked as a houseman and his mother worked as a housekeeper in a hotel. He is proud of his upward mobility and accomplishments. He has worked in the real estate industry; he spoke of how he had benefited from the housing boom. Martín described himself as an "in-between" in the real estate industry; he liaised between buyers and banks. On his best month, he made $31,000. He made about $1,000 on each sale, but he was vague with the details of the operation.

When we spoke about the founding of his organization, Martín emphasized the significance of image and appearance, or cultural capital. Soon after the conversation began, he pointed out the Cuban restaurant next door, the location of one of the "Business After Hours" events he and his board of directors sponsor. He proudly noted that the sidewalk was adorned with a luxury vehicle and a red carpet for the event. These are examples of objectified cultural capital; they symbolically signaled the organization's prestigious status and the elite class position of the membership. Martín saw his organization as different from other business networking groups: "My organization is professional. These types of events commonly have raffles, and we give away quality prizes like radio time for advertising or free membership." Access to these forms of objectified cultural capital signal the class position of the individuals who participate in Martín's business networking organization. Although he struggled to get his organization off the ground, Martín felt that he had succeeded. He told me that restaurants that initially wouldn't host their business networking events were now calling and trying to do business with his organization.

When we talked about the growing number of Latino-owned businesses in the region, Martín said that Latino business owners didn't think they needed marketing. "They come with mami's recipe for rice and beans and think that they are going to make a killing here. It's not cheap to start a business. You need one year of resources in advance to pay expenses for each month or you're guaranteeing failure." Martín's aim was to create an organization that would bring together Latinos like him: people who had money, who dressed the part, and who were interested in working together to help each other generate more economic capital. Martín told me why he founded his organization: "I started because I saw the need. In 2007 the economy was diminishing and professionals were not coming out to network. I was the only one at some networking events wearing a suit. It was too social. People had on tennis shoes and I asked myself, 'Where are the professionals, the people with money to do business with?' I knew doctors and lawyers that I went to school with, but they didn't know each other so I created my organization." Martín emphasized the importance of dressing the part at business networking events, noting that "image is number one." He mentioned how people looked each other up and down at the events the *Orlando Business Journal* hosted. He told me a story about how he engages in this type of social scrutiny. He once saw a woman who was dressed nicely in a suit. He watched her as she walked to her car, then saw that her vehicle was a pickup truck. "My demeanor changed," he admitted. He judged her.

Martín admitted that he has turned people down at the door of his events because of how they were dressed. At his board meetings, which take place at various locations, he requires everyone to dress professionally. "Hispanics like to dress up, but the young people like to wear jeans," he said. To be accepted into this circle of professionals and entrepreneurs, to literally walk through the door, a businessperson needs to embody and perform professionalism through the clothing they wear. They must also pay a fee for participation and membership. Although one person had complained about that, Martín feels that the services members receive justify the fee. These include free business advising, free legal advice, a magazine column once a year, and a table at one of their mini-expos one time a year. At the time of our interview, he estimated that his group had sixty members, 10 percent of which were Anglos. However, more than 150 individuals attended his events. "Latinos don't like to commit. Why become a member if you can come to the events without being a member? They have a different mentality than Anglos." His goal was to bring the organization to the level of professionalism that Anglos expect. He mentioned Anglos telling him they want to tap into the Hispanic market. Anglo hotel managers wanted their hotels to be the hotel of choice in the Hispanic community, for example.

Martín described how he interacts with other members and assists individuals as they network with other professionals. He emphasized that he offers "warm," not "cold" business leads to members. At events he asks members, "Who do you want to meet?" Then he facilitates the introduction or makes a phone call to introduce that member to a potential client. He compared his approach to business networking with the practices of other organizations that simply provide a name and phone number, leaving the member to facilitate their own introduction.

While my discussion with Martín initially focused on one particular form of embodied cultural capital, image and appearance, he addressed the significance of other forms of cultural capital, most notably language. He mentioned the language ideologies non-Hispanic whites articulate in opposition to the use of Spanish in public spaces.[31] However, instead of challenging opponents of bilingualism, he instructs his Spanish-speaking board members to speak in English when they want to network with non-Latino entrepreneurs and professionals. Much like some of my other interviewees who identified as middle or upper-middle class, he wanted to avoid offending or excluding non-Spanish speakers. He believed that this would foster Latinos' integration in the region instead of anti-immigrant backlash.

Derek Martínez

Derek Martínez and I met at a leads meeting in downtown Kissimmee in 2011. The Hispanic Area Council, part of the Kissimmee/Osceola Chamber of Commerce, sponsored the leads group at the Puerto Rican Cultural Center. Each week, professionals met to network and help each other generate new business through referrals. At the beginning of the meeting, everyone had an opportunity to say a few words about their company and the types of clients they were marketing to. Martínez seemed like the last person to participate in my ethnographic study. At first he was skeptical about my research as a cultural anthropologist and my role as a participant observer. He saw this as "studying everyone in the room." However, when we crossed paths at another networking event hosted by Amigos Profesionales, he gave me an opportunity to explain the project in more detail. After that, he agreed to participate in an interview with me and soon he was introducing me to his contacts and "marketing" my project by suggesting that they participate in an interview about their experiences of living and working in Greater Orlando. He had been attending events sponsored by business organizations for fourteen years.

One morning in June 2011, Derek gave me permission to shadow him for a day as he worked as a sales consultant. This gave me an opportunity to interview him and chat with him more informally while we drove to real estate agencies and insurance companies to inform them about the services of his employer, a national corporation that restores homes damaged by fire, flooding, or other accidents.

Derek, a Cuban American in his 40s, is originally from Boston. He earned a bachelor's degree at Northeastern University and a master's degree at Franklin College. As we drove around Greater Orlando, Derek and I spoke about his experience of living and working in Florida. He mentioned the variety of interesting jobs he has had at various times in his life: photographing models, working as a martial arts instructor, working at Hewlett-Packard, and owning his own business. He described the darker side of Orlando's labor market. When he arrived in Orlando with his wife, a scientist whom he later divorced, they "came with money." In Boston, his wife had done molecular research for a company funded by German investors. Derek said that he had a "good, well-paid job" at Hewlett-Packard. This led both of them to believe, like so many others, that they would find a job in Orlando "in about 10 minutes." The couple purchased a house in Orange County and began searching for jobs. However, Derek and his wife could not find steady work and burned through their entire savings over the next two years. Since that time, Derek has worked at many jobs and had been laid off many times. "There is no job security," he said. "Those days are long gone everywhere."

Derek's move from Boston to Orlando led to downward mobility: he depleted his savings and was forced to accept less income. He said that he used to be "upper class" and used to make "very good money." However, he said, "life throws curve balls, especially if someone steals from you." He was referring to a woman he got involved with after his divorce, "a con woman" who stole $50,000 from him. When I asked him why he identified as upper class, he replied, "Because I fit better in an environment that is driven by highly educated or financially well-off people." Derek emphasized how comfortable he was at country clubs and the invitations he received to visit the Citrus Club, an exclusive business and social club in downtown Orlando.

When I asked Derek, "How do you determine an individual's class position?"

he responded, "By their mannerisms, what they drive, where they live, their education, although sometimes that doesn't mean diddly squat. You can tell by their attitude and how they carry themselves, although this can be very deceiving." He described how he determined an individual's class position and how he interacts with people on the basis of certain factors. Two issues for him are appearance and language usage:

> For example, with white trash everything is F-that. They can be the best wife or husband, but to me, stay away. I don't want to be associated. I judge people by how I see them and I make my own calls. If every word out of your mouth is a curse or you dress poorly, I don't want to talk to you. But sometimes you can't help it. I've been this close to being homeless.

Derek lives in Winter Park. He told me how his place of residence is perceived and about his conscious attempt to use his place of residence to elevate his status:

> Where I live is more Anglo. If you say you live in Winter Park, people think you have money. I wouldn't mind living in Orlando, but I couldn't find an affordable place. I'm middle class, sorta kinda, but if you say you live in Winter Park, you get the "oh wow, excuse me." People automatically put you in another category, and I want people to see me that way.

This is an example of performing and defending an economic position through the accumulation of social, cultural, and symbolic capital. It also illustrates Ortner's conceptualization of class as always being made, defended, and desired.[32] My early encounters with Derek and other members of Orlando's business networking organizations brought my attention to the social class distinctions within Orlando's Latino community and to the significance of cultural capital for access to resources that gatekeepers control in order to maintain exclusive social spaces.

Ron Ramírez

Ron Ramírez, a native Puerto Rican who is a commercial banker, was one of the elected leaders of the Puerto Rican Chamber of Commerce.[33] He attended law school but entered the banking industry before he completed his degree. He migrated from Puerto Rico in October 2005 to improve his quality of life. He chose to live in Volusia County because of its school system. He ranked the counties by the quality of education they offered. In his opinion, Seminole County offered the best education, followed by Volusia, Orange, and Osceola. He also mentioned a big difference in housing prices in the counties, even though the houses are constructed by the same builder. His children had attended a bilingual school in Puerto Rico, so the transition was easy for them. He joked that they did not speak English with an accent.

When I brought up the topic of anti-immigrant sentiments and discrimination against Latinos, he couldn't recall any instances of discrimination directed at him while working in Orlando, although he admitted that "things still happen." He said, "It's hard to be Hispanic. You get compared to Mexicans and other communities, but Puerto Ricans have the same rights as Americans." He surprised me, though. Instead of criticizing the second-class citizenship of Puerto Ricans and blaming it on the colonial relationship between the island and the states, xenophobia and nativism, or other forms of discrimination, Ron blamed other Puerto Ricans. "If you are a professional versus a laborer," he explained, "how you act in the community is totally different." He explained his theory about why there is prejudice against Puerto Ricans: "Most [Puerto Ricans and Latinos] think they are in Puerto Rico or in their country." Although Ron chose not to go into detail about which practices and behaviors he considered unacceptable, he did say, "Well, whites have white trash and the rednecks, and we have ours." His attitude fits with a dynamic anthropologist Jorge Duany writes about. He found that it was "typical" for middle-class legal immigrants to look down on lower-class undocumented immigrants.[34] While the individuals I interviewed emphasized social class distinctions because of my line of questioning, other researchers have found tensions and divisions between island-born and diasporic Puerto Ricans and between Puerto Ricans and other Latinos.[35] These tensions were not as clearly evident in business networking organizations.

Miranda Otero

For Miranda Otero, another banker, class distinctions were part of her daily life experiences.[36] Miranda was part of the Hispanic Chamber of Commerce for four years, where she developed close relationships with other members and served as a chamber ambassador. As a result of her involvement, she attended many of the networking events in Greater Orlando. She admitted that many of her evenings are filled up with these networking events. "Sometimes," she said, "it is absolutely exhausting." But she does it for the exposure. "As a Hispanic," she explained, "you have to prove yourself. You have to work hard and you have to prove yourself even more." When I asked her if there was a Hispanic middle class in Orlando, she responded, "Hispanics in a certain tax bracket stick together. At the events you can tell the high rollers because they stick together." She gave me an example: "If you are at a business networking event and you are an entry-level employee, you won't feel like the group opens up to you as much in comparison to if you are a president of a company. It is all about your title and how much money you have. Physically, though, you can tell who is who just by looking at them."

Making judgments about class positionality based on appearances is possible because we embody and perform our class position through our mannerisms, how we use language, the clothing we wear, and other bodily dispositions. She talked about how her parents like to go to Asociación Borinqueña, a Puerto Rican cultural organization, because they can relate to the people there. However, she knows that they would not be comfortable at an event that included more affluent, younger people. "Based on your status, you stick together, you aren't going to go to dinner with people that are more affluent because you won't be able to afford the places they go," Miranda maintained.

When we discussed Miranda's experiences of class exclusivity, she mentioned the house she owns. She lives in "a very nice home," but she bought it because she saved a lot of money for the down payment. Most of her neighbors are professors, doctors, or lawyers. When she invites people to her house, their faces light up: "They say oh my god, your house is sooo nice." Miranda said that her visitors expect her to live in a less affluent area. However, even though she lives in that community, her neighbors no longer includer her in their social circles. Initially, she was invited over for dinner and her family would do things together with their neighbors. Little by little, however, they distanced themselves. They say hello, but they don't get together anymore. Then she will hear from another friend about who is going to dinner together or traveling together and she realizes she has been excluded. "I have the house," she said, "but I don't have the money to go on the trips. People think if you have the big house, you have the money." Miranda explained that she lives comfortably but does not splurge on big expenditures.

Jennifer González

Jennifer González is an executive in an Osceola County corporation and is on the board of one of the business networking organizations.[37] She told me that

Hispanic professionals are more visible in Orlando than in other places. Jennifer, who is of Colombian descent, said Orlando has a professional class of Latinos and a more corporate setting than her previous place of residence in Houston, Texas. She mentioned that she had been asked to sit on corporate or organizational boards to create gender diversity but never to create ethnic diversity. Hispanics are well represented on the boards she is a member of. She also felt there wasn't a backlash due to the influx of Latinos. The Hispanic Chamber of Commerce, she said, has a very positive reputation. "Hispanics are not seen as a detriment. Florida is welcoming to Hispanic immigrants." She mentioned that she has not felt discrimination but admitted that this is perhaps because she has a big company behind her. According to Jennifer, Orlando is filled with Hispanic professionals. She said that all of her mother's doctors in Orlando have been Puerto Rican or Dominican. Jennifer was keen to emphasize the existence of a Hispanic professional class.

Magna Rodrigo

Magna, an employee at the Hispanic Chamber of Commerce, was born and raised in Puerto Rico and attended the University of Puerto Rico, where she earned her bachelor's and master's degrees.[38] She first moved to Washington, DC, with her husband, but after they divorced she left the city to be with her parents and sister in southeast Orlando. In Washington, she had been a stay-at-home mom, but in Greater Orlando, she needed an income. At the time of our interview she had been in Orlando for thirteen years and had worked at several jobs. She said that finding a job "is all about who you know." She was a member of the Hispanic Chamber of Commerce through a company that previously employed her and thus knew the chamber staff and members. That is how she landed the job at the Hispanic Chamber of Commerce after four months of unemployment.

When we discussed the changes in Greater Orlando, she mentioned the Semoran Corridor, a commercial strip in Greater Orlando. She described the area as "Puerto Rico, it's Latin. It's like going to Santurce or Bayamón." When people from Puerto Rico come to visit her, they are surprised by the resemblance to parts of Puerto Rico because of the Spanish-language signage, for instance. She has noticed a change in language use over the last ten years. "There are areas where the owners of stores don't speak English; they don't have to." She said that even though these business owners might not know English, they still can thrive. She also noted that government offices in the area always have someone who speaks Spanish. Government offices and businesses have a "token Spanish person to do the translating," she added. She served in this role at her first job with an insurance company. She was always called in to translate, especially with customers from Miami. A well-known developer in the area confirmed Magna's observation about having a token Hispanic employee. Ron explained to me that "gringos don't realize that you can't market to Hispanics the same as everyone else." He gave me the example of real estate. "You need to have a Spanish speaker to sell [Hispanics] the house, for trust. It might just be to say hello and greet them. In fact it doesn't matter that the buyers probably speak English as well. What's important is that the seller speaks the language."[39]

Magna mentioned during our interview that everything is in English at the Hispanic Chamber of Commerce. When I asked why, she responded that it is "because they want Americans to do business with Hispanics. American companies." The chamber's magazine is also in English because it wants to be "inclusive." At the time of our interview, the Hispanic Chamber of Commerce had "a membership of 535 companies, of which 60 percent were Latino and 40 percent non-Latino." When I asked her how Latinos have been received in Orlando, she started by saying, "it's so sad, but" and then began describing two types of Hispanics that can be found in Orlando, "Hispanics that are professional and want to blend in versus those that are in your face and react like 'are you looking at me ugly?'" She described the second type of Latino as "having a chip on their shoulder" and "always wanting to scream discrimination."

She described her mother as a "Nuyorican who was very corporate" because she "knew how to dress and her English was perfect." She was successful, Magna claimed, because she had the ability to move in two worlds: "She could talk pasteles and arroz con gandules with the residents she was selling homes to," but she was able to turn that on and off and return to her corporate persona. Her mother was acceptable in two coexisting social spaces. Her mother's success and financial stability were based on her ability to navigate various spaces and either accentuate her Latina identity or perform an Anglo corporate persona.

Some migrants involved in networking organizations are interested in more than assimilating into the dominant, mainstream culture. They want the skills and the flexibility to move in two worlds. These individuals, like Magna's mother, can comfortably communicate and interact with consumers based on their ethnic identity but they are also comfortable in elite spaces where their employers value their ability to generate business from the Latino community. However,

sometimes other Latinos challenge and critique their strategic display of multiple competencies and the exclusivity of Latino business networking organizations. When these other Latinos challenge the behaviors and attitudes of elite
members of their community, they are displaying a form of everyday activism.[40]

Everyday Activism: Contesting Exclusivity and Digital Dissent

From my interviews, I learned that individuals were able to identify and distinguish Latino professionals from the other Puerto Ricans and Latinos who
migrated to the region based on their cultural, social, symbolic, and economic
capital. Interviewees emphasized the significance of image and appearance. How
individuals spoke, dressed, and carried themselves was key to being accepted in
business networking organizations that brought together highly educated and
financially well-off Latinos and those who wanted to be. However, participation in networking organizations meant being judged by others. Interviewees
connected social class to references to place, like the Winter Park residential
community, or the ability to attend prestigious social clubs. Through references
to various forms of capital, my interviewees distinguished between themselves
and working-class Latinos.

In Greater Orlando, participation in membership-based business organizations generated multiple forms of capital. This created a visible cohort of Latino
entrepreneurs and professionals. The founders, board members, and individuals
who coordinated leads groups within these organizations sometimes functioned
as gatekeepers who determined how much access an individual could have to
the group's resources. One leads group that met every week to share contacts
and business-generating strategies engaged in such gatekeeping before they
agreed to let me join the group. Derek, who had been an active member for
years, told me later about that conversation. "Well, what can she do for us?" they
asked. Only Derek's status in the group enabled me to have access; he explained
that I was making a contribution to the larger Latino community through my
research.

On another occasion when I was attending a Hispanic Area Council–led
meeting at the Puerto Rican Cultural Center, group members quietly criticized
two women who were presenting their jewelry business for speaking in Spanish. Individuals usually spoke in English, but those who felt more comfortable
speaking in Spanish or whose English was limited would present to the group
in Spanish. I recorded the comments of the woman sitting next to me in my

fieldnotes. "This is the US, they should really be speaking English," one woman said, characterizing the language use of the two presenters as rude. When the presenters mentioned their Puerto Rican identity and said that the jewelry they sell is shipped from Puerto Rico, the woman whispered to me, "then she should know English." On another occasion, Derek made a comment about a presentation made in Spanish. He too thought business should be conducted in English and remarked that the Hispanic Chamber of Commerce, which he characterized as a five-star group, was more professional than the Hispanic Area Council leads group. "They are too religious," he said of the Hispanic Area Council. He mentioned the presence of pastors in the group and a "remembrance walk" a church was encouraging us to participate in when it was time for its members to present. However, the exclusivity of these spaces for professionals was not uncontested.

The Don Quijote Awards

Each year the Hispanic Business Initiative Fund of Florida and the Hispanic Chamber of Commerce of Metro Orlando sponsored the Don Quijote Award ceremony to celebrate the achievements and contributions of Latino entrepreneurs, professionals, and activists. This event was an opportunity to bestow symbolic capital upon individuals by honoring and recognizing their accomplishments in a public forum. The award ceremony was intended to serve three primary objectives for the sponsoring organizations: 1) recognize top Hispanic entrepreneurs, professionals, and leaders of the community; 2) be the premier business recognition event for the Hispanic community; and 3) serve as a fund raiser for the Hispanic Business Initiative Fund and the Hispanic Chamber of Commerce. In December 2009, journalist Victor Manuel Ramos posted a story about the twelfth annual ceremony on the *Hispanosphere* blog. The post immediately generated a critique of the elitism members of the chamber displayed, the exclusivity of their events, and the chamber's lack of outreach to the larger Latino community. Nineteen people contributed to the conversation, some more than once. Six of the responses spoke positively about the event and/or chamber, eleven were negative, and eighteen were either neutral or were about an unrelated topic. "Maria rosario Gomez," commented that "the Hispanic chamber has become more of a social club for those people who you mentioned, always the same faces. They are very selective and protective of their recognition and unless you have done your deeds and kissed the pope's ring, you won't get any recognition from them." The next respondent agreed with Maria, stating, "I think this is a scam! What does the Hispanic Chamber do except throw expensive parties on rooftops? Nothing! . . . Same faces! So they can say 'they are the masters of their own little world' It is just sick what they are doing." That commenter also criticized the cost of attending some of the chamber's celebratory events, mentioning the fee of $100 per plate at the gala the Hispanic Chamber of Commerce sponsored at a World Showcase Pavilion at the Epcot Center.

The thread continued for months and in March 2010 individuals were still commenting on and questioning the inequalities these events and organizations fostered and maintained. Commenters questioned the selection process for choosing award recipients. They also questioned the membership and event fees. Others recounted experiences when they were "brushed off" or someone "blew [them] off." These experiences led those commenters to conclude that the chamber was not community friendly, inclusive, or diverse. "I don't see what this does except have an open bar with food for the so called Hispanic elite," "Daniela Torres" wrote. "You as a representative of the press should represent us better than through coverage of these events that do nothing than promote a private social club." One respondent posted a sarcastic remark directed at the Hispanic Chamber of Commerce's president: "Ramon, I love your 1957 Type W180 220S cabriolet Mercedes, very fitting for a chamber president. Congrats!" The comment ended with a link that showed a photograph of a Mercedes. Clearly the broader Hispanic community is very aware of displays of objectified cultural capital.

Several months later, in February 2010, Victor Manuel Ramos posted another blog entry on *Hispanosphere* to follow up on the debate about the role of the chamber. He had interviewed the chamber president, Ramón Ojeda, a Venezuelan immigrant. "Some of our Hispanic blog readers have criticized you and the chamber's events at times, saying the chamber's work doesn't benefit the small businesses. How do you respond to those complaints?" Ojeda immediately mentioned the criticism he had received about his car and said that he has worked hard for everything he owns. Then he defended the chamber. But the comments that followed the February post continued to criticize the chamber for its exclusivity and lack of support for the larger Latino community. In an especially powerful and sarcastic post, an individual referred to the benefits and privileges of membership in the chamber such as business contracts and employment opportunities, revealing a sharp awareness of how membership could convert social capital into economic resources:

Enough! Enough to all you criticizing our American way of life. We came here and we conquered. Like it or not, we, at the Hispanic Chamber, are a different kind of Latinos, most of us have married Anglos and you will never see us at a "bodege," "baile" or public event were regular Latinos congregate. By the way, we spic English well. We have worked so hard to create our "click," developed relationship with the establishment; without our membership we have people in key position that by a secret hand-shake, phone call or text message we acquire contracts, get business done, and find employment for friends/relatives. Conversely, we can cut people's legs as easy as 1, 2, 3. We have prominent members always on the lookout for own benefits. Linda Ladman Gonzalez (you see how we can use the last name thing? Depending if she want to work in a position that has to do with Latinos, then she uses the Gonzales last name).

Participation in business networking organizations gave members access to resources and expanded their networks, which enabled them to build so-cial capital that could ultimately be converted to economic capital. These privileges, however, did not go unrecognized by members of the larger La-tino community who were excluded from the benefits that came along with participation.

The Amigos Award

In September 2010, Victor Manuel Ramos posted a story on the *Hispanosphere* blog about Linda Landman-Gonzalez, vice-president of community relations for the Orlando Magic, who had received the Amigo Award at the 2010 Gala Osceola. According to Ramos, she had received the award "for having excelled at celebrating the diversity of Hispanic culture."[41] Earlier that year, the Orlando Magic, the city's NBA team, had worn "Hispanic-themed T-shirts" that read "El Magic" for one game to show their appreciation of their Hispanic fan base. Over the next five days, sixteen comments were posted: one congratulated Linda, nine criticized her, and six suggested that other individuals should have won or com-mented on another aspect of social and political life. Commenters also chal-lenged the organization that sponsored these exclusive events:

I met Ms Landman at the Hispanic Metro group and SHE REALLY is plastic woman who plays only with certain elite groups of people. You are not one of them, that is for sure.

I feel that community groups like these do a poor job of finding hard working people that do honor helping the community. They go after the big donors because they can buy a sponsorship that way, especially from big business like the Magicos. . . . Besides it is always the same individuals over and over. The Kissimmee council is a smaller copy of the Hispanic Chamber but they don't want to associate because they live from the membership fees and sponsorship opportunities.

While many of the posts on the *Hispanosphere* site ignited heated debates among anonymous commenters, this was one of the few times when the majority of respondents reached a consensus about the exclusion of "regular people" from these organizations. One person wrote, "For the first time in many 'blogposts,' I think there's some common ground regarding the issue: Hispanic groups should be open to give this type of 'awards' to regular people, everyday heroes in our growing community raising kids, opening businesses, volunteering their time, helping others."

Golfing among the Wealthy Whites of Mickeyland

In April 2007, the *Orlando Sentinel* featured an article about the first Latino Open, an Orlando fund raiser that hoped to involve the more affluent members of the Latino community in a sport that is "favored by company executives and high-income professionals alike."[42] The event attracted more than 100 golfers and offered prizes that included a two-year lease for a new BMW. Nancy Sharifi, a manager at a financial firm, and Patricia Urban, who sells luxury homes, were featured in the article as women who sometimes feel excluded when their colleagues take clients out to play golf. According to Latino Leadership, a local organization, Hispanics have lost out on networking opportunities "because they are unfamiliar with the game—not the most popular recreational outlet in any minority community."[43] Sharifi, who is Puerto Rican, said that playing golf is essential for a person in the business community and that she felt that she had lost opportunities to be better known in the banking and financial industry because she was excluded. Urban, who is Dominican, had purchased golf clubs and golfing attire for the Open even though she did not know how to play yet. She said that golf has been "a good old boys club" but that she was determined to change that.[44]

According to the National Golf Foundation, an individual's class, ethnicity, and gender are related to knowledge of and access to the sport.[45] This limits the cultural capital a person can acquire through playing golf to those who are already on the higher end of the economic spectrum, largely non-Hispanic white upper-class males. The exclusivity of the sport limits the social and economic capital—the socialization, networking, and deal making—that takes place on the green to individuals who already have the most capital. The National Golf Foundation reports that Hispanics play golf less often than non-Hispanic whites, Asian Americans, and non-Hispanic blacks and that golfers come from the upper echelons of income and professional achievement.[46] This matches what Ramos found in Orlando: "Among Hispanic households . . . most of those who play golf make more than $150,000 a year." In Metro Orlando, "nearly 2,500 Hispanic households fall in that income category."[47]

Much like the responses to the contested Don Quijote Award ceremony, some Hispanics criticized Latino Leadership for hosting an exclusive event that, ironically, was intended to raise funds for low-income Latinos in a venue that was not accessible to that group. In 2007, Latino Leadership changed its fund-raising strategies in an attempt to garner corporate sponsorship and appeal to a select group of Latino golfers. In previous years, the organization had sponsored an annual community fair with music and food to raise funds, but according to the Latino Leadership president, "'In the fair we realized that when you attract so many people, the music, the loud crowd, you don't have an environment that is conducive to educating people."[48] According to Marucci Guzmán, Latino Leadership's former vice-president, "corporate sponsors were more willing to participate and sponsor golfing events, but showed much less interest in participating in the other charity events."[49] While Latino Leadership is committed to assisting low-income Latinos, its leaders realized that they were able to better serve this population by sponsoring fundraisers that generated the most possible revenue among a segment of the community that was financially well off.

In April 2010, the comments on the *Hispanosphere* blog revealed the polarized perception of the event.[50] "Lisa" posted the following response to the blog's coverage of the golf tournament: "I am excited that Latinos are doing something that is not a festival this is an event for a professional sector of the community Congratulations to the organizers, you are helping us gain equal respect Kudos!!!"[51] This comment implied that elite Latinos value playing golf—a form of cultural capital that can increase social and economic capital—but not activities at community fairs. josua posted a response that connected the success of the event and the organization to the "quality," value, or capital of the participants and highlighted the opportunity to generate business: "I was a player in their first event and I was really impressed with the organization and the quality of people there I got a lot of business from that event please join the event I am a GRINGO and I recommend it, the place is a great and the food and drinks are worth it."[52] The third respondent was much more critical of the event's exclusivity: "a game for pretenders is what golf is . . . they should hold a dominoes tourney, with a $50 entry they could more hispanics to participate, but they don't want hispanics, they cater to whites and other wealthy people in this community . . . we the economically challenged cant afford to pay $150 to show off among the wealthy whites of mickeyland."[53] The opportunity to increase social and economic capital through participation in an activity like a golf tournament was limited to those who had the largest amounts of capital. This shut working-class Hispanics out.

The lower numbers of golfers among the poor most likely reflects the inability of working-class people to afford the costly country-club membership fees and expensive equipment the sport requires. Working-class neighborhoods also generally lack the space needed to construct a golf course. Because playing golf has social meaning and is an indicator of economic capital, Latinos make judgments about each other's social class based on whether a person plays golf or plays dominoes. The judgment of tastes and the stratification that results from those distinctions is possible because of our ability to acknowledge our place in stratified social spaces and to articulate distinctions between, as one of my informants put it, "those with money and those without."[54] Markers of class distinctions can be arbitrary, but they become meaningful differentiators because the significance of driving a BMW or playing golf, for instance, is widely agreed upon.

During my two years of ethnographic fieldwork, I interviewed owners of small businesses, attorneys, corporate representatives, politicians, and other Latino professionals and entrepreneurs who participated in networking events and activities. I asked them how they described their class position, what factors led them to their conclusions, and how they determined other people's class position. I wanted to document how they understood and articulated the class-based distinctions they drew during everyday conversations and social encounters in Greater Orlando.

Several commonalities became evident. Interviewees consistently referred to the three forms of cultural capital—objectified, institutionalized, and embodied—in response to my questions about class. They often emphasized the importance of "image," taste in clothing, "how you act," mannerisms, attitudes, how someone speaks, how someone "carries themselves," or their "comfort" in the elite spaces of private social clubs, country clubs, and golf courses. These are all examples of embodied cultural capital. They unapologetically used these factors to construct their own class identity and determine the class position of others. For example, it was clear that the cultural capital Derek Martínez possessed—his education, the ease with which he socialized and interacted with well-educated or well-off people, and the other embodied tastes and dispositions he used to draw class distinctions—were enough to maintain his upper-class identity, although he was downwardly mobile in Orlando.

While the media was supportive of elite Hispanics and their organizations and consistently covered their activities and events in the local newspaper and on blogs, the responses to media coverage made it clear that members of the larger Latino community contest this exclusivity. Some individuals criticized the cost of participation and the types of events elite groups sponsored such as cocktail parties and golf tournaments. These individuals preferred domino tournaments and community fairs. And some people protested that annual award ceremonies, which bestowed institutionalized cultural capital, always rewarded the same people, the members of an inner circle.

Juanita Ramiréz, who was born in Puerto Rico, felt that "there is only some degree of unity among Puerto Ricans." Juanita had worked for the Disney Corporation and then as a sales associate at a Lowe's store. In her experience, class unity trumped ethnic-based solidarity. She said that people like her boss, who is also Puerto Rican, "do not care if you are another Puerto Rican or not. The rich stay together." That desire to "stay together" with other upwardly mobile individuals, both Latino and non-Latino, is evident in the social spaces of business networking organizations and other elite places. I am not suggesting that the social class distinctions Juanita and other people expressed are unique to the Latino population. However, Greater Orlando allows us to observe the process of social class formation among Latinos and how class identities are articulated, performed, and contested within that population. The exclusive spaces where upwardly mobile Latinos congregate and network reveal the divisions and inequalities within a migrant population.

5

The Encargado System

During my fieldwork, when I wasn't conducting interviews or engaging in participant observation around Greater Orlando, I spent time with people in the homes where I rented rooms. The lives of these individuals were drastically different from those of the professionals in business networking organizations. The people I lived with worked in low-paid jobs in the hospitality industry. The sample size of this group was small because I lived in only three houses. Still, the man and the two women who rented rooms to me were entrepreneurs who were participating in what Sarah Mahler has described as an encargado system.[1]

In her account of Salvadorian migration to suburban Long Island, Mahler discussed the formation of a housing rental market that operated on the margins of the mainstream housing market. Immigrants, encargados or encargadas, sublet space to other migrants in order to pay the rent or the mortgage. In Greater Orlando, sometimes these rooms were unadvertised and information was exchanged through social networks. In other instances, posters on a front lawn, a local newspaper, or a website such as Craigslist advertised available rooms. I found my first room through a Craigslist advertisement. The second and third were unadvertised; I learned about them through the social networks of my first two roommates, Marco and Pedro.

The practice of renting rooms and other spaces in a house has transformed what appear to be single-family suburban homes into small businesses operating in an informal ethnic market. The encargado system has helped some migrants who have low-wage, insecure jobs survive and has helped others become upwardly mobile. I never encountered rooms rented to vacationers; the encargado system functioned differently from companies like Airbnb. Mahler notes that in the past, although boarding in urban spaces "was a particularly helpful strategy historically among newly arriving [European] immigrants," this practice preceded "zoning laws and regulations that currently limit the flexibility of families to rent rooms, apartments, or houses to non-family."[2]

In Mahler's study, encargados and encargadas did not view themselves as exploitative. The same was true in Greater Orlando. People who rented rooms in their houses viewed the practice as a good financial strategy. At a minimum they hoped to pay the rent or the mortgage and utilities. However, as Mahler found among the Salvadorian tenants in Long Island, tenants in Greater Orlando felt resentment. One of the major differences between Mahler's study and mine is the current condition of the housing. While her informants were forced to live in substandard conditions, the homes where I rented or visited were usually in good condition and at times even had amenities like a pool.

Migrants in other areas have struggled to find affordable housing in decent condition. Angela Stuesse found that migrants in Mississippi lived in substandard housing. In these communities, "immigrants face housing discrimination from white residents and predatory practices of unscrupulous landlords of all backgrounds."[3] However, some immigrants have "gained a foothold into the privileges of whiteness" and have been able to rent houses or apartments that are closed to African Americans.[4] Stuesse concluded that "across Central Mississippi migrants are pushing at the boundaries of locally engrained patterns of spatial segregation, which has given rise to tensions as well as opportunities."[5] A similar dynamic was under way in Greater Orlando. Latinos had moved into predominantly non-Hispanic white suburbs, challenging spatial segregation. In suburbs like Buenaventura Lakes, they have created a sense of belonging by Latinizing the landscape and the soundscape.

Marco

Marco came to the United States from Venezuela on a temporary visa. In his early 20s, he married a Puerto Rican woman, which gave him the right to live and work in the United States. Marco was in his late 20s when I began my fieldwork. He had become a US citizen shortly before I moved in and on several occasions he expressed his pride about that. I first met Marco because he had posted an advertisement on Craigslist for a room rental in his Buenaventura Lakes home. Marco had lived in Miami and Sarasota before he purchased two houses in Osceola County with his Puerto Rican wife. They lived in Buenaventura Lakes for seven years and then went through a turbulent divorce. The court awarded Marco both houses. Marco was working at a General Mills warehouse when I moved in, but to maintain his mortgage payments he rented out two of the three bedrooms in the house.

When Marco wasn't busy working, maintaining the house, or participating in his Pentecostal church, he spent time with Paz, his Colombian girlfriend. He gave me his "testimony" one evening, explaining how he became involved with the church at a desperate time in his life. He was facing criminal charges after being accused of stealing from the Home Depot where he was working. He claimed to be innocent of the charges and said that a manager had set him up. Marco's experiences with the criminal justice system put him in contact with a Pentecostal preacher who helped him straighten his life out and find God. When I met Marco he was deeply religious; he attended services at least three times a week and was committed to living his life according to the guidelines of his church. Marco preached to me at times, frequently mentioned God, and sometimes read me passages from the Bible. He expressed a desire to help people and always insisted that he, Pedro, and I were a family, calling us "brother" or "sister."

At times, however, Marco's religiosity was overshadowed by his preoccupation with finances. His job was unstable and he constantly worried that he would be laid off. This economic insecurity made him very dependent on his houses, which he often referred to as his business. The rent Marco collected from Pedro and me was enough to cover his mortgage payment and most of the utility bills. But he often complained that he wasn't making any money on his second property, $40 profit a month at most. That house was rented to a non-Hispanic white family in a rural part of Osceola County that was approximately forty minutes from Buenaventura Lakes.

On one occasion Marco described the family who was renting his other house as "dirty" and "dysfunctional" and admitted that he had called social services about them since he did not think they took proper care of their child. He claimed the parents left dog feces around the house and the property and were constantly late with the rent. He whispered to me that they were "white trash" but immediately expressed his guilt for using the term. He said that God would not like him to say bad things about people.

Pedro

In Buenaventura Lakes I had a second roommate, Pedro, who introduced me to his network of friends at his hotel job. This network became very important because it helped me secure my third room rental in Kissimmee with Pedro's co-worker María. When I first met Pedro he was 18 years old and was working as a houseman in the housekeeping division of a hotel located ten minutes from our house. Pedro crossed the border into Texas when he was 16 years old with the help of coyotes, individuals who help guide migrants across the border. He traveled to Florida to meet his uncle and father, who had migrated years earlier. He was traumatized by his experience because the group he traveled with to cross the border got lost in the desert for several days. In tears one evening he shared a poem he had written about his experience and recounted the death of a woman while her baby lay crying. When I asked him what had happened to the baby, he continued to sob, unable to reply. Pedro spent a few months living in Georgia and then moved from place to place in parts of north and central Florida, following family members and work opportunities. His mother, his brother, and many members of his extended family were still in Puebla, Mexico. Pedro said he earned the most money picking watermelons in Florida, but he had also worked a variety of construction jobs and had spent a brief time in the kitchen of a local Colombian restaurant with several other undocumented Mexican workers. Paz's brother owned the restaurant.

Pedro had many dreams and aspirations for his life and expressed interest in becoming an auto mechanic, learning more about the construction industry, learning English, writing songs and poetry, having a family one day, and owning his own home. Over time, however, his hope dwindled and it became clear that Pedro was psychologically broken. He often cried for his family in Mexico, longing to see his grandmother and grandfather again before they died. He lived in fear, constantly concerned about his lack of documentation and what would happen if his undocumented status was discovered. Pedro had only fake identification and his original birth certificate; he did not have a Mexican passport.

During my fieldwork I watched Pedro slip deeper and deeper into depression as he battled alcoholism and his conflicting emotions about life in the United States and Mexico. "Why don't you just go back home?" I once asked him, thinking life in Mexico couldn't be much worse than what he was experiencing in the United States. He told me that he was accustomed to the material comforts of life in the United States and the spending money his small salary provided. For the first time in his life he had a cell phone, a television, a bicycle, and an Xbox. He could buy clothes, shoes, and jewelry for himself and he loved being able to buy pizza from Domino's and hamburgers from Wendy's. He told me that as a child in Mexico, he had to steal food for him and his brother. He couldn't afford to go to school, he lived in the streets, and he went barefoot. I had no idea how to help him and it saddened me to observe his suffering while I took for granted the privileges I enjoyed as a US citizen.

Pedro's life in the United States was marked by economic insecurity and a constant struggle for survival. His undocumented status prevented him from obtaining a driver's license and severely limited his work opportunities. He had no opportunity for upward social mobility. I met several undocumented immigrants at Pedro's hotel who were suffering the same fate. They had gotten their jobs from a contractor who provided the hotel with housekeeping staff. The contractor took $2.50 per hour from Pedro's check as a fee, so Pedro earned only $7.76 per hour after the deductions. He wasn't able to cash the paper check he received each week and relied on others with bank accounts to do him the favor of cashing his check, which was usually for a little over $300 per week. Pedro's job was always insecure and he worried about being fired when the peak tourist season ended and staff was drastically cut. Most of the workers I met in the housekeeping division of the hotel rarely received wages for forty hours of work per week. They described themselves as full-time workers during our conversations, but their work hours and daily schedules fluctuated from week to week. When I looked at the weekly schedules of the housekeeping division for May 29 through June 4 and July 31 to August 6 of 2011, for example, I realized that occupancy rates in the hotel were extremely low. The housekeepers, all of whom were female, consistently received the fewest hours, no more than twenty-seven per week, and when the peak tourist season ended many of these employees lost their jobs. The hotel was their sole employer.

Paz

After living in Buenaventura Lakes for several months with Pedro and Marco, I moved to Hunters Creek to rent a room in the house of Paz, Marco's girlfriend. Her house in Orange County was a 20-minute drive from Buenaventura Lakes. According to the 2016 census, the Latino population in Hunters Creek had grown to approximately 40 percent of the total population.[6] Paz, who was 49, had moved to the United States from Colombia in her early 20s to find better work opportunities. She had come to the United States by crossing the Mexican border with the help of a coyote. Paz came with $2,000 in her pocket. A few friends who had also migrated to the United States had promised to help her when she arrived. However, she ended up alone and slept in a park for days. A

woman approached her in the park and asked her if she was crazy, then offered
to help her. She helped her get a domestic service job with a wealthy New Jersey
family. Paz left the position a month later. The husband in the family was trying
to touch her and kept making inappropriate advances. Paz then worked two jobs
cleaning office buildings.

Paz spent eleven years as an undocumented worker until she married a US
citizen. During our conversations she told me about run-ins with immigration
officials and her various attempts to obtain papers. She attributes her success
to a Jewish lawyer who was good to her. Over the years she traveled back and
forth to Colombia to visit her daughters, who remained with her parents. Two
times she was caught by immigration officers, once in Mexico and once in the
United States, but they let her go. One time she was trying to travel to and
from Colombia to visit her daughters by assuming the identity of a Puerto Rican woman. They asked her questions about Puerto Rico, inquiring about the
name of a historic place and the Spanish word for the frogs found in Puerto
Rico. She failed the question about the frogs, using the term rana instead of
coqui. She told me about an incident that continues to traumatize her. As she
and her sister were trying to bring their daughters to the United States via
Mexico, they were almost kidnapped by men who stole their money and their
passports. She talked about the women and children who are kidnapped and
raped as they are attempting to cross the border and felt fortunate to have nar-
rowly escaped such a fate. Time after time I was shocked by the challenges she
has faced and overcome.

Paz described her family in Colombia as very poor. When I met her she was
a wealthy restaurant owner living in a luxurious five-bedroom, three-bathroom
home with an enclosed pool. The house was next to a small lake. She was well
traveled, kind, religious, worldly, and quite opinionated, although she had no
formal education. She dreamed of returning to school to become a nurse but
her restaurant kept her busy. She had owned the restaurant for eleven years and
hoped to sell it and move to North Carolina. Her two daughters had bachelors'
degrees from the University of Central Florida. One daughter was in medical
school when Paz and I first met and her second daughter was working as a
therapist after finishing a master's degree. Both of her daughters were married
to non-Hispanic white males. Paz's brother and sister were also successful restaurant owners who owned chains in New York, North Carolina, and Florida.
Despite her wealth, Paz participated in the encargado system to pay her mortgage and live for free. I paid $450 per month for a room, which included utili-

ties. She charged the other tenants $500 for their rooms. Paz rented one of the bedrooms on the first floor to a Hispanic male who appeared to be in his late 20s or early 30s. He worked long hours and I rarely saw him or spoke to him. A young Mexican couple who worked in Paz's restaurant rented a bedroom on the second floor and a young man in his early 20s, a friend of the couple, rented the bedroom next to theirs. Paz occupied the master bedroom down the hall from my room on the second floor. I left Paz's house after a few months. Despite the luxurious interior of the house, I found the living situation challenging because of a lack of privacy. I stayed with Paz in November and December of 2010, then I rented an apartment in a gated community ten minutes from Buenaventura Lakes to take a break from the encargado system. Finally I moved in with María, a room inspector in Pedro's hotel.

María

María, who was 40 years old, was from an upper-class Guatemalan family. Her mother had owned a clothing factory in Guatemala until the family lost the business because of financial difficulties. Soon after that, María's mother left for New York City and became a seamstress and a designer for a major clothing label. María joined her in New York while she was still a young child and lived in Queens for twenty-five years. María eventually married a Colombian man she met in the city and had three children. After they divorced, she moved to Kissimmee with her second husband, also a Colombian she had met in New York City. María described the life of luxury she once lived many times. After she took a few courses at New York's Fashion Institute of Technology, she and her mother operated a small boutique in Queens. Her first husband was a businessman who owned real estate in Florida and Colombia, and she described her many shopping sprees on Fifth Avenue in New York City nostalgically. However, when I met her, her life was dominated by financial insecurity, marginality, and the struggle to care for herself and her three children on her low salary. At the hotel, she earned less than $10 per hour inspecting rooms. When it was possible to do so, she took on extra hours cleaning rooms.

María said that her misfortune began when she caught her first husband having an affair and he chose to be with the other woman. When I met her she was separated from her second husband because he was in jail for selling drugs. María lived in two homes in Kissimmee during the course of my field-work. She had a large house with a pool and later a smaller townhouse in a gated community, both of which had rooms that she rented out. I lived in her second home. María charged $300 a room to supplement her income.

The Encargado "Family"

My experiences in the first two houses I lived in were fraught with tension. The challenges of living communally, particularly with people who were not family, were quite evident. However, Marco, my roommate in Buenaventura Lakes, often said that we "were all a family." He called me sister and my other roommate carnal (brother). Paz and María made the same references to family when I lived in their homes. Marco and his girlfriend often involved Pedro and me in conversations about God and invited us to their respective churches. They spoke often of giving and hospitality. When Pedro's bike was stolen, Paz and Marco surprised him with a new one. Nonetheless, I always knew if someone couldn't pay their rent, they would be thrown out. Payments were expected in cash. There was no credit and there was no working off the rent through service. Marco often reminded me that his house was his business, and he was indeed an entrepreneur. He referred to the house as his "restaurant" and pointed out that it was no different than Paz's restaurant business. Still, in some ways we were like a family. We talked to each other about our lives and our problems and saw each other every day.

However, when you live communally, you sacrifice the privilege of privacy. Discourses that emphasized a familial bond contrasted sharply with the many instances when I felt taken advantage of or when I lacked control over my living conditions. When I rented rooms, the homeowner always lived in the house. This meant that they managed the care of the home, regulated the air conditioning and heating to keep their electric bills down, and generally set the pace of life in the house. Alejandro, for example, who had rented my room in Marco's house before I moved in, was not entitled to change the setting on the air conditioner when he slept at night. This often caused problems with Marco, who wanted to keep the temperature between 76 and 77 degrees Fahrenheit. When I changed the temperature one time, Marco confronted me in a passive-aggressive way. Such incidents, which seem minor and petty, often caused tensions in the home and eventually led renters to seek another room, as Alejandro had done.

I decided to leave Marco's house when his girlfriend Paz revealed to me that he went into my room when I was not there to check things out. I had also seen him go into Pedro's room on numerous occasions and he had scolded Pedro, in front of me, for being messy and leaving his clothes thrown around the room. Pedro always accepted the way he was treated and silently nodded his head. At times it felt like Marco treated Pedro like a child or took advantage of him. He referred to him as "those people" when he wasn't present. One time Pedro complained that Marco made him pay half for all of the groceries he bought even if Pedro didn't eat anything or didn't want those particular items. But he didn't want problems, so he just paid. Pedro ate fast food or ate at other local restaurants since he only had a bicycle and Buenaventura Lakes had limited public transportation. One day, Pedro said that there were two groups or types of people in the world: those with money and those trying to get it. He described himself as poor. He described Marco as having ambition. He described Paz as rich.

The second room I rented was even a worse situation. I liked to keep my bedroom door closed, but every time I returned to the house I found the door wide open, indicating that someone could have entered the room. This is just one of the minor problems that arose while I lived in Paz's house. During the winter months the house was excessively cold and I was frequently sick. One time I returned after a visit to New York to find everything in my closet reorganized and all of the furniture in my room rearranged. Paz called it a Christmas present. That pushed me over the edge. It was clear who controlled the living space.

The homeowners who rent out rooms do not think of the arrangement as exploitative. They see it as a way of improving their financial situation and helping someone, particularly if they rent a room to family or friends. After all, renting a room, which cost from $300 to $500 a month including utilities, was substantially cheaper than renting an apartment, which started at around $600 and required a security deposit. Renting a room usually required a small down payment of less than $400 and there were minimal credit and security checks, if any at all.

For María Martínez, who had had many tenants over the years, renting rooms provided an important part of her income. When I met her in 2010, she was living in a large, luxurious home in Kissimmee that was undergoing foreclosure. Her job at the hotel with Pedro was not enough to maintain the house she had shared with her husband before their separation. Maria was not making payments on the mortgage but was charging rent to Miguel, an undocumented Guatemalan hotel worker, and to Alejandro, an undocumented Colombian hotel worker. María's three sons were also living with them. Her tenants supplemented the cost of utilities and living expenses. However, everyone was struggling financially and it was common for someone to pay their rent days or weeks late. María was always accommodating and socialized with her tenants as if they were close friends or family. She was more accepting of late payments since she wasn't making mortgage payments. For $50 more per month she would even provide the tenant with meals and include the tenant when she cooked large dinners for her three children.

María developed familial bonds with her tenants and began referring to one particular renter as her son. When his cousin arrived suddenly from Texas with no place to stay and no money, María allowed him to stay out of generosity. However, María also had a reputation for being manipulative and using people for favors and money. As a result, she had issues with several tenants over money. When some personal items were stolen from my room, for example, she blamed her youngest teenage son but didn't offer any compensation.

Another time, María and her tenant Miguel found out that Alejandro had been "ripping them off." Alejandro had agreed to open cell phone lines for María and Miguel under his name since neither of them had good credit. However, the monthly phone bill cost substantially less than he told them it did; Alejandro was pocketing the difference. They found out about this by invading his privacy and opening his mail to review the billing statement from the phone company. María asked Alejandro to leave her house, saying that she felt like she could no longer trust him. She was especially hurt because Alejandro knew she was struggling to manage the house and support her three children. In another example, Miguel and Alejandro had a falling out when Miguel stole a television from Alejandro before returning to Guatemala. Alejandro had purchased the TV through a Rent-A-Center, which allows customers to pay for furniture and other items in installments. Miguel was responsible for making payments on the TV that Alejandro had put under his name, but when Miguel left for Guatemala he failed to pay the balance he owed. María continued to run into issues with her tenants; they did not keep their rooms clean or they were unable to pay their rent on time. Still, her goal was to purchase a new home of her own and continue to rent out rooms when the bank seized her current home.

During the two years of my ethnographic fieldwork, Alejandro, Miguel, and I each rented three different rooms and Pedro lived in six different rooms. While renting rooms certainly has financial benefits for both the tenant and the encargado, there are always the dangers of bringing a stranger into one's home, the discomforts that result from overcrowding and the invasion of privacy, and the compromises that communal living requires. The encargado system gave me the opportunity to observe and hear about individuals' everyday activities and their interactions with friends and family. The daily conversations and comments that I recorded in my fieldnotes helped me learn more about racial identities, categorizations, and ideologies. These themes emerged during informal, unprompted conversations.

Identities, Categorizations, and Interethnic Relations

My roommates identified themselves based on national origin: they were Colombian, Mexican, or Venezuelan. They rarely used the terms Latino, Hispanic, black, or white as identifiers. On one occasion as I was eating dinner with Paz and Marco, we started talking about racial identities and racial discrimination. Paz mentioned a time when a principal tried to have her two daughters moved to a school with a larger Hispanic population. She told him, "I'm white! No one is going to discriminate against me!" and refused to have her children moved. In response, Marco jokingly said, "Well, I'm black. Look at my hair." I asked him if he was serious, if he really identified as black and he kept repeating, "I'm black" and pointing to his curly brown hair. Paz rolled her eyes at him and said, "He's just joking," although Marco never did respond to my question.

Paz told me that she always responds with "I'm from Florida" when people ask her where she is from or about her ethnic background. She always receives confused looks, she says, because she speaks English with a strong Spanish accent. However, she refuses to admit that she was born and raised in Colombia when she is asked and explains to the person questioning her that people from Florida speak like this too. On many occasions she told me that she identifies as an American from Florida. She no longer saw Colombia as her home; she expressed no desire to return and she had little desire to even visit. Many times Paz and Marco expressed their pride about being American citizens and both of them said that America is their country too. In contrast, Pedro often referred to himself as part of the population of ilegales (illegals) or as a fantasma (ghost). When I asked him what term he uses to describe his background, he said "Mexican." But when I inquired about his race, he described himself as indio because he speaks Nahuatl in addition to Spanish and has features that reveal his indigenous Mexican ancestry. María identified as Guatemalan and white.

In the houses lived in, interethnic relations were marked by contradictions. At times I observed a solidarity among the Hispanics who interacted with my roommates based on their shared economic position and similar circumstances.

The Puerto Rican women who were working in the hotel who were married to undocumented Mexican men helped their husbands and their husbands' friends navigate life in the United States without documentation. However, during spontaneous conversations it became clear that some of the Hispanics I met had a low opinion of other ethnic and racial groups, particularly Puerto Ricans and African Americans. On one occasion, Paz mentioned that the Puerto Ricans who lived in Buenaventura Lakes were "very poor people" and were not well educated about homeownership; this was her explanation for the high number of foreclosures in the suburb. Although she did not know any of the Puerto Rican residents of Buenaventura Lakes personally, she made judgments based on what she saw as she drove through the suburb to visit Marco almost every day. Paz also differentiated the Mexican workers in her family's restaurant based on class, referring to their poverty and lack of education and making comments about "that kind of people" in our casual conversations. Still, because of her generosity and deep religious beliefs she felt it was her duty to help others. She employed undocumented workers in her restaurant and she rented them rooms in her house. When one of her workers was arrested for driving without a license, she paid all of the legal fees and he returned to work at her restaurant when the proceedings finished. She also helped other undocumented immigrants find work and housing and expressed a genuine interest in the well-being of others. African Americans, however, were absent from her social networks and the social spaces she frequented.

Similarly, Marco surrounded himself with very few Puerto Ricans and African Americans. His girlfriend Paz once suggested to me that he had married his Puerto Rican wife for papers. However, Marco never spoke negatively about Puerto Ricans in front of me. When Pedro's bicycle was stolen from in front of our house, his first instinct was to blame the child of a Puerto Rican family living across the street. He began criticizing the family, mentioning that the father is always blasting loud Spanish music and working on his car in the driveway. But he stopped himself and told me that he knows I am Puerto Rican and didn't want to say anything bad about Puerto Rican people. I encouraged him to go on, but he said that he needed to go across the street and introduce himself so he could build a relationship with our Puerto Rican neighbors.

Pedro built his social network primarily from the hotel. He communicated in broken English with the Eastern Europeans he considered acquaintances and he befriended several of the South and Central American workers. He also developed familial bonds with a few of the older Puerto Rican housekeepers who treated him like a son. He referred to them as madrazas (devoted mothers). These co-workers were the closest thing he had to a family in the United States. However, he often made fun of the way Puerto Ricans spoke Spanish and would emulate their accent jokingly. He would also express jealousy when he would see a Puerto Rican male drive by in a sports car, calling them gandayas or presumidos to communicate that they were arrogant and conceited. He desperately wanted a Honda sports car of his own but could not obtain a license or afford a car. He felt that Puerto Ricans were very privileged to have American citizenship but that they were conceited, entitled, and lazy as a result. However, he later married a Puerto Rican woman and they now have two children.

Another time when Pedro and I went to the Publix Sabor supermarket, a man from HOGAR Crea, Inc. approached us in the parking lot.[7] He asked us to purchase one of the flans he and another person from the organization were selling from their car for $5. Pedro asked if the money and the place they represented was for Puerto Ricans only or if Mexicans would benefit too. When the man told Pedro that he was half Mexican and half Puerto Rican and that the money would help both groups, Pedro purchased two flans. As we walked away, Pedro whispered that he wouldn't have bought any flans if the money was just for Puerto Ricans. He explained that it is harder for Mexicans in the United States since they don't have papers and that Puerto Ricans shouldn't need the help. He walked away happy that he was able to help other Mexicans in need.

During informal conversations, María also expressed negative feelings toward Puerto Ricans. On one occasion she told me that all of the Puerto Rican women in the area take advantage of the welfare system. She told me that they put their children on medication for attention deficit disorder in order to increase their welfare benefits. She also expressed her distaste for Puerto Rican men, saying that she could never be romantically involved with a Puerto Rican male since she does not like the way they talk, dress, and behave. She made a similar comment about black men when she told me why she would not get involved romantically with a close Afro Cuban friend. He was a great person and a great friend, she said, but "I just don't like black men." She told me that she does not find the black skin color attractive.

Angela Stuesse argues that in Mississippi, instead of reconfiguring the rigid social hierarchies of race, immigrants arriving in new destinations reinforce "a system in which whiteness maintains its privilege and Blackness persists at the very bottom."[8] This dynamic seemed to be present in Greater Orlando. During my fieldwork, I met very few Hispanics who were involved romantically with African Americans or Afro-Latinos. I recall only one Puerto Rican woman who was married to an African American man; she was an attorney from the Northeast. However, I did meet Puerto Rican women from the island who were married to and had children with undocumented Mexican men. In many of those relationships I observed that the Puerto Rican women were displaying greater awareness of and involvement with Mexican culture than their husbands were with Puerto Rican culture. The women learned how to cook Mexican food and frequently prepared homemade tacos, tamales, taquitos, mole, guacamole, salsa verde, enchiladas, and other traditional Mexican dishes. Additionally, the homes of these women contained visible displays of Mexican symbols such as the Virgen de la Guadalupe and/or Mexican flags. The women also listened to and enjoyed music by famous Mexican musicians such as Espinoza Paz. Of course, I heard other genres of music like salsa and reggaeton in their homes; their children were exposed to Puerto Rican and Mexican culture simultaneously. I was always fascinated by how willing these women were to embrace Mexican cultural practices as their own.

In all of these relationships, the women had the responsibility of caring for their children and at times for also managing the household finances. Their husbands' undocumented status meant that the women often earned higher wages and had more secure employment. Additionally, as citizens of the United States, the Puerto Rican women could access various social services to help support their families. Pedro's father has two children with Alma, who is originally from Puerto Rico. Alma was also employed at the hotel. When Pedro and his father were out of work, the family of five lived together in a single hotel room and Alma provided everyone with food using her welfare benefits. In June 2010, Pedro introduced me to Natalia and her husband Roberto. They also lived in Buenaventura Lakes and I visited their house frequently during my fieldwork. Pedro had once rented a room from them. Pedro, Natalia, and Roberto initially met at the hotel, where they worked in the housekeeping division. Natalia has two children from her previous marriage to a Puerto Rican man from the island and became pregnant a third time soon after she and Roberto started dating. A woman from Mexico watches their youngest child while they work. Natalia is originally from Puerto Rico, but she had lived in Texas with her husband before she divorced him and moved to Kissimmee.

One day in August 2010, Natalia texted me to ask me to go with her to the Department of Children and Family Services office to take care of her food stamp paperwork. She said that food stamps help her a lot because her three sons are constantly eating. She can budget only about $300 per month to feed her family of five. She was anxious on the drive to the office, explaining that they make you show proof of everything: income, rent, etc. "Maybe I make too much now," she worried, "but my rent went up $50." As we drove, she talked about the couple's legal and financial troubles and described a time when she and her husband were discriminated against. They were driving down Royal Palm Drive in Buenaventura Lakes when they passed a police car. Roberto, an undocumented Mexican immigrant without a Florida license, was driving. Natalia had a feeling the officer was going to pull them over, so they turned into a development, pulled over, and quickly switched places. Even though they were going the speed limit, the officer found them moments later and pulled them over. "We were treated like criminals," she said. "The car was searched and everything." They were lucky; in the end, they were only fined $1,000. She did not elaborate about the court proceedings or the charges.

As we passed the villas where Natalia and Roberto used to live, Natalia mentioned the bed bugs and roaches that infested the house. "Before," she said, "things were really bad, but now in comparison we are rich." Natalia said that she prepares breakfast, lunch, and dinner for Roberto every day to save money. "Once I gave him only rice, beans, and corn for lunch and he made a comment about us being poor. If I don't prepare a lunch for him and he doesn't have money then he won't eat, plus he knows the money can be used for bills," she told me. When I met Natalia her financial situation was better than it had been in previous years. She was employed as a room inspector in Pedro's hotel and her husband had found work painting houses. The couple was living in a large three-bedroom, two-bathroom house in Buenaventura Lakes that cost $900 per month. At times they struggled to come up with all of the rent money, but the modern interior was nicely decorated and was always immaculately clean. Initially, the interior of the home did not have anything that was distinctly Mexican or Puerto Rican, but they eventually placed a large portrait of the Virgen de la Guadalupe on their living room wall.

On one occasion Natalia proudly told me how she had bargain-hunted for all of their beautiful furniture and had spent only $700 for their very large flat-screen television. Another time she showed me her $2,000 set of cooking pots as I stared at her in shock. They have a lifetime guarantee, she explained, and nothing ever sticks to them. This was her one splurge and it was for a material item that she used more than anything and that would last her a lifetime. They forewent all other luxuries, such as getting her hair done or going out to dinner, unless there was a little extra money after the necessary expenses were covered. Everyone agreed that Natalia was an amazing mother and wife and an extremely hardworking and dedicated employee. But many of the other women I met in the hotel complained about Natalia's attitude, saying that she was a gossip and was cruel to the housekeepers she oversaw. She eventually got María fired, for example. María, who was unable to afford medical care, had taken some antibiotics from the lost and found to help her get over a cold. Natalia told their supervisor, who terminated María's employment.

The study of workplace interactions is an area for future research in Greater Orlando. Vanesa Ribas recommends "situating the study of intergroup relations in the crucial social domain of the workplace, a context in which Latino/a migrants and African Americans encounter one another in structured ways that are likely to be meaningfully related to how they think about and act toward each other."[9] Workplace interactions are also important for understanding interethnic relations among Latinos of different nationalities. In the houses I lived in or visited, a diverse group of Latinos from different countries often lived under one roof. However, non-Latino whites racialized Latinos as a homogenous group even though they had distinct experiences of migration and different positions in Greater Orlando's class hierarchy.

The Latino migration to Greater Orlando contained both professionals and low-paid service sector workers whose lives differed because of their socioeconomic status, citizenship status, and access to resources such as capital-building social networks. However, different forms of entrepreneurship were evident in Latino-concentrated communities and the encargado system enabled some migrants to profit from the housing needs of their co-ethnics. By renting out rooms in the houses where they live, the encargados and encargadas I lived with were able to generate economic capital. While the encargado system makes upward mobility possible for some migrants, it exploited others who have to relinquish control of their living environment. Although discourses about family circulated among residents and familial terms such as "brother" and "sister" were sometimes used, occupancy was based on one's ability to pay and relationships between tenants could be complex.

Through the encargado system I observed the daily struggles of some Latinos to find transportation and earn enough money for food and housing. I realized how much migrants' lives are impacted by their legal status and their dependency on the low-wage, insecure jobs that are available in the hospitality industry. Economic struggles fostered other social problems. Theft and drug dealing were the most common criminal actions individuals resorted to in an effort to make ends meet. The financial burden some members of the Latino community bore helps explain the decline of suburbs and increasing crime in Osceola County. When I first met María, her large suburban home was undergoing foreclosure. She anticipated losing the house eventually, so she did not invest money in maintenance or landscaping. She even sold the fence that enclosed her swimming pool for the extra cash, which resulted in a ticket from code enforcement since that was a violation in her development.

Financial struggles strained familial relations and friendships since individuals were constantly forced to borrow money from one another and at times take advantage of or manipulate others for financial gain. Erratic work schedules also meant that children were neglected, and renting out rooms led to crowded houses and a number of distractions for younger and older children alike. Additionally, children were exposed to and sometimes got involved with criminal practices and destructive habits. I came to realize that many of the people I lived with were barely scraping out a living. The encargados welcomed me into their lives and homes because they needed the steady source of income my rent money provided. One of the benefits of living with other Latinos, however, was the opportunity to learn during daily interactions how they self-identify and perceive other Latinos.

Conclusion

In August 2011, I attended a seminar for local businesses entitled "Hispanics: A Market Revolution" that the Hispanic Chamber of Commerce of Metro Orlando had advertised on its website. During the one-hour session, a variety of speakers from the business community emphasized the consumer power of Hispanics and the importance of adjusting advertising and marketing campaigns to target that population. I was struck by a presentation given by Geoscapes International Inc., a firm that provides data, technology, and analytic services to businesses to help them stay competitive as an emerging American mainstream consumer is created by the increasing presence and economic power of immigrants.[1]

The representative began with a PowerPoint slide of a map that showed the concentration of Hispanics in the United States in the 1990s. The second slide showed projections for 2017. The caption on the first slide highlighted the gateway states bordering Mexico that were the primary destinations of Hispanic migration. The second slide pointed out that "major metro areas outside border states are now gateway cities too." The slides made it clear that Hispanics can now be found in urban, suburban, and rural communities throughout the nation. But more important, the speaker was conveying that Hispanics have already arrived in Greater Orlando, that they are a force to be reckoned with, and that the population will only continue to grow. These visuals were a powerful reminder of the overall "browning of America" and the position of Hispanics as a majority minority.[2] The Hispanic population has surpassed the African American population in the United States; according to the US census estimates for July 1, 2018, African Americans were 13.4 percent of the total US population and Hispanics were 18.1 percent.[3]

The Latino population continues to grow in Buenaventura Lakes, Osceola

County, and other parts of Greater Orlando where I conducted fieldwork. According to the American Community Survey's estimates for 2012–2016, the Latino population in Buenaventura Lakes grew to 74.2 percent, up from 69.6 percent at the time of the 2010 US census.[4] The Puerto Rican population grew to 49.4 percent, up from 44.6 percent.[5] In Osceola County, the Latino population grew to 50.2 percent, up from 45.5 percent at the time of the 2010 US census.[6] In 2017, Hurricane Maria devastated the island of Puerto Rico, prompting an exodus to the states. At the time of this writing it was not clear how many newly arriving migrants would make Greater Orlando their permanent home.

The political, economic, and cultural impact of Latino migrants cannot be ignored in the parts of Osceola County where they are concentrated because of the changes they have brought to the landscape and soundscape. Tensions have grown between Latinos and non-Latino whites because of the growing economic and political influence of migrants and the widespread use of Spanish in the Orlando area. Some non-Latino whites oppose this change and have made attempts to restrict the use of Spanish because they have language ideologies that equate English with Americanness. In communities like Buenaventura Lakes, non-Latino whites have become a minority, many for the first time in their lives. This had led to the development of a stronger white racial consciousness and to allegations of reverse discrimination and exclusion. Often non-Latinos perceived Latinos as a distinct racial group because of linguistic and other cultural differences. They racialize Latinos as a separate, nonwhite race despite Latinos' claims to a white racial identity. Latinos are challenging the South's historic black-white racial binary as they carve out a space for themselves in Greater Orlando. However, Latino-concentrated spaces are often perceived negatively.

Several factors are responsible for the changes in the Buenaventura Lakes suburbs. When I analyzed my data from interviews, newspapers, and online material, a long list emerged that included crime, concerns about safety, ageing homes that have not been maintained, and the absence of homeowners' associations. The loss of amenities like the country club and the golf course changed the class status of the suburb and the foreclosure crisis exacerbated the community's economic problems. Some residents no longer perceived Buenaventura Lakes as a good investment.

I began my fieldwork in Buenaventura Lakes in search of upwardly mobile, middle-class homeowners. However, Puerto Ricans and other Latinos in that community were perceived as working-class or low-income people. Where I found upwardly mobile Latinos was in business networking organizations. Newspaper articles revealed how professionals, entrepreneurs, and other wealthy Puerto Ricans had established organizations such as the Puerto Rican Chamber of Commerce, the Hispanic Chamber of Commerce, and the Puerto Rican Professional Association. These individuals distinguished themselves from the working-class migrants who had settled in New York and Chicago in the 1940s through the 1960s.

Professionals and entrepreneurs in Greater Orlando worked together to generate social and economic capital through events that fostered networks and new business opportunities. Those who participated in these business networking organizations drew strong distinctions between themselves and other Latinos based on their possession of the cultural and symbolic capital that was important to their class identities. They formed a visible Latino elite with clear social boundaries. Cultural capital functioned as a mechanism of power that helped create and maintain exclusive elite spaces. The cross-class nature of this migration has created obstacles to the development of an ethnic-based solidarity.

The people I lived with rarely talked about racial and ethnic identities and categories during everyday conversations. They referred to blackness or whiteness only rarely. The vast majority preferred to identify by national origin instead of as Latino, Hispanic, or white. Interethnic relations varied. Some Latinos were prejudiced against Puerto Ricans, but I also met Puerto Rican women who had married undocumented Mexican men and who supported and aided other undocumented workers. These women embraced Mexican traditions and cultural practices and raised their children as proud "Mexi-Ricans."

The Racialization of Latinos

Researchers who study new and maturing destinations of migration have explored the role of Latinos in challenging the South's historic black-white racial binary. How have Latinos been incorporated into the racial hierarchy and will they "become white" like the European immigrants who migrated to this country decades ago? Future research is needed to document the place-specific experiences of Latinos in order to answer the central questions Angela Stuesse posed in her book *Scratching Out a Living*: how will the growing presence of Latino communities transform social hierarchies of race in the South? How will new migrants identify and be identified racially? Will the category of whiteness expand to include some Latinos? Will another racial category, Latino or Hispanic, emerge to categorize those who don't fit into the classifications of white or black? In her study of new destinations, Helen Marrow asks questions that came to shape my research: "How will Hispanic newcomers' identities affect their incorporation into this largely binary region; will racial discrimination prevent their incorporation; and how might southern notions of race be ultimately reformulated by their incorporation?"[7] These are the questions I began to ask about Greater Orlando as I analyzed my data, although they are not the research questions I set out to study. After relocating to the Mississippi-Tennessee border in 2013, another destination with an influx of Latinos, I decided to continue my study of Latinos in the South to compare two distinct locales. I plan to focus on the research questions Angela Stuesse and Helen Marrow have posed using a methodology similar to the one I used in my Orlando fieldwork.

In Greater Orlando, social class position and language usage mediated the relationships of Hispanics with other Hispanics and with non-Hispanics. My fieldwork provides evidence of the social construction of a distinct Hispanic race that is situated hierarchically between whites and blacks; non-Hispanics talked about and perceived Hispanics as a nonwhite, "Hispanic race" of people. This is similar to what Helen Marrow found in a case study in North Carolina: "My data . . . do not show that Hispanics have yet become 'whites.' Strong linguistic, cultural, and racial boundaries continue to separate the two groups, and discrimination by whites is indeed harming Hispanics' wellbeing in fundamental ways."[8] Patricia Silver has also found that "Central Floridians racialize Puerto Ricans in general as a non-white group."[9]

Marrow found that Hispanics challenged the black-white racial binary in favor of a tripartite model: "Hispanic respondents both self-identified and reported external identification by southern natives most strongly as something other than whites or blacks—particularly as Hispanics, Latinos, or people of some 'other race.'"[10] In many instances, non-Hispanic whites in North Carolina referred to Hispanics as "Spanish people" or people of the "Spanish race." In Greater Orlando, there was evidence that a growing portion of Hispanic elites were on the path to becoming honorary whites, particularly among the second and third generations who are assimilating and are not as easily identified as Hispanic. Nevertheless, non-Hispanic whites saw the vast majority of Hispanics as a distinct Hispanic race because of their linguistic practices, their national origins, and other cultural identifiers. Eduardo Bonilla-Silva has found that while for most Latinos, integrating into mainstream US culture has meant becoming "nonwhite," for a few select groups migration has meant becoming "honorary" whites; that is, "becoming almost white."[11] Researchers doing case studies in North Carolina are documenting "the erosion of the historical racial binary between African Americans and whites and the development of an even more complex system of race relations."[12]

In Greater Orlando, many Latinos identified as white in the census, while in Memphis, the site of my current research, more Latinos identified as "some other race." In fact, in their answer to the census question about race, most narrators of an oral history project in Memphis wrote in "Hispanic." What does this mean? To what extent are Latinos dissenting from categories of racial and ethnic identification that have been created and imposed? Future research should certainly investigate the conflation of the terms "race" and "ethnicity" in the minds of the larger Latino and non-Latino population.

In 2015, the Pew Research Center conducted research that asked whether being Hispanic is a matter of race, of ethnicity, or both. Latinos stand out from other Americans when they report their racial identity, the report claims. In the 2010 census, 94 percent of the US population selected "at least one of the five standard, government-defined racial categories-white, black, Asian, American Indian or Pacific Islander." Only 63 percent of Latinos selected one of those categories; the other 37 percent selected "'only some other race,' with many offering write-in responses such as 'Mexican,' 'Hispanic' or 'Latin American.'"[13] While the government defines "Hispanic" as an ethnicity and not a race, "these census findings suggest that standard U.S. racial categories might either be confusing or not provide relevant options for Hispanics to describe their racial identity." A Pew Research Center survey found that "for two-thirds of Hispanics, their Hispanic background *is* a part of their racial background—not something separate. This suggests that Hispanics have a unique view of race that doesn't necessarily fit within the official U.S. definitions."[14]

This book has begun to grapple with the complexity of ethnoracial identities and categorizations by examining how Hispanics are being racialized, how they self-identify, and the extent to which the racial schema of the United States Census Bureau are being enacted or challenged in everyday interactions. I have drawn particular attention to the ways that language ideologies are connected to racialization processes and how they impact residents' racial understandings, classifications, and residential preferences. Some of the Hispanic residents I met were difficult to place in a racial category based on phenotype alone. Elizabeth Aranda and Guillermo Rebollo-Gil point out that "when racial markers such as skin color, hair texture, and eye shape are not enough to identify the other, ethnoracial markers such as language, accent, culture and national origin serve as proxies." They note that while the appearance of light-skinned Puerto Ricans can shape their experience with racism and enable them to pass for white in some instances, "their white privilege is surrendered when considering other factors such as accents" or their Puerto Rican ancestry.[15] This is why I have focused on how language usage is racialized and how language ideologies impact racial understandings.

Racial Consciousness

In an article titled "The Myth of Majority-Minority America: I Have One Cuban Grandparent. Why Does the Census Count Me as Hispanic?" Matthew Yglesias challenges the census bureau's racial and ethnic categories. He asks whether the United States will become a majority-minority nation or if the white racial category will just expand to include Hispanics. In May 2012, in a rare occasion, a census bureau press release dominated the media with a claim that most children younger than age one are minorities. According to Yglesias, the press interpreted the shortage of white Anglo babies as a foreshadowing of things to come in America's future majority-minority nation. In response, Yglesias said, "I have my doubts. . . . I suspect an awful lot of these 'minority' babies are going to be white when they grow up."[16]

Yglesias explained his own confusion as he filled out the 2010 census form. The census bureau's extension of the one-drop rule to Hispanic identity seemed ridiculous. Yglesias suspects that the white racial category will indeed evolve to include Asians and Latin Americans since there is already a great deal of ambiguity about racial and ethnic identities. In answer to the question that asked if he was of Hispanic, Latino, or Spanish origin, he responded "yes." His grandfather José Yglesias immigrated to Ybor City in Tampa, Florida, and grew up speaking Spanish in a Hispanic-concentrated community. Since he is a descendent of his grandfather, he must be of Hispanic origin. However, Yglesias noted that "back in the real world, though, I'm just another white dude. My three other grandparents are all of Eastern European Jewish extraction."[17] He grew up speaking English and recalls taking a Spanish class only once. It seemed ridiculous that a single Hispanic ancestor would make him part of the Hispanic minority population. Whiteness, he points out, has always been an "elastic concept" in America. He suggests that if whiteness has always defined the sociocultural majority, than the only way to maintain that power "is to recruit large swathes of the Hispanic and fractionally Asian population into whiteness."[18] Yglesias points out that assimilation and interracial and interethnic marriages has the potential to whiten the Hispanic population.

In February 2012, the Pew Research Center released a report on interracial marriage that revealed that 26 percent of Hispanics marry non-Hispanics.[19] These Hispanics are more likely to have a college education than those who married within their group, pointing to the potential links between upward mobility and "becoming" white. White-Hispanic couples accounted for more than 43 percent of approximately 275,500 new interracial or interethnic marriages in 2010; white-Asian couples accounted for 14 percent and white-black couples accounted for 12 percent. Intermarriage rates among blacks are somewhat lower: 17 percent of black newlyweds had married nonblacks. Only 9 percent of whites had married someone who is not white, the lowest percentage among all the groups. Marriages between whites and Hispanics are the most common type of intermarriage. How will the children of those white and Hispanic couples identify? As academics continue to examine Hispanic migration and race relations in the South, the third generation will be of increasing importance, as will interracial and interethnic families and upwardly mobile Hispanics.

In 2013, when I moved to the northern Mississippi/Tennessee border I planned to continue my research on Latinos in the South. The migratory experience is place-specific and I wanted to learn about the racialization experiences of other Latinos in the South. I immediately found the story of Ginny, a "Mississippi dame with a Puerto Rican name," who chose to share her experiences of racialization in the South via a self-reflexive Internet blog. Her parents, who were born and had been raised in Puerto Rico, moved to the Mississippi Gulf Coast in the 1990s. According to Ginny,

> It was in living here that I became acutely, and painfully, aware that I was different and was always going to be. My skin was dark, "black" as some of the other kids at my predominately-white Catholic school said. This, along with my mother's constant worry that something terrible would happen to us because the South did not have a history of being kind to dark-skinned people, made the navigation of my identity in southern Mississippi confusing and difficult.

Ginny rejected a black racial identity, like so many other Hispanics, and hoped that she could cross to the white side of the color line. She longed to be perceived as white by other southerners. Her father always referred to her as a "Puerto Rican southern belle." However, Ginny explains that

I was in constant worry through my adolescence that I looked "too black," that I would be confused for anything other than Latin American, or maybe just a dark-complected white person. I used to ask my friends in high school what race they would think I am, fearing that they would say black. I never had the luxury to live without thinking constantly about my race and how it played a part in how others saw me in the South. This consciousness manifested itself in a strong desire to not be seen as the other, to somehow develop into a light-skinned, European-featured woman, because that is desirable. If that could somehow happen, I would be acceptable, easy to befriend by the white people I was surrounded by.

The devastation of Hurricane Katrina in 2005 altered Ginny's racial consciousness and her desire to assimilate and be accepted into the white race. Houses were destroyed and schools were closed for almost a month. When Ginny returned to school, "there was a lot of talk about the influx of Latin American workers entering the state to work on rebuilding homes and businesses. Many were roofers, and I remember kids talking about the 'Mexicans' who were rebuilding their homes and working on their roofs." The presence of these "Mexican" laborers bothered "these white kids so much and I would constantly hear them talk about how these people were weird or scary or dirty or stupid because they spoke little or no English." For the first time, she was confronted with blatant racism against a population that looked like her. Yet Ginny escaped the racist, stereotypical responses in her own life. "I was safe and good to these white people because I assimilated; I spoke English, I 'passed' in appearance, and I had accepted mainstream interests that I never thought critically about."

As Ginny came to realize that her Americanized culture, her English-language skills, and her class position helped her pass for white, she was able to think about the implications of passing with a critical lens for the first time: "I thought, 'I've been spending almost my entire life trying to fit in with people who would just as soon dehumanize and diminish me if I were more closely tied to a certain culture and language and economic situation.'" Ginny came to the realization that "there was never going to be any space made for my difference and the differences of people of color, racialized by skin color and language." She would have to start accepting herself and start making a space for herself in the South. This has been a struggle:

There are so many seen and unseen forces in this society, this southern culture, in the United States, that makes it incredibly hard sometimes to care for myself and love myself and my roots the way they are meant to be loved by me. I'm not Puerto Rican enough, I'm not mainstream enough, I talk about race too much. . . . I have been told countless times that "it's not always about race" and "you don't need to question everything" and "it's not always like that." I've figured out that these phrases are one way people can feel comfortable about the world we live in. It's an acceptance of the status quo, and it's a strategy to keep you from "bitching" about the conditions of oppression and marginalization.

Ginny's commentary about the responses to talk about race and racism reflects the color-bind ideologies and white privilege I documented in Greater Orlando.

Many of my non-Hispanic white informants did not have to think about their racial identity. Before the Latinization of Greater Orlando, they could deny the significance of race in their everyday lives. However, the Hispanic population entered their suburban communities and challenged ideas about what is normal, mainstream, and American. In many instances, the non-Hispanic whites I met had far less capital than some of the upwardly mobile Hispanics I interacted with. These are poor and working-class whites and they are marginalized economically, so they feel victimized when they can't get a job because they don't speak Spanish or can't order food because all of the employees are speaking Spanish. While Hispanics have been living with these experiences for generations, the feelings that result from being a minority or the Other is new to the non-Hispanic white population. Their ideologies and belief systems tell them that they are the true Americans, that the United States is becoming more foreign, and that these Hispanics are the newcomers as they "forget" Florida's Spanish past.

Ginny claims that she is "done with this socialization of neglect and internalized racism and misogyny that I learned in Mississippi, and which is constantly reinforced wherever I go." The South both frustrates and fascinates her, so she created a virtual space, which she calls *Mississippi Goddam*, where she could share her experiences in the hope of creating a semblance of progress and justice:[20]

I'm not done with Mississippi. I'm not done with Alabama. I'm not done with Florida. I grew up in these places, and my home for now is the Gulf

Coast. My childhood was difficult in many ways because of the culture of the south, but I think that's a culture that can change. Mississippi is not a lost cause. Alabama and Florida aren't either.

There is a fear of change, and if demography is destiny, the "browning" of America that is under way means that we will need to rethink our understandings of race, of ethnicity, and of what it means to be American.

NOTES

Prologue

1. Flores, *Divided Borders*, 189.
2. Flores, *Divided Borders*, 182.
3. Duany and Matos-Rodriguez, "Puerto Ricans in Orlando and Central Florida."
4. Duany, *Blurred Borders*. Duany, "The Orlando Ricans: Overlapping Identity Discourses Among Middle-Class Puerto Rican Immigrants."
5. Duany, "The Orlando Ricans: Overlapping Identity Discourses Among Middle-Class Puerto Rican Immigrants," 98.

Introduction: New Destinations

1. A metropolitan statistical area is defined as a region with a high population density and close economic ties throughout the geographic area. The metropolitan statistical areas are defined by the U.S. Office of Management and Budget and are used by government agencies for statistical purposes.
2. See Portes and Stepick, *City on the Edge*; Sánchez-Korrol, *From Colonia to Community*; and Pedraza and Rumbaut, *Origins and Destinies*.
3. Ribas, *On the Line*, 32. For the presence of migrants in suburbs, see Rodriguez, Saenz, Rodriguez, and Menjivar, *Latinas/os in the United States*; Mantero, *Latinos and the U.S. South*; Massey, *New Faces in New Places*; Mahler, *Salvadorans in Suburbia*; and Falcón, *Atlas of Stateside Puerto Ricans*.
4. See Zuñiga and León, *New Destinations*; Murphy, Blanchard, and Hill, *Latino Workers in the Contemporary South*; Furuseth, *Latinos in the New South*; and Millard and Chapa, *Apple Pie and Enchiladas*.
5. Winders and Smith, "Excepting/Accepting the South," 225.
6. Winders and Smith, "Excepting/Accepting the South," 225.
7. Ribas, *On the Line*, 32.
8. Ribas, *On the Line*, 32.
9. Stuesse, *Scratching Out a Living*, 4.
10. Weise, *Corazón de Dixie*, 1.
11. Weise, *Corazón de Dixie*, 4.

12. Weise, "Dispatches from the 'Viejo' New South," 14.

13. Silver, "Culture Is More Than Bingo and Salsa," 69.

14. The largest population is still in the New York metropolitan statistical area.

15. Vélez, "A New Framework for Understanding Puerto Ricans' Migration Patterns and Incorporation," 128.

16. Sánchez-Korrol, *From Colonia to Community*. Operation Bootstrap was a set of policies and incentives developed jointly by the Puerto Rico Industrial Development Company and the US government that sought to industrialize Puerto Rico by attracting companies from off the island, primarily from the United States, through tax exemptions, industrial services, lower labor costs, and other forms of special assistance.

17. Morales, *Puerto Rican Poverty and Migration*, 35.

18. Morales, *Puerto Rican Poverty and Migration*, 35.

19. Vélez, "A New Framework for Understanding Puerto Ricans' Migration Patterns and Incorporation," 128.

20. Vélez, "A New Framework for Understanding Puerto Ricans' Migration Patterns and Incorporation," 128.

21. Sánchez-Korrol, *From Colonia to Community*.

22. Sánchez-Korrol, *From Colonia to Community*.

23. Meléndez, *Sponsored Migrations*.

24. Silver and Vélez, "'Let Me Go Check Out Florida.'"

25. Silver and Vélez, "'Let Me Go Check Out Florida.'"

26. Duany and Silver, "The 'Puerto Ricanization' of Florida: Historical Background and Current Status," 17.

27. Schneider, "Puerto Ricans Increasingly Calling Florida Home."

28. Silver and Vélez, "'Let Me Go Check Out Florida,'" 102.

29. Silver and Vélez, "'Let Me Go Check Out Florida,'" 102.

30. Martínez-Fernández, "Orlando: The Puerto Rican Frontier."

31. Silver and Vélez, "'Let Me Go Check Out Florida,'" 101.

32. Silver and Vélez, "'Let Me Go Check Out Florida,'" 102.

33. See Brodwin, *Everyday Ethics*, for a discussion of the value of unprompted conversations and remarks as part of fieldwork methodology.

34. Boellstorf, *Coming of Age in Second Life*, 61.

35. Oboler, *Ethnic Labels, Latino Lives*, 4.

36. Ennis, Ríos-Vargas, and Albert, "The Hispanic Population: 2010."

37. Rumbaut, "Pigments of Our Imagination," 23.

38. Cobas, Duany, and Feagin, *How the United States Racializes Latinos*.

39. Rumbaut, "Pigments of Our Imagination, 23.

40. Rumbaut, "Pigments of Our Imagination, 23.

41. Lavenda and Schultz, *Anthropology: What Does It Mean to Be Human?* 533.

42. Lavenda and Schultz, *Anthropology: What Does It Mean to Be Human?* 538.

43. Omi and Winant, *Racial Formation in the United States*, 5.

44. Hxrguitar, comment on city-data.com forum, January 2, 2010.

45. United States Census Bureau, "Profile of General Population and Housing Characteristics: 2010: Buenaventura Lakes."

46. United States Census Bureau, "Profile of General Population and Housing Characteristics: 2010: Osceola County."

47. Rumbaut, "Pigments of Our Imagination," 24.

48. Cobas, Duany, and Feagin, *How the United States Racializes Latinos*, 1.

49. Aranda and Rebollo-Gil, "Ethnoracism and the 'Sandwiched' Minorities," 913.

50. Aranda and Rebollo-Gil, "Ethnoracism and the 'Sandwiched' Minorities," 913.

51. Aranda and Rebollo-Gil, "Ethnoracism and the 'Sandwiched' Minorities," 911.

52. Cobas, Duany, and Feagin, *How the United States Racializes Latinos*, 40.

53. Rumbaut, "Pigments of Our Imagination."

54. Humes, Jones, and Ramirez, "Overview of Race and Hispanic Origin."

55. Loue and Sajatovic, *Determinants of Minority Health and Wellness*, 368.

56. Cobas, Duany, and Feagin, *How the United States Racializes Latinos*, 46.

57. United States Census Bureau, "Census Bureau Statement on 2020 Census Race and Ethnicity Question."

58. United States Census Bureau, "Census Bureau Statement on 2020 Census Race and Ethnicity Question."

59. Rumbaut, "Pigments of Our Imagination," 29.

60. Silver, "Latinization, Race, and Cultural Identification in Puerto Rican Orlando."

61. Silver, "Latinization, Race, and Cultural Identification in Puerto Rican Orlando," 68.

62. Language ideologies are ideas, perceptions, and beliefs about the nature and usage of languages that become naturalized, shared, commonsense understandings that connect language to identities, values, morals, and to popular perceptions of "race." See Rumsey, "Wording, Meaning, and Linguistic Ideology."

Chapter 1. Buenaventura Lakes

1. "Osceola County History."

2. Mahler, *American Dreaming*.

3. Social Explorer, "Census 1980 [Osceola County, Florida]"; Social Explorer, "Census 1990 [Osceola County, Florida]"; Social Explorer, "Census 2000 [Osceola County, Florida]"; Social Explorer, "Census 2010 [Osceola County, Florida]."

4. Social Explorer, "Census 1980 [Osceola County, Florida]"; Social Explorer, "Census 1990 [Osceola County, Florida]"; Social Explorer, "Census 2000 [Osceola County, Florida]"; Social Explorer, "Census 2010 [Osceola County, Florida]."

5. Social Explorer, "ACS 2016 (5-Year Estimates) [Hispanic or Latino by Race and Specific Origin, Buenaventura Lakes]."

6. Fernandez, "Family Born in America, Still Faithful to Puerto Rican Roots."

7. Ramos, "1986: Couple Escape New York for Central Florida Retirement."

8. Ramos, "1986: Couple Escape New York for Central Florida Retirement."

9. "Mexican Millionaires Build City."

10. "Landstar Homes: A Quarter Century of Milestones."

11. During the 1970s and 1980s, economic activity in Mexico was characterized by spurts of rapid growth followed by depressions, most notably in 1976 and 1982. President Luis Echeverría Álvarez's (1970–1976) leftist rhetoric and actions—for instance, his support of peasants' illegal land seizures—diminished the confidence of investors and alienated private sector developers. Falling oil prices, higher world interest rates, rising inflation, the overvaluation of the peso, and the deterioration of balance-of-payment accounts continued into the 1980s. This resulted in massive capital flight. In August 1982, President José López Portillo y Pacheco (1976–1982) declared an involuntary moratorium on debt payments; one month later, he announced the nationalization of the private banking system.

12. John Wright, interview by Simone Delerme, July 28, 2010.

13. "Mexican Millionaires Build City."

14. "Mexican Millionaires Build City."

15. John Wright interview.

16. "Options Are a Given at Landstar."

17. "Another Florida Builder Opens Sales Office on L.I."

18. Straight, "Landstar Lures Northern Buyers."

19. Kilsheimer, "Orlando's Overseas Attraction International Appeal Shows Up in Newcomers."

20. Snyder, "Developments Are Gems for Landstar, BVL, Meadow Woods Score in Sales."

21. Fernandez and Conway, "Osceola Hispanics Blend of Cultures, Traditions, Food."

22. Ross, "Landstar Capitalizes on Puerto Rican Exodus."

23. Chediak, "Booming Enclave Remains Affordable."

24. María García, interview by Simone Delerme, July 23, 2007.

25. Holton, "Many Seek a New Life in Orlando."

26. Pico, "Out-of-State Property Scams Nothing New in P.R."

27. Holton, "Many Seek a New Life in Orlando."

28. Holton, "Many Seek a New Life in Orlando."

29. Holton, "Many Seek a New Life in Orlando."

30. Brewington, "A New Home."

31. Ross, "Landstar Capitalizes on Puerto Rican Exodus."

32. Ross, "Landstar Capitalizes on Puerto Rican Exodus." The oral history project is titled "Puerto Ricans in Central Florida from 1940s to 1980s: A History." See http://www.digitalethnography.dm.ucf.edu/pr/community.html.

33. Silver, "Latinization, Race, and Cultural Identification in Puerto Rican Orlando," 63.

34. Duany and Silver, "The 'Puerto Ricanization' of Florida," 16.

35. Firpo, "Forming a Puerto Rican Identity in Orlando."

36. Silver, "Culture Is More Than Bingo and Salsa."

37. The General Development Corporation was registered in Puerto Rico to sell property in Port St. Lucie, Port Malabar, Port La Belle, Port Charlotte, and Silver Spring Shores.

38. Duany and Silver, "The 'Puerto Ricanization' of Florida," 17.

39. Duany and Silver, "The 'Puerto Ricanization' of Florida," 17.

40. Holton, "Many Seek a New Life in Orlando."

41. Two of my interviewees from New York mentioned that a newspaper ad drew them to Central Florida. However, most of my sources focused on Puerto Ricans migrating from the island. The individuals from the Northeast or Midwest were mentioned far less frequently. This is somewhat surprising; according to the 2000 census, 55.1 percent of Central Florida's residents of Puerto Rican origin were born in Puerto Rico, while 44.9 percent were born in the US mainland.

42. Hunt, "County Looks More Latin—Hispanic Population Is Up 294%."

43. Collazo, Ryan, and Bauman, "Profile of the Puerto Rican Population in the United States and Puerto Rico: 2008."

44. Fernandez, "Hispanic Population Surges in Osceola."

45. Ramos, "Central Florida Top Region for Puerto Ricans."

46. Ross, "Landstar Capitalizes on Puerto Rican Exodus."

47. Chediak, "Booming Enclave Remains Affordable."

48. Chediak, "Booming Enclave Remains Affordable."

49. Ramos, "Between 2 Worlds." Levittown, a suburb of San Juan, is one of the largest planned communities on the island. The first Levittown was built in New York in the period 1947–1951 for returning World War II veterans.

50. Ramos, "Between 2 Worlds."

51. Holton, "Many Seek a New Life in Orlando."

Chapter 2. Latinization, Landscapes, and Soundscapes

1. Davíla and Laó-Montes, *Mambo Montage*, 3.

2. Torres, "Latin Beat Is a Definite Part of Local Entertainment."

3. Fernandez, "Hispanic Population Surges In Osceola."

4. Mitchell, "Hispanics' Quiet Migration Is Making Area More Diverse."

5. Mitchell, "Hispanics' Quiet Migration Is Making Area More Diverse."

6. "They Are Citizens."

7. Suris, "Focusing on Hispanics."

8. Fernandez, "Hispanic Population Surges in Osceola."

9. Fernandez, "Hispanic Population Surges in Osceola."

10. Fernandez, "Hispanic Population Surges in Osceola."

11. McLeod, "Diversity 101."

12. Feigenbaum, "It's No Party for Fest Goers."

13. Flynn, "Banco Popular Expanding on Plans for Central Florida."

14. Flynn, "Banco Popular Expanding on Plans for Central Florida."

15. Burnett, "R-G Crown Branches Out across Florida."

16. Fernandez, "Hispanic Population Surges in Osceola"; Ramos, "Between 2 Worlds."

17. Arreola, *Hispanic Spaces, Latino Places.*

18. Duany, "The Orlando Ricans," 89.

19. Social Explorer, "Census 2010 [Hispanic or Latino by Specific Origin, Buenaventura Lakes]"; Social Explorer, "Census 2010 [Osceola County, Florida]."

20. Fieldnotes, December 19, 2010.

21. United States Census Bureau, "Quick Facts: St. Cloud, Florida."

22. Cruz, "Barriers to Political Participation of Puerto Ricans and Hispanics in Osceola County," 272.

23. Cruz, "Barriers to Political Participation of Puerto Ricans and Hispanics in Osceola County," 272.

24. Cruz, "Barriers to Political Participation of Puerto Ricans and Hispanics in Osceola County," 265.

25. Cruz, "Barriers to Political Participation of Puerto Ricans and Hispanics in Osceola County," 265.

26. Cruz, "Barriers to Political Participation of Puerto Ricans and Hispanics in Osceola County," 267.

27. *United States v. Osceola County, Florida and Donna Bryant*, 475 F.Supp.2d 1220 (2006).

28. Cruz, "Barriers to Political Participation of Puerto Ricans and Hispanics in Osceola County," 255.

29. Cruz, "Barriers to Political Participation of Puerto Ricans and Hispanics in Osceola County," 257.

30. Jacobson, "Osceola Avoids Suit on Voting.

31. Cruz, "Barriers to Political Participation of Puerto Ricans and Hispanics in Osceola County." A consent decree is an agreement or settlement resolving a dispute between two parties without admission of guilt or liability.

32. Cruz, "Barriers to Political Participation of Puerto Ricans and Hispanics in Osceola County," 264.

33. Cruz, "Barriers to Political Participation of Puerto Ricans and Hispanics in Osceola County," 262.

34. Cruz, "Barriers to Political Participation of Puerto Ricans and Hispanics in Osceola County," 270, Cruz's italics.

35. Cruz, "Barriers to Political Participation of Puerto Ricans and Hispanics in Osceola County," 270.

36. Fernandez and Conway, "Hispanic Boom Is Rare Chance to Track Change."

37. Ibid.

38. Owens, "Don't Trash Historic Puerto Rican Regiment."

39. Franqui-Rivera, "The Borinqueneers."

40. Franqui-Rivera, "The Borinqueneers."

41. John Quiñones, statement made at 65th Infantry Veterans Park Press Conference, Buenaventura Lakes, Florida, April 21, 2011.

42. "Ernest Acosta," comment on *Hispanosphere*, April 21 2011.

43. "Frente Unido436," comment on *Hispanosphere*, April 20, 2011.

44. "Frente Unido436," comment on *Hispanosphere*, April 20, 2011.

45. "luis Martinez," comment on *Hispanosphere*, April 21, 2011.

46. "Curiouser," comment on *Hispanosphere*, April 25, 2011.

47. "Gay_Rights_Are_HUMAN_RIGHTS," comment on *Hispanosphere*, April 27, 2011.

48. Ramos-Zayas and De Genova, *Latino Crossings*.

49. Rumsey, "Wording, Meaning, and Linguistic Ideology."

50. Woolard, "Introduction: Language Ideology as a Field of Inquiry."

51. Martínez-Fernández, "Orlando Develops Hispanic Accent"; Ramos, "Latinos at the Helm of Orlando's Public Broadcasting"; Martínez-Fernández, "Ever Wonder Why ATMs in Central Florida Speak Spanish?"; Ramos, "Seminole to Offer Ballots in Spanish"; Brewington, "A New Home."

52. Chris Williams, interview by Simone Delerme, July 27, 2010.

53. Unmuth, "More Puerto Ricans Make County Home."

54. Ramos, "Central Florida Top Region for Puerto Ricans."

55. Martínez-Fernández, "Orlando Develops Hispanic Accent."

56. Pedicini, "New Grocer in Town."

57. Sandra López, interview by Simone Delerme, June 9, 2011.

58. Low, "Maintaining Whiteness."

59. In 1990, a judge from the US District Court, Southern District of Florida signed a consent decree that gave the court the power to enforce an agreement between the Florida State board of Education and a coalition of eight groups. The groups were the League of United Latin American Citizens, ASPIRA of Florida, The Farmworkers' Association of Central Florida, Florida State Conference of NAACP Branches, Haitian Refugee Center, Spanish American League Against Discrimination, American Hispanic Educators' Association of Dade, and the Haitian Educators' Association. The eight organizations were represented by Multicultural Education, Training, and Advocacy, Inc. (META) and Florida legal services attorneys. The consent decree settlement focused on six core issues: identification and assessment, equal access to appropriate programming, equal access to appropriate categorical programming for English limited learner students, personnel, monitoring, and outcome measures.

60. Workforce Central Florida is a non-profit 501(c)3 that helps the unemployed find work. The agency connects employers to job seekers, provides worker resources and training, and prepares residents for careers that meet the needs of local businesses. They are responsible for workforce planning in five counties, including Orange and Osceola.

61. Ramos, "Workforce Central Florida Had an English-Only Policy," *Hispanosphere*, October 5, 2011.

62. "Ruffus," comment on *Hispanosphere*, October 5, 2011.

63. "Rocket City," comment on *Hispanosphere*, October 6, 2011.

64. "Manny," comment on *Hispanosphere*, October 6, 2011.

65. Cruz, "Barriers to Political Participation of Puerto Ricans and Hispanics in Osceola County," 253.

66. Cruz, "Barriers to Political Participation of Puerto Ricans and Hispanics in Osceola County," 253.

67. Cruz, "Barriers to Political Participation of Puerto Ricans and Hispanics in Osceola County," 253.

68. Cruz, "Barriers to Political Participation of Puerto Ricans and Hispanics in Osceola County," 257.

69. Cruz, "Barriers to Political Participation of Puerto Ricans and Hispanics in Osceola County," 257.

70. Urciuoli, *Exposing Prejudice*, 2.

71. Fieldnotes, August 2, 2010.

72. "Publius," comment on *Hispanosphere*, December 21, 2009.

73. Tom Thornburg, comment on *Hispanosphere*, December 22, 2009.

74. "tim," comment on *Hispanosphere*, December 22, 2009.

75. "poor taxpayer," comment on *Hispanosphere*, December 22, 2009.

76. "Barton," comment on *Hispanosphere*, December 24, 2009.

77. In "Returned Migration, Language, and Identity," Ana Celia Zentella highlights the many dialects of English that diversified the California region, including the English spoken by African American ex-slaves, gold seekers, and the "Okies" who escaped the dust bowl.

78. Silverstein, "Monoglot 'Standard' in America," 295.

79. Silverstein, "Monoglot 'Standard' in America," 285.

80. Urciuoli, "Containing Language Difference," 176.

81. Lewis, "'What Group?'" 628.

82. Urciuoli, *Exposing Prejudice*, 36.

83. "Slap Maxwell," comment on *Hispanosphere*, September 8, 2009.

84. "Ed," comment on *Hispanosphere*, September 9, 2009.

Chapter 3. The Fractured American Dream

1. Michael's description of the local economy was consistent with how the county's website describes it: "Osceola County's economic base is dominated by tourism, serving as a gateway to Walt Disney World and other Central Florida attractions. The area's historical investments in ranching and citrus are still very strong, while light industry and service enterprises are growing." "Osceola County History."

2. Rivera-Lyles, "Osceola Unveils BVL Rescue Plan."

3. Rivera-Lyles, "Osceola Unveils BVL Rescue Plan."

4. Rivera-Lyles, "Osceola Unveils BVL Rescue Plan."

5. Steirer, "It's Time to Clean Up This Neighborhood."

6. Steirer, "It's Time to Clean Up This Neighborhood."

7. Sandra López, interview by Simone Delerme, June 9, 2011.

8. Acevedo, "Crime Worries Vex BVL Residents."

9. "Eighty Three (83) Arrested in 3-Day Operation."

10. Leusner, "I-75 Stop Leads to Osceola Coke Bust."

11. Jacobson, "BVL Resident Charged in Fatal Beating."

12. Clarke, "2 Men Accused of Shooting at Osceola cops."

13. Pacheco, "Deputies Explore Trio's Ties to Burglaries."

14. Clarke, "Man Jailed in Stabbing at Party."

15. Curtis, "Osceola Sheriff's Office Ties 3 Killings to Gang."

16. Rivera-Lyles, "Residents' Crime Watch on Patrol."

17. See Ramos-Zayas, *National Performances*; Zentella, "Returned Migration, Language, and Identity"; and Grosfoguel, Maldonado-Torres, and Saldivar, *Latin@s in the World-System*.

18. Duany, "The Orlando Ricans," 107.

19. Duany, "The Orlando Ricans," 107.

20. Social Explorer, "ACS 2014 (5-Year Estimates) [Household Income, Buenaventura Lakes]."

21. The doctor did not specify when he bought the house.

22. Rivera-Lyles, "Judge: Mediation Not Needed in Osceola Home Foreclosures."

23. Shanklin, "Who Are Region's Biggest Losers in Housing Freefall?"

24. National Council of Negro Women, "Assessing the Double Burden," 5.

25. National Council of Negro Women, "Assessing the Double Burden," 5.

26. Sabogal, "Viviendo en la Sombra," 126.

27. "Assessing the Double Burden," 10.

28. McClure and Shanklin, "The Subprime Mess."

29. McClure and Shanklin, "The Subprime Mess."

30. For example, in 2007, middle- and upper-income Hispanic females were more than twice as likely to receive high-cost loans than middle- and upper-income white females in almost 62 percent of the metropolitan areas the NCRC examined. In that same year, low- and moderate-income Hispanic females were 1.5 times more likely than low- and moderate-income white females to receive high-cost loans in 32 percent of the metropolitan areas examined.

31. Newman et al., "Cities Destroyed (Again) for Cash."

32. Murphy, "The Suburban Ghetto," 22.

33. Neighborhood Scout, "Kissimmee, FL (Buenaventura Lakes)."

34. Murphy, "The Suburban Ghetto," 18.

35. Murphy, "The Suburban Ghetto," 28.

36. Murphy, "The Suburban Ghetto," 28.

37. Patton "Down and Out in Suburbia," 29.

38. Suro, Wilson, and Singer, "Immigration and Poverty in America's Suburbs." The Brookings Institution counted Puerto Ricans as part of the native-born population.

39. Suro, Wilson, and Singer, "Immigration and Poverty in America's Suburbs," 1.

40. "Annerk," comment on city-data.com forum, November 4, 2009.

41. "don macauley," comment on city-data.com forum, November 20, 2009.

42. "ComSense," comment on city-data.com forum, November 21, 2009.

43. "lifelongMOgal," comment on city-data.com forum, November 28, 2009.

44. "Hxrguitar," comment on city-data.com forum, January 2, 2010.

45. "Duttygal86," comment on city-data.com forum, January 2, 2010.

46. United States Census Bureau, "Profile of General Population and Housing Characteristics: 2010: Buenaventura Lakes."

47. United States Census Bureau, "Profile of General Population and Housing Characteristics: 2010: Osceola County."

48. Aranda and Rebollo-Gil, "Ethnoracism and the 'Sandwiched' Minorities."

49. "The pinksquid," comment on city-data.com forum, February 12, 2009.

50. "GinnyFavers," comment on city-data.com forum, July 21, 2010.

51. "Metrowester," comment on city-data.com forum, July 21, 2010.

52. "Ir5497," comment on city-data.com forum, July 22, 2010.

53. "Infinite loop," comment on city-data.com forum, July 22, 2010.

54. "Watchdaride," comment on city-data.com forum, July 28, 2010.

55. "DavieJ89," comment on city-data.com forum, July 28, 2010.

56. Low, "Maintaining Whiteness," 88; italics in original.

57. Low, "Maintaining Whiteness," 79.

58. Low, "Maintaining Whiteness," 79. The term white privilege describes a structural position of social privilege and power that has identifiable advantages. Whiteness "refers to the systematic advantage of one group over another" whereby a white racial identity becomes an advantaged, unmarked racial category (81).

59. Carpio, Abal, and Pulido, "Right to the Suburb?" 16.

60. Carpio, Abal, and Pulido, "Right to the Suburb?" 15.

61. Pulido, "Rethinking Environmental Racism," 16.

62. Pulido, "Rethinking Environmental Racism," 16.

63. Pulido, "Rethinking Environmental Racism," 16.

64. Silver and Velez, "'Let Me Go Check Out Florida.'"

65. Rumbaut, "Pigments of Our Imagination," 24.

66. Cruz, "Barriers to Political Participation of Puerto Ricans and Hispanics in Osceola County, Florida."

67. Cruz, "Barriers to Political Participation of Puerto Ricans and Hispanics in Osceola County, Florida," 249.

Chapter 4. Social Class Distinctions and the Latino Elite

1. Duany and Matos-Rodriguez, "Puerto Ricans in Orlando and Central Florida."

2. Duany and Matos-Rodriguez, "Puerto Ricans in Orlando and Central Florida"; Nader, "Up the Anthropologist."

3. Marquez, "Pride, Potential Swell as Hispanic Chamber Showcases Solidarity."

4. Feigenbaum, "Radio with a 'Titi' Spin."

5. Silver, "Latinization, Race, and Cultural Identification in Puerto Rican Orlando."

6. Delgado, "New Agency Will Guide Hispanic Entrepreneurs."

7. Delgado, "New Agency Will Guide Hispanic Entrepreneurs."

8. Delgado, "New Agency Will Guide Hispanic Entrepreneurs."

9. Delgado, "Hispanic Community Is Growing."

10. López, "Lack of Cuban–Puerto Rican Solidarity?"

11. Holton, "Many Seek a New Life in Orlando."

12. Pacheco, "Puerto Rican Group to Start Local Chapter."

13. Pacheco, "Puerto Rican Group to Start Local Chapter."

14. Martínez-Fernández, "Orlando: The Puerto Rican Frontier."

15. Yasuda, "Minorities Make Mark on Business Financial Strength Needed to Add to Successes."

16. Taylor, "Puerto Rican Chamber Expects to Expand."

17. Silver, "Latinization, Race, and Cultural Identification in Puerto Rican Orlando," 62–63.

18. Silver, "Sunshine Politics," 15.

19. Silver, "Sunshine Politics," 20.

20. Silver, "Sunshine Politics," 15.

21. Sabogal, "Viviendo en la Sombra," 125.

22. Marrow, "New Immigrant Destinations and the American Colour Line," 1040.

23. López-Sanders, "Bible Belt Immigrants," 147.

24. See Scott and Leonhardt, Class Matters; Newman, Falling from Grace; Bourdieu, Distinctions; Veblen, Conspicuous Consumption; Ortner, New Jersey Dreaming.

25. Ridgeway, "Why Status Matters for Inequality."

26. Bourdieu, Distinctions.

27. Ortner, New Jersey Dreaming, 12–14.

28. Lamont and Lareau, "Cultural Capital," 587.

29. Lareau and Weininger, "Cultural Capital in Educational Research," 587.

30. Martín Rodríguez, interview by Simone Delerme, August 13, 2010.

31. Delerme, "The Latinization of Orlando."

32. Ortner, New Jersey Dreaming.

33. The quotes and material in this section are from my interview with Ron Ramírez on January 23, 2011.

34. Duany, "The Orlando Ricans," 104.

35. Silver, "Sunshine Politics"; Duany, "The Orlando Ricans."

36. The quotes and material in this section are from my interview with Miranda Otero on June 23, 2011.

37. The quotes and material in this section are from my interview with Jennifer González on January 20, 2011.

38. The quotes and material in this section are from my interview with Magna Rodrigo on January 13, 2010.

39. Ron Harrison, interview by Simone Delerme, April 21, 2011.

40. Mansbridge, "Everyday Activism."

41. Victor Emmanuel Ramos, "Orlando Magic Executive Recognized by Hispanic Group," Hispanosphere, September 2, 2010.

42. Ramos, "Despite Their Differences They Have 3 Things in Common."

43. Ramos, "Despite Their Differences They Have 3 Things in Common."

44. Ramos, "Despite Their Differences They Have 3 Things in Common."

45. Ramos, "Despite Their Differences They Have 3 Things in Common."

46. Ramos, "Despite Their Differences They Have 3 Things in Common."

47. Ramos, "Despite Their Differences They Have 3 Things in Common."

48. Ramos, "Despite Their Differences They Have 3 Things in Common."

49. Ramos, "Despite Their Differences They Have 3 Things in Common."

50. Ramos, "Latino Leadership Brings Back Golf Tournament."

51. Lisa, comment on Hispanosphere, April 22, 2010.

52. Lisa, comment on Hispanosphere, April 22, 2010.

53. Cubanaso, comment on Hispanosphere, April 23, 2010.

54. Pedro Ramos, interview by Simone Delerme, August 9, 2010.

Chapter 5. The Encargado System

1. Mahler, *American Dreaming*.

2. Mahler, *American Dreaming*, 201.

3. Stuesse, *Scratching Out a Living*, 100.

4. Stuesse, *Scratching Out a Living*, 100.

5. Stuesse, *Scratching Out a Living*, 104.

6. United States Census Bureau, "Quick Facts: Hunters Creek CDP, Florida."

7. HOGAR Crea, Inc. is a nonprofit organization dedicated to the prevention and treatment of alcohol and substance abuse.

8. Stuesse, *Scratching Out a Living*, 95.

9. Ribas, *On the Line*, 186.

Conclusion

1. Geoscapes International Inc. was acquired by another company, Claritas, after I finished my fieldwork.

2. Rodriguez, *Brown*; Sundstrom, *The Browning of America and the Evasion of Social Justice*.

3. United States Census Bureau, "Quick Facts: United States."

4. Social Explorer, "ACS 2016 (5-Year Estimates) [Hispanic or Latino by Race and Specific Origin, Buenaventura Lakes, Florida]"; Social Explorer, "Census 2010 [Osceola County, Florida]."

5. Social Explorer, "ACS 2016 (5-Year Estimates) [Hispanic or Latino by Race and Specific Origin, Buenaventura Lakes, Florida]"; Social Explorer, "Census 2010 [Osceola County, Florida]."

6. Social Explorer, "ACS 2016 (5-Year Estimates) [Hispanic or Latino by Race and Specific Origin, Osceola County, Florida]"; Social Explorer, "Census 2010 [Osceola County, Florida]."

7. Marrow, "New Immigrant Destinations and the American Colour Line," 1037–1038.

8. Marrow, "New Immigrant Destinations and the American Colour Line," 1052.

9. Silver, "Latinization, Race, and Cultural Identification in Puerto Rican Orlando," 68.

10. Marrow, "New Immigrant Destinations and the American Colour Line," 1043.

11. Bonilla-Silva, "We Are All Americans!" 9.

12. Ribas, *On the Line*, 11.

13. Gonzalez-Barrera and Lopez, "Is Being Hispanic a Matter of Race, Ethnicity or Both?" 1.

14. Gonzalez-Barrera and Lopez, "Is Being Hispanic a Matter of Race, Ethnicity or Both?" 2; Gonzalez-Barrera and Lopez's italics.

15. Aranda and Rebollo-Gil, "Ethnoracism and the 'Sandwiched Minorities,'" 926.

16. Yglesias, "The Myth of Majority-Minority America."

17. Yglesias, "The Myth of Majority-Minority America."

18. Yglesias, "The Myth of Majority-Minority America."

19. Wang, "The Ruse of Intermarriage."

20. The phrase "Mississippi Goddam" is from a song written and performed by Nina Simone in response to the murder of Medgar Evers in Mississippi and the 16th Street Baptist Church bombing in Alabama.

BIBLIOGRAPHY

"Another Florida Builder Opens Sales Office on L.I." *Daily News*, May 13, 1978.

Acevedo, Alsy. "Crime Worries Vex BVL Residents." *Orlando Sentinel*, July 20, 2008.

Aranda, Elizabeth, and Guillermo Rebollo-Gil. "Ethnoracism and the 'Sandwiched' Minorities." *American Behavioral Scientist* 47, no. 7 (2004): 910–927.

Arreola, Daniel, ed. *Hispanic Spaces, Latino Places: Community and Cultural Diversity in Contemporary America*. Austin: University of Texas Press, 2004.

Boellstorff, Tom. *Coming of Age in Second Life: An Anthropologist Explores the Virtually Human*. Princeton, NJ: Princeton University Press, 2008.

Bonilla-Silva, Eduardo. 2002. "We Are All Americans! The Latin Americanization of Racial Stratification in the USA." *Race & Society* 5 (2002): 3–16.

Bourdieu, Pierre. *Distinctions: A Social Critique of the Judgment of Taste*. Cambridge, MA: Harvard University Press, 1986.

Brewington, Kelly. "A New Home—One of Every Three Puerto Ricans in the State Calls Central Florida Home, Giving the Region a Bilingual Flair." *Orlando Sentinel*, July 21, 2002.

Brodwin, Paul. *Everyday Ethics: Voices from the Frontline of Community Psychiatry*. Berkeley: University of California Press, 2012.

Burnett, Richard. "R-G Crown Branches Out across Florida." *Orlando Sentinel*, July 28, 2003.

Carpio, Genevieve, Clara Iraz Abal, and Laura Pulido. "Right to the Suburb? Rethinking Lefebvre and Immigrant Activism." *Journal of Urban Affairs* 33, no. 2 (2011): 185–208.

Chediak, Mark. "Booming Enclave Remains Affordable." *Orlando Sentinel*, January 1, 2006.

Clarke, Sara. "Man Jailed in Stabbing at Party." *Orlando Sentinel*, October 12, 2009.

———. "2 Men Accused of Shooting at Osceola Cops." *Orlando Sentinel*, August 18, 2008.

Cobas, José, Jorge Duany, and Joe Feagin, eds. *How the United States Racializes Latinos: White Hegemony and Its Consequences*. Boulder, CO: Paradigm Publishers, 2009.

Collazo, Sonia, Camille Ryan and Kurt Bauman. "Profile of the Puerto Rican Population in the United States and Puerto Rico: 2008." US Census Bureau. https://www.census.gov/content/dam/Census/library/working-papers/2010/demo/collazo-ryan-bauman-paa2010-paper.pdf.

Cruz, José. "Barriers to Political Participation of Puerto Ricans and Hispanics in Osceola County, Florida: 1991–2007." *Centro Journal* 22, no. 1 (2010): 242–285.

Curtis, Henry Pierson. "Osceola Sheriff's Office Ties 3 Killings to Gang." *Orlando Sentinel*, April 3, 2010.

Davíla, Arlene, and Agustin Laó-Montes, eds. *Mambo Montage: The Latinization of New York*. New York: Colombia University Press, 2001.

Delerme, Simone. The Latinization of Orlando: Language, Whiteness, and the Politics of Place. *Centro Journal* 25, no. 2 (2013): 60–95.

Delgado, Dora. "Hispanic Community Is Growing." *Orlando Sentinel*, April 7, 1988.

———. "New Agency Will Guide Hispanic Entrepreneurs." *Orlando Sentinel*, October 5, 1986.

Duany, Jorge. *Blurred Borders: Transnational Migration between the Hispanic Caribbean and the United States*. Chapel Hill, NC: University of North Carolina Press, 2011.

———. "The Orlando Ricans: Overlapping Identity Discourses among Middle-Class Puerto Rican Immigrants." *Centro Journal* 22, no. 1 (2010): 84–115.

Duany, Jorge, and Félix Matos-Rodriguez. "Puerto Ricans in Orlando and Central Florida." *Centro de Estudios Puertorriquenos Policy Report* 1, no. 1 (2006). Accessed May 3, 2019. http://www.latinamericanstudies.org/puertorico/Puerto_Ricans_in_Orlando. pdf.

Duany, Jorge and Patricia Silver. "The 'Puerto Ricanization' of Florida: Historical Background and Current Status." *Centro Journal* 22, no. 1 (2010): 4–31.

"Eighty Three (83) Arrested in 3-Day Operation." *Orlando Sentinel*, November 2, 2007.

Ennis, Sharon, Merarys Rios-Vargas, and Norma Albert. "The Hispanic Population: 2010." *2010 Census Briefs* (May 2011), 1. Accessed April 9, 2013, http://www.census. gov/prod/cen2010/briefs/c2010br-04.pdf.

Falcón, Angelo. *Atlas of Stateside Puerto Ricans*. Washington, DC: Puerto Rico Federal Affairs Administration, 2004.

Feigenbaum, Nancy. "It's No Party for Fest Goers." *Orlando Sentinel*, September 12, 1994.

———. "Radio with a 'Titi' Spin: Kids' Show Host Finds 2nd Career in Talk Radio." *Orlando Sentinel*, May 13, 1994.

Fernandez, Phil. "Family Born in America, Still Faithful to Puerto Rican Roots." *Orlando Sentinel*, May 12, 1991.

———. "Hispanic Population Surges in Osceola." *Orlando Sentinel*, March 9,1991.

Fernandez, Phil, and John Conway, "Hispanic Boom Is Rare Chance to Track Change." *Orlando Sentinel*, May 14, 1991.

———. "Osceola Hispanics Blend of Cultures, Traditions, Food." *Orlando Sentinel*, May 14, 1991.

Firpo, Julio. "Forming a Puerto Rican Identity in Orlando: The Puerto Rican Migration to Central Florida, 1960–2000." Thesis, University of Central Florida, 2012.

Flores, Juan. *Divided Borders: Essays on Puerto Rican Identity*. Houston, TX: Arte Público Press, 1993.

Flynn, Barry. "Banco Popular Expanding on Plans for Central Florida." *Orlando Sentinel*, December 31, 1996.

Franqui-Rivera, Harry. "The Borinqueneers: The Forgotten Heroes of a Forgotten War." *Centro Voices*, n.d. Accessed January 10, 2019, https://centropr.hunter.cuny.edu/centrovoices/chronicles/borinqueneers-forgotten-heroes-forgotten-war.

Furuseth, Owen, and Heather Smith. *Latinos in the New South: Transformations of Place.* Burlington, VT: Ashgate Publishing, 2006.

Gonzalez-Barrera, Ana, and Mark Hugo Lopez. "Is Being Hispanic a Matter of Race, Ethnicity or Both?" Pew Research Center, June 15, 2015. Accessed May 3, 2019. http://www.pewresearch.org/fact-tank/2015/06/15/is-being-hispanic-a-matter-of-race-ethnicity-or-both/.

Grosfoguel, Ramón, Nelson Maldonado-Torres, and José Saldivar, eds. *Latin@s in the World-System: Decolonization Struggles in the 21st Century U.S. Empire.* Boulder, CO: Paradigm Publishers, 2005.

Hill, Jane. *The Everyday Language of White Racism.* Hoboken, NJ: Wiley-Blackwell, 2008.

Holton, Sean. "Many Seek a New Life in Orlando." *Orlando Sentinel*, November 14, 1993.

Humes, Karen, Nicholas Jones, and Roberto Ramirez, "Overview of Race and Hispanic Origin: 2010, US Census Reports." *2010 Census Briefs*, March 2011. Accessed May 15, 2019. https://www.census.gov/prod/cen2010/briefs/c2010br-02.pdf.

Hunt, April. "County Looks More Latin—Hispanic Population Is Up 294%" *Orlando Sentinel*, March 28, 2001.

Jacobson, Susan. "BVL Resident Charged in Fatal Beating." *Orlando Sentinel*, July 26, 2008.

———. "Osceola Avoids Suit on Voting," *Orlando Sentinel*, June 26, 2002.

Kilsheimer, Joe. "Orlando's Overseas Attraction International Appeal Shows Up in Newcomers." *Orlando Sentinel*, October 2, 1988.

Lamont, Michele, and Annette Lareau. "Cultural Capital: Allusions, Gaps and Glissandos in Recent Theoretical Developments." *Sociological Theory* 6, no. 2 (1988): 153–168.

"Landstar Homes: A Quarter Century of Milestones." Accessed January 13, 2010, http://www.landstarhomes.com/corporate/milestones.html.

Lareau, Annette, and Elliot Weininger. "Cultural Capital in Educational Research: A Critical Assessment." *Theory and Society* 32, nos. 5–6 (2003): 567–606.

Lavenda, Robert, and Emily Schultz, *Anthropology: What Does It Mean to Be Human?* New York: Oxford University Press, 2017.

Leusner, Jim. "I-75 Stop Leads to Osceola Coke Bust." *Orlando Sentinel*, December 21, 2007.

Lewis, Amanda. "'What Group?' Studying Whites and Whiteness in the Era of 'Color-Blindness.'" *Sociological Theory* 22, no. 4 (2004): 623–646.

Loue, Sana, and Martha Sajatovic, eds. *Determinants of Minority Mental Health and Wellness.* New York: Springer Publishing, 2009.

Low, Setha. "Maintaining Whiteness: The Fear of Others and Niceness." *Transforming Anthropology* 17, no. 2 (2009): 79–92.

López, Miguel A. "Lack of Cuban-Puerto Rican Solidarity?" *Orlando Sentinel*, September 22, 1989.

López-Sanders, Laura. "Bible Belt Immigrants: Latino Religious Incorporation in New Immigrant Destinations." *Latino Studies* 10, nos. 1–2 (2012): 128–154.

Mahler, Sarah. *American Dreaming: Immigrant Life on the Margins*. Princeton, NJ: Princeton University Press, 1995.

———. *Salvadorans in Suburbia: Symbiosis and Conflict*. Boston: Allyn and Bacon, 1996.

Mansbridge, Jane. "Everyday Activism." In *The Wiley-Blackwell Encyclopedia of Social and Political Movements*. Accessed January 10, 2019. https://onlinelibrary.wiley.com/doi/abs/10.1002/9780470674871.wbespm086.

Mantero, Jose Maria. *Latinos and the U.S. South*. Westport, CT: Praeger Publishers, 2008.

Marquez, Myriam. "Pride, Potential Swell as Hispanic Chamber Showcases Solidarity." *Orlando Sentinel*, February 17, 1995.

Marrow, Helen. "New Immigrant Destinations and the American Colour Line." *Ethnic and Racial Studies* 32, no. 6 (2009): 1037–1057.

Martínez-Fernández, Luis. "Orlando: The Puerto Rican Frontier." *Orlando Sentinel*, December 16, 2004.

———. "Orlando Develops Hispanic Accent." *Orlando Sentinel*, July 26, 2005.

———. "Ever Wonder Why ATMs in Central Florida Speak Spanish?" *Orlando Sentinel*, January 1, 2007.

Massey, Douglas. *New Faces in New Places: The Changing Geography of American Immigration*. New York: Russell Sage Foundation, 2008.

McClure, Vicki, and Mary Shanklin. "The Subprime Mess: It's All Around You." *Orlando Sentinel*, May 18, 2008.

McLeod, Michael. "Diversity 101: Variety and Just a Pinch of Trouble Is the Spice of Life at Gateway High-School, a Cosmopolitan Enclave in the Middle of Once-Rural Osceola County." *Orlando Sentinel*, March 13, 1994.

Meléndez, Edgardo. *Sponsored Migrations: The State and Puerto Rican Postwar Migration to the United States*. Columbus: Ohio State University Press, 2017.

"Mexican Millionaires Build City: Mickey Mouse Gets Neighbors." *Fort Lauderdale News and Sun-Sentinel*, November 23, 1974.

Millard, Ann and Jorge Chapa. *Apple Pie and Enchiladas: Newcomers in the Rural Midwest*. Austin: University of Texas Press, 2004.

Mitchell, Renee. "Hispanics' Quiet Migration Is Making Area More Diverse." *Orlando Sentinel*, September 10, 1989.

Morales, Julio. *Puerto Rican Poverty and Migration: We Just Had to Try Elsewhere*. Westport, CT: Praeger Publishers, 1986.

Murphy, Arthur, Colleen Blanchard, and Jennifer Hill. *Latino Workers in the Contemporary South*. Athens: University of Georgia Press, 2001.

Murphy, Alexandra. "The Suburban Ghetto: The Legacy of Herbert Gans in Understanding the Experience of Poverty in Recently Impoverished American Suburbs." *City and Community* 6, no. 1 (2007): 21–37.

Nader, Laura. "Up the Anthropologist—Perspectives Gained from Studying Up." In *Reinventing Anthropology*, edited by Dell H. Hymes, 284–311. New York: Pantheon Books, 1972.

National Council of Negro Women. "Assessing the Double Burden: Racial and Gender

Disparities in Mortgage Lending." June 2009. Accessed July 16, 2018. https://ncrc.org/wp-content/uploads/2009/07/ncrc%20nosheild%20june%2009.pdf.

Neighborhood Scout. "Kissimmee, FL (Buenaventura Lakes, FL)." Accessed February 18, 2016. http://www.neighborhoodscout.com/fl/kissimmee/buenaventura-lakes/.

Newman, Katherine. *Falling from Grace: Downward Mobility in the Age of Affluence.* Berkeley: University of California Press, 1999.

Newman, Katherine, Jeff Crump, Eric Belsky, Phil Ashton, David Kaplan, and Daniel Hammel. "Cities Destroyed (Again) for Cash: Forum on the U.S. Foreclosure Crisis." *Urban Geography* 29, no. 8 (2006):745–784.

Oboler, Suzanne. *Ethnic Labels, Latino Lives: Identity and the Politics of (Re)Presentation in the United States.* Minneapolis: University of Minnesota Press, 1995.

Omi, Michael, and Howard Winant. *Racial Formation in the United States: From the 1960s to the 1980s.* New York: Routledge, 1986.

"Options Are a Given at Landstar." *Daily News*, February 3, 1979.

Ortner, Sherry. *New Jersey Dreaming: Capital, Culture, and the Class of '58.* Durham, NC: Duke University Press, 2003.

"Osceola County History." Accessed October 18, 2010. http://www.osceola.org/about_osceola_county/157-428-784/osceola_county_history.cfm.

Owens, Darryl. "Don't Trash Historic Puerto Rican Regiment." *Orlando Sentinel*, April 23, 2011.

Pacheco, Walter. "Puerto Rican Group to Start Local Chapter." *Orlando Sentinel*, November 24, 2002.

———. "Deputies Explore Trio's Ties to Burglaries." *Orlando Sentinel*, July 11, 2009.

Patton, Zach. "Down and Out in Suburbia." *Governing* 23, no. 8 (2010): 28.

Pedraza, Silvia, and Ruben Rumbaut. *Origins and Destinies: Immigration, Race, and Ethnicity in America.* Belmont, CA: Wadsworth Publishing, 1995.

Pedicini, Sandra. "New Grocer in Town." *Orlando Sentinel*, December 29, 2009.

Pico, Maria. "Out-of-State Property Scams Nothing New in P.R." *San Juan Star*, April 22, 1990.

Portes, Alejandro and Alex Stepick. *City on the Edge: The Transformation of Miami.* Berkeley: University of California Press, 1994.

Pulido, Laura. "Rethinking Environmental Racism: White Privilege and Urban Development in Southern California." *Annals of the Association of American Geographers* 90, no. 1 (2000): 12–40.

Ramos, Victor Manuel. "Between 2 Worlds: Puerto Ricans Remember Roots as They Sink New Ones." *Orlando Sentinel*, February 5, 2006.

———. "Central Florida Top Region for Puerto Ricans." *Orlando Sentinel*, March 4, 2005.

———. "Despite Their Differences They Have 3 Things in Common: They Are Latinas, Successful and Want to Golf." *Orlando Sentinel*, April 20, 2007.

———. "Latino Leadership Brings Back Golf Tournament." *Hispanosphere*, April 22, 2010.

———. "Latinos at the Helm of Orlando's Public Broadcasting." *Orlando Sentinel*, December 11, 2008.

———. "1986: Couple Escape New York for Central Florida Retirement." *Orlando Sentinel*, February 5, 2006.

———. "Seminole to Offer Ballots in Spanish." *Orlando Sentinel*, February 10, 2009.

Ramos-Zayas, Ana. *National Performances: The Politics of Class, Race, and Space in Puerto Rican Chicago*. Chicago: University of Chicago Press, 2003.

Ramos-Zayas, Ana Yolanda, and Nicholas De Genova. *Latino Crossings: Mexicans, Puerto Ricans, and the Politics of Race and Citizenship*. Chicago: University of Chicago Press, 2007.

Ribas, Vanesa. *On the Line: Slaughterhouse Lives and the Making of the New South*. Oakland: University of California Press, 2016.

Ridgeway, Cecilia. "Why Status Matters for Inequality." *American Sociological Review* 79, no. 1 (2014): 1–16.

Rivera-Lyles, Jeannette. "Judge: Mediation Not Needed in Osceola Home Foreclosures." *Orlando Sentinel*, March 14, 2009.

———. "Osceola Unveils BVL Rescue Plan." *Orlando Sentinel*, April 2, 2009.

———. "Residents' Crime Watch On Patrol." *Orlando Sentinel*, April 5, 2009.

Rodriguez, Richard. *Brown: The Last Discovery of America*. New York: Penguin Books, 2002.

Rodriguez, Havidan, Rogelio Saenz, Clara Rodriguez, and Cecilia Menjivar. *Latinas/os in the United States: Changing the Face of America*. New York: Springer, 2007.

Ross, Karl. "Landstar Capitalizes on Puerto Rican Exodus." *Orlando Sentinel*, August 7, 1994.

Rumbaut, Rubén. "Pigments of Our Imagination: On the Racialization and Racial Identities of 'Hispanics' and 'Latinos.'" In *How the United States Racializes Latinos: White Hegemony and Its Consequences*, edited by José A. Cobas, Jorge Duany, and Joe R. Feagin, 15–36. Boulder, CO: Paradigm Publishers, 2009.

Rumsey, Alan. "Wording, Meaning, and Linguistic Ideology." *American Anthropologist* 92 (1990): 346–361.

Sabogal, Elena. "Viviendo en la Sombra: The Immigration of Peruvian Professionals to South Florida." *Latino Studies* 3 (2005): 113–131.

Sánchez-Korrol, Virginia. *From Colonia to Community: The History of Puerto Ricans in New York City, 1917–1948*. Berkeley: University of California Press, 1994.

Schneider, Mike. "Puerto Ricans Increasingly Calling Florida Home." *Ocala Star-Banner*, March 4, 2005. Accessed May 3, 2019. https://www.ocala.com/article/LK/20050304/News/604224094/OS/.

Scott, Janny, and David Leonhardt. *Class Matters*. New York: Henry Holt and Company, 2005.

Shanklin, Mary. "Who Are Region's Biggest Losers in Housing Freefall?" *Orlando Sentinel*, February 23, 2010.

Silver, Patricia. "Culture Is More Than Bingo and Salsa: Making Puertorriqueñidad in Central Florida." *Centro Journal* 22, no. 1 (2010): 57–83.

———. "Latinization, Race, and Cultural Identification in Puerto Rican Orlando." *Southern Cultures* 19, no. 4 (2013): 55–75.

——. "Sunshine Politics: Puerto Rican Memory and the Political in New Destinations." *Centro Journal* 29, no. 2 (2017): 4–37.

Silver, Patricia, and William Vélez. "'Let Me Go Check Out Florida': Rethinking Puerto Rican Diaspora." *Centro Journal* 29, no. 3 (2017): 98–125.

Silverstein, Michael. "Monoglot 'Standard' in America: Standardization and Metaphors of Linguistic Hegemony." In *The Matrix of Language: Contemporary Linguistic Anthropology*, edited by Donald Brenneis and Ronald K. S. Macaulay, 284–306. Boulder, CO: Westview Press, 1996.

Snyder, Jack. "Developments Are Gems for Landstar, BVL, Meadow Woods Score in Sales." *Orlando Sentinel*, January 9, 1989.

Social Explorer. "ACS 2009 (5-Year Estimates) [House Value for All Owner-Occupied Housing Units, Buenaventura Lakes, Florida]." Accessed June 9, 2019. https://www.socialexplorer.com/tables/ACS2009_5yr/R12188131.

——. "ACS 2011 (5-Year Estimates) [House Value for All Owner-Occupied Housing Units, Buenaventura Lakes, Florida]." Accessed June 9, 2019. https://www.socialexplorer.com/tables/ACS2011_5yr/R12188132.

——. "ACS 2014 (5-Year Estimates) [Household Income, Buenaventura Lakes, Florida]." Accessed June 8, 2019. https://www.socialexplorer.com/tables/ACS2014_5yr/R12188116.

——. "ACS 2016 (5-Year Estimates) [Hispanic or Latino by Race and Specific Origin, Buenaventura Lakes, Florida]." Accessed May 24, 2019, https://www.socialexplorer.com/tables/ACS2016_5yr/R12169756.

——. "ACS 2016 (5-Year Estimates) [Hispanic or Latino by Race and Specific Origin, Osceola County, Florida]." Accessed June 23, 2019. https://www.socialexplorer.com/tables/ACS2016_5yr/R12205288.

——. "ACS 2016 (5-Year Estimates) [House Value for All Owner-Occupied Housing Units, Buenaventura Lakes, Florida]." Accessed June 9, 2019. https://www.socialexplorer.com/tables/ACS2016_5yr/R12188137.

——. "ACS 2017 (5-Year Estimates) [Household Income, Buenaventura Lakes, Florida]." Accessed June 9, 2019. https://www.socialexplorer.com/tables/ACS2017_5yr/R12188126.

——. "ACS 2017 (5-Year Estimates) [House Value for All Owner-Occupied Housing Units, Buenaventura Lakes, Florida]." Accessed June 9, 2019. https://www.socialexplorer.com/tables/ACS2017_5yr/R12188141.

——. "Census 1980 [Orange County, Florida]." Accessed July 18, 2019. https://www.socialexplorer.com/tables/C1980/R12231074.

——. "Census 1980 [Osceola County, Florida]." Accessed February 5, 2016. http://www.socialexplorer.com/tables/C1980/R11109024.

——. "Census 1990 [Hispanic Origin by Race, California, Illinois, New Jersey, New York]." Accessed June 3, 2019. https://www.socialexplorer.com/tables/C1990/R12205330.

——. "Census 1990 [Hispanic or Latino by Specific Origin, Alabama, Arkansas, Georgia,

Kentucky, Minnesota]." Accessed June 3, 2019. https://www.socialexplorer.com/tables/C1990/R12205847.

———. "Census 1990 [Hispanic or Latino by Specific Origin, Nebraska, Nevada, North Carolina, South Carolina, Tennessee]." Accessed July 18, 2019. https://www.socialexplorer.com/tables/C1990/R12230986.

———. "Census 1990 [Orange County, Florida]." Accessed July 18, 2019. https://www.socialexplorer.com/tables/C1990/R12231069.

———. "Census 1990 [Osceola County, Florida]." Accessed February 5, 2016. http://www.socialexplorer.com/tables/C1990/R11109030.

———. "Census 2000 [Hispanic Origin by Race, California, Illinois, New Jersey, New York]." Accessed June 3, 2019. https://www.socialexplorer.com/tables/C2000/R12205331.

———. "Census 2000 [Hispanic or Latino by Specific Origin, Alabama, Arkansas, Georgia, Kentucky, Minnesota]." Accessed June 3, 2019. https://www.socialexplorer.com/tables/C2000/R12205840.

———. "Census 2000 [Hispanic or Latino by Specific Origin, Nebraska, Nevada, North Carolina, South Carolina, Tennessee]." Accessed July 18, 2019. https://www.socialexplorer.com/tables/C2000/R12230961.

———. "Census 2000 [Orange County, Florida]." Accessed July 18, 2019. https://www.socialexplorer.com/tables/C2000/R12231056.

———. "Census 2000 [Osceola County, Florida]." Accessed February 5, 2016. http://www.socialexplorer.com/tables/C2000/R11109033.

———. "Census 2010 [Hispanic Origin by Race, California, Illinois, New Jersey, New York]." Accessed June 3, 2019. https://www.socialexplorer.com/tables/C2010/R12205332.

———. "Census 2010 [Hispanic or Latino by Specific Origin, Alabama, Arkansas, Georgia, Kentucky, Minnesota]." Accessed June 3, 2019. https://www.socialexplorer.com/tables/C2010/R12205839.

———. "Census 2010 [Hispanic or Latino by Specific Origin, Buenaventura Lakes, Florida]." Accessed June 3, 2019. https://www.socialexplorer.com/tables/C2010/R12181988.

———. "Census 2010 [Hispanic or Latino by Specific Origin, Nebraska, Nevada, North Carolina, South Carolina, Tennessee]." Accessed July 18, 2019. https://www.socialexplorer.com/tables/C2000/R12230961.

———. "Census 2010 [Orange County, Florida]." Accessed July 18, 2019. https://www.socialexplorer.com/tables/C2010/R12231027.

———. "Census 2010 [Osceola County, Florida]." Accessed February 5, 2016. http://www.socialexplorer.com/tables/C2010/R11109037.

Straight, Harry. "Landstar Lures Northern Buyers." *This Week*, February 11, 1979.

Steirer, Larry. "It's Time to Clean Up This Neighborhood." *Orlando Sentinel*, May 16, 2009.

Stuesse, Angela. *Scratching Out a Living: Latinos, Race, and Work in the Deep South*. Oakland: University of California Press, 2016.

Sundstrom, Ronald. *The Browning of America and the Evasion of Social Justice*. Albany: State University of New York Press, 2008.

Suris, Oscar. "Focusing on Hispanics—Advertisers, Retailers Prepare for More Moves into Orlando." *Orlando Sentinel*, February 6, 1989.

Suro, Roberto, Jill Wilson, and Audrey Singer. "Immigration and Poverty in America's Suburbs." Metropolitan Policy Program at Brookings. August 2011. Accessed May 3, 2019. https://www.brookings.edu/wp-content/uploads/2016/06/0804_immigration_ suro_wilson_singer.pdf.

Taylor, Gary. "Puerto Rican Chamber Expects to Expand." *Orlando Sentinel*, March 9, 2002. "The Florida Consent Decree: A Summary Background." Accessed June 6, 2019. https://www.scps.k12.fl.us/_resources/documents/ESOLMETAConsentSummary.pdf.

"They Are Citizens." *Orlando Sentinel*, August 13, 1989.

Torres, Agnes. "Latin Beat Is a Definite Part of Local Entertainment." *Orlando Sentinel*, August 29, 1986.

United States Census Bureau. "Census Bureau Statement on 2020 Census Race and Ethnicity Question." Press Release CB18-RTQ.02. January 26, 2018. Accessed January 3, 2019. https://www.census.gov/newsroom/press-releases/2018/2020-race-questions. html.

———. "Profile of General Population and Housing Characteristics: 2010: Buenaventura Lakes." Accessed February 2, 2016. https://factfinder.census.gov/faces/tableservices/ jsf/pages/productview.xhtml?src=CF.

———. "Profile of General Population and Housing Characteristics: 2010: Osceola County." Accessed February 2, 2016. https://factfinder.census.gov/faces/tableservices/jsf/ pages/productview.xhtml?src=CF.

———. "Quick Facts: Hunters Creek CDP, Florida." Accessed June 14, 2018. https://www. census.gov/quickfacts/fact/table/hunterscreekcdpflorida/PST045216.

———. "Quick Facts: St. Cloud City, Florida." Accessed January 5, 2019. https://www.census.gov/quickfacts/fact/table/stcloudcityflorida/PST045218.

———. "Quick Facts: United States." Accessed January 10, 2019. https://www.census.gov/ quickfacts/fact/table/US/PST045218.

Unmuth, Katherine Leal. "More Puerto Ricans Make County Home." Orlando Sentinel, April 24, 2002. Accessed May 3, 2019. https://www.orlandosentinel.com/news/os-xpm-2002-04-24-0204240021-story.html.

Urciuoli, Bonnie. *Exposing Prejudice: Puerto Rican Experiences of Language, Race, and Class*. Boulder, CO: Westview Press, 1996.

———. "Containing Language Difference: Advertising in *Hispanic* Magazines." In *Language and Social Identity,* edited by Richard Blot, 171–198. Westport, CT: Prager Publishers, 2003.

Veblen, Thorstein. *Conspicuous Consumption*. London: Penguin Books, 2006.

Vélez, William. "A New Framework for Understanding Puerto Ricans' Migration Patterns and Incorporation." *Centro Journal* 29, no. 3 (2013).

Wang, Wendy. "The Ruse of Intermarriage: Rates Characteristics Vary by Race and Gender." Pew Research Social and Demographic Trends, February 16, 2002. Accessed May 5, 2013. http://www.pewsocialtrends.org/2012/02/16/the-rise-of-intermarriage/2/.

Weise, Julie. "Dispatches from the 'Viejo' New South: Historicizing Recent Latino Migrations." *Latino Studies* 10, nos. 1–2 (2012): 41–59.

———. *Corazón de Dixie: Mexicanos in the U.S. South since 1910*. Chapel Hill: University of North Carolina Press, 2015.

Winders, Jaime, and Barbara Smith. "Excepting/Accepting the South: New Geographies of Latino Migration, New Directions in Latino Studies." *Latino Studies* 10, nos. 1–2 (2012): 220–245.

Woolard, Kathryn. "Introduction: Language Ideology as a Field of Inquiry." In *Language Ideologies: Practice and Theory*, edited by Bambi B. Schieffelin, Kathryn A. Wollard, and Paul V. Kroskrity, 3–47. New York: Oxford University Press, 1998.

Yasuda, Gene. "Minorities Make Mark on Business Financial Strength Needed to Add to Successes." *Orlando Sentinel*, February 17, 1991.

Yglesias, Matthew. "The Myth of Majority-Minority America." *Slate.com*, May 22, 2012. Accessed May 5, 2013, https://slate.com/news-and-politics/2012/05/majority-minority-america-will-more-hispanics-and-asians-become-white.html.

Zentella, Ana Celia. "Returned Migration, Language, and Identity: Puerto Rican Bilinguals in Dos Worlds/Two Mundos." In *Perspectives on Las Americas: A Reader in Culture, History and Representation*, edited by Matthew C. Gutmann, Felix V. Matos Rodriguez, Lynn Stephen, and Patricia Zavella, 245–258. Malden, MA: Blackwell, 2003.

Zentella, Ana Celia, ed. *Multilingual San Diego: Portraits of Language Loss & Revitalization*. San Diego, CA: University Readers, 2009.

Zuñiga, Víctor, and Rubén Hernández-León. *New Destinations: Mexican Immigration in the United States*. New York: Russell Sage Foundation, 2006.

INDEX

SIMONE DELERME is McMullan Associate Professor of Southern Studies and Anthropology at the University of Mississippi.

Southern Dissent

EDITED BY STANLEY HARROLD AND RANDALL M. MILLER

The Other South: Southern Dissenters in the Nineteenth Century, by Carl N. Degler, with a new preface (2000)

Crowds and Soldiers in Revolutionary North Carolina: The Culture of Violence in Riot and War, by Wayne E. Lee (2001)

"Lord, We're Just Trying to Save Your Water": Environmental Activism and Dissent in the Appalachian South, by Suzanne Marshall (2002)

The Changing South of Gene Patterson: Journalism and Civil Rights, 1960–1968, edited by Roy Peter Clark and Raymond Arsenault (2002)

Gendered Freedoms: Race, Rights, and the Politics of Household in the Delta, 1861–1875, by Nancy D. Bercaw (2003)

Civil War on Race Street: The Civil Rights Movement in Cambridge, Maryland, by Peter B. Levy (2003)

South of the South: Jewish Activists and the Civil Rights Movement in Miami, 1945–1960, by Raymond A. Mohl, with contributions by Matilda "Bobbi" Graff and Shirley M. Zoloth (2004)

Throwing Off the Cloak of Privilege: White Southern Women Activists in the Civil Rights Era, edited by Gail S. Murray (2004)

The Atlanta Riot: Race, Class, and Violence in a New South City, by Gregory Mixon (2004)

Slavery and the Peculiar Solution: A History of the American Colonization Society, by Eric Burin (2005; first paperback edition, 2008)

"I Tremble for My Country": Thomas Jefferson and the Virginia Gentry, by Ronald L. Hatzenbuehler (2006; first paperback edition, 2009)

From Saint-Domingue to New Orleans: Migration and Influences, by Nathalie Dessens (2007)

Higher Education and the Civil Rights Movement: White Supremacy, Black Southerners, and College Campuses, edited by Peter Wallenstein (2008)

Burning Faith: Church Arson in the American South, by Christopher B. Strain (2008)

Black Power in Dixie: A Political History of African Americans in Atlanta, by Alton Hornsby Jr. (2009; first paperback edition, 2016)

Looking South: Race, Gender, and the Transformation of Labor from Reconstruction to Globalization, by Mary E. Frederickson (2011; first paperback edition, 2012)

Southern Character: Essays in Honor of Bertram Wyatt-Brown, edited by Lisa Tendrich Frank and Daniel Kilbride (2011)

The Challenge of Blackness: The Institute of the Black World and Political Activism in the 1970s, by Derrick E. White (2011; first paperback edition, 2012)

Quakers Living in the Lion's Mouth: The Society of Friends in Northern Virginia, 1730–1865, by A. Glenn Crothers (2012; first paperback edition, 2013)

Unequal Freedoms: Ethnicity, Race, and White Supremacy in Civil War–Era Charleston, by Jeff Strickland (2015)

Show Thyself a Man: Georgia State Troops, Colored, 1865–1905, by Gregory Mixon (2016)

The Denmark Vesey Affair: A Documentary History, edited by Douglas R. Egerton and Robert L. Paquette (2017)

New Directions in the Study of African American Recolonization, edited by Beverly C. Tomek and Matthew J. Hetrick (2017)

Everybody's Problem: The War on Poverty in Eastern North Carolina, by Karen M. Hawkins (2017)

The Seedtime, the Work, and the Harvest: New Perspectives on the Black Freedom Struggle in America, edited by Jeffrey L. Littlejohn, Reginald K. Ellis, and Peter B. Levy (2018; first paperback edition, 2019)

Fugitive Slaves and Spaces of Freedom in North America, edited by Damian Alan Pargas (2018)

Latino Orlando: Suburban Transformation and Racial Conflict, by Simone Delerme (2020)

CPSIA information can be obtained
at www.ICGtesting.com
Printed in the USA
JSHW020756111022
31406JS00001B/9